The Parental Child-Support Obligation

The Parental Child-Support Obligation

Research, Practice, and Social Policy

Edited by
Judith Cassetty
The University of Texas at Austin

LexingtonBooks
D.C. Heath and Company
Lexington, Massachusetts
Toronto

604092

Library of Congress Cataloging in Publication Data

Main entry under title:
  The Parental child-support obligation.

  1. Child support—Law and legislation—United States. 2. Child support—
Law and legislation. 3. Child support—United States. 4. Child support.
I. Cassetty, Judith.
KFS47.P37 1982   346.7301′72   81-48464
ISBN 0-669-05376-7   347.306172

Published simultaneously in Canada

Printed in the United States of America

International Standard Book Number: 0-669-05376-7

Library of Congress Catalog Card Number: 81-48464

*To
the pursuit of justice and
equity for the benefit
of our children*

Contents

Contents

Figures and Tables

Preface

Recently a number of scholars from diverse disciplines and professional backgrounds have begun to turn their attention to a previously neglected area of social inquiry: the economic consequences of a rapidly growing number of female-headed families in the United States. These scholars and social scientists have explored this phenomenon from such perspectives as the law, sociology, economics, psychology, social-work practice, and public administration. Several have taken a comparative view, seeking insight from the experiences of other developed countries that face similar problems. Most, however, have confined their attention to domestic laws, institutions, and practices. Their concerns have been directed at the macro-level issues, such as the economic and social consequences of this phenomenon, and at the microlevel issues, such as the individual and interpersonal consequences to those families affected by family dissolution. The issue of parental liability for support of the children of such families has begun to emerge as a focal point of interest to many of these social scientists, public officials, scholars, and professionals.

Although reasons for being concerned with the ramifications of the growing incidence of female-headed families may differ, those who have contributed to this book share a basic commitment to the pursuit of social justice. This book represents the culmination of what is believed to be the first interdisciplinary effort directed at identifying the fundamental issues associated with the parental child-support obligation. In addition to differences arising from professional and academic distinctions, research scientists and scholars who have concerned themselves with this issue have approached each topic differently as a consequence of their own philosophical, professional, and personal concerns. Among those whose work is represented in this book, for instance, research has been based upon the following broad questions:

What is the actual scope of the problem of nonsupport by parents of children with whom they do not live or, conversely, to what extent is this child-support obligation being met by the parents of these children?

What relative share of support needs of children are being met by each parent and the public, and what are the implications of these patterns in terms of issues of interpersonal and social responsibility and equity?

What is the appropriate mechanism and institutional structure for effecting the changes suggested by the answers to these questions?

The conference of scholars that ultimately resulted in the chapters in this book raised more questions than were answered. Although this is usually the case with early forays into areas of inquiry not previously explored, the contributors to this book have succeeded in identifying a number of salient issues that, it is hoped, will be pursued in greater depth by others who share their concerns.

Acknowledgments

The contributions of numerous people and organizations have made this book possible.

First and foremost, the Institute for Research on Poverty (IRP) at the University of Wisconsin at Madison provided both financial and nonfinancial support for the larger child-support research and reform project out of which this book developed. Beginning in the summer of 1979, the IRP provided support for preliminary research activities, which led to the development and funding of the Wisconsin Child Support Project, which continues.

Through the combined efforts of the institute, the Division of Economic Assistance of the Wisconsin Department of Health and Social Services, the Graduate School of the University of Wisconsin, and the Ford Foundation, a conference of scholars was held in the spring of 1981 in Madison, Wisconsin. The preliminary papers prepared for and presented at this conference—The Wisconsin Workshop on Child Support Research and Public Policy—were revised and edited over the following months for this book. Although the views of the editor and the contributors are solely their own, all owe a debt to the vision and commitment of the people within these organizations who provided the necessary support for the scholarly exchange of views. In particular, we wish to express our gratitude to: Eugene Smolensky, director of the Institute for Research on Poverty; Bernard Stumbras, administrator of the Division of Economic Assistance, Wisconsin; Irwin Garfinkel, principal investigator, Wisconsin Child Support Project; and Sherwood Zink, project manager, Wisconsin Child Support Project.

In addition, I wish to express my thanks to the Resource Center on Child Abuse and Neglect at the School of Social Work, University of Texas at Austin, Michael Lauderdale, director, for providing support for the preparation of the manuscript for this book. Also, I wish to thank the administration of the University of Texas at Austin for their gracious accommodation to the demands upon my time entailed in the planning and organization of the workshop and the manuscript preparation.

Many others have contributed to this effort, often without remuneration. They include Susan Cunningham, Suzette La Vigne, Joan Priest, Vicki Rebisz, Mickey Russel, and Pat Wall. Very special gratitude is extended to Robert Nissenbaum and the Tarlton Law Library at the University of Texas at Austin.

Finally, several contributing authors owe debts of gratitude to other organizations for support of various basic research activities that contributed to the development of their respective chapters; these are noted at appropriate points in the book.

The Institute for Research on Poverty at the University of Wisconsin at Madison; the Division of Economic Assistance of the Department of Health and Social Services, State of Wisconsin; the Graduate School of the University of Wisconsin; and the Ford Foundation provided major funding for the conference out of which this book grew.

**Part I
The Child-Support System
Today: Laws, Practice, and
Patterns of Support**

1 Emerging Issues in Child-Support Policy and Practice

Judith Cassetty

The issue of child support—that is, the economic support of children by their natural or adoptive parents with whom they do not reside—is suddenly emerging as one of great concern to social scientists, public officials, and the average citizen. Until very recently, the problem of nonsupport of children by their parents was thought to be one that touched very few lives. With the growing recognition of the scope of the problem of nonsupport, together with the problem of inadequate parental support, lawmakers and others have begun to address the question of how best to improve the system for establishing and enforcing the parental-support obligation and collecting reasonable amounts of support for the benefit of children who, for reasons outside of their control, must live with only one or neither of their parents.

The Importance of Economic Support for Children

Until recently, public concern with enforcing the parental child-support obligation was confined to issues related to the reduction of welfare costs. In fiscal year 1981, for instance, the states collected child support from parents who did not reside with their children in only 10.8 percent of all Aid to Families with Dependent Children (AFDC) cases.[1] Research data suggest also that nonsupport is a serious problem for children who do not benefit from welfare payments. Estimates of nonsupport for all children who are eligible for it range from 60 to 80 percent.[2] Information from the 1980 census is expected to show more precisely how widespread is this problem. Although estimates of the extent of nonsupport may vary a great deal, the implications of even the most conservative of these are appalling in a society that purports to place such high value on the welfare of its children. Moreover among the small proportion of parents who do contribute to the support of their children who reside elsewhere, the amounts contributed average only two thousand to three thousand dollars per family per year.[3] While the exact reason for the magnitude of the problem of nonsupport is unclear, it is likely a combination of factors, including a general rejection of the notion of personal responsibility for the consequences of one's procreative activities together with the belief that children are the responsibility only of their mothers or other adults with whom they reside. Thus, when

3

marriages or adult relationships end, the persons with whom the children continue to reside are presumed to be solely responsible for their economic well-being, especially if these persons are held responsible for the demise of the relationship.[4]

Gradually the long-range consequences of permitting this notion of unilateral freedom on the part of parents—freedom to choose not to take economic responsibility for their children—are becoming clearer. Aside from the inequity of shifting this responsibility to one parent, grandparents, stepparents, or society, children who are the victims of economic abandonment cannot be expected to mature into adults who will take personal responsibility for the economic consequences of their own sexual activities and personal commitments. Second, a growing body of evidence supports the conclusion that the social and economic success (or failure) of adults is, in very large measure, the consequence of the economic opportunities from which they benefited as children. Social scientists have concluded that children from broken homes are no more likely to become juvenile or adult criminals or academic failures, for instance, than their counterparts from intact families, if their economic status does not suffer as a consequence of divorce or separation.[5] Unless child-support payments from the parent who lives elsewhere are adequate, however, a serious decline in the standard of living of these children is inevitable. This result is the consequence, generally, of the inability of women—with whom most children in single-parent households reside—to earn nearly as much as their former husbands earned. The results of research in recent years have shown that women and children suffer by far the greater economic decline at the time of divorce and over subsequent years than do former husbands.[6] While few women recover their predivorce economic status until they remarry—often several years later, if at all—their former husbands recover their predivorce standard of living or above within two to three years following divorce. Research findings indicate that many of these women are likely to become increasingly depressed, some quite seriously, especially those whose predivorce incomes were high. This result, together with frequent changes in residence—usually to steadily poorer neighborhoods—contributes to social instability and stress in children's lives.[7]

Current Issues in Child Support

Standards for Child-Support Payments

Due to the growing awareness of the scope of the problem of nonsupport and inadequate support of children by parents who do not reside with them and the short- and long-term consequences of this problem, a number of issues have recently emerged as topics of public discussion. Among these is the debate over the development and adoption of standards for setting appropriate levels of child-support payments. Basically there are two approaches to this problem: the cost-sharing approach and the resource-sharing approach.[8] The cost-sharing approach begins with the assumption that there are rather fixed and measurable costs associated with raising a child and that once known, they can be apportioned in some way between a child's parents. A major problem with this approach is that the cost of a child is largely a function of the resources available to the parents. Thus, the cost of a child in a poor household is different from the cost of a child in a moderate- or high-income family. Because the problem of estimating the costs of raising a child is an inherently endogenous one, the application of child-support standards based upon the cost-sharing approach can lead to serious inequities. If children reside with their mother whose earning power is limited, for instance, their standard of living may be quite low, and the cost-sharing approach to setting child support may lead to a relatively meager contribution from the father, though his earnings may be substantial. On the other hand, if the children reside with their father in this example, the strict application of the cost-sharing approach would lead to child-support payments from the mother that may represent a disproportionately large share of her income.

The resource-sharing approach, on the other hand, is based on the belief that children should benefit proportionately from the resources of each parent. In other words, children would not suffer a decline in their standard of living in the event of the parents' divorce. In most cases, this approach would lead to a larger contribution to the children's household than most divorced fathers (or those never married to the mothers of their children) are willing to make. While most legal scholars interpret the law as favoring this approach, an analysis of formulas designed to set support liability suggests that an approximation of the cost-sharing approach is that which may actually prevail.

For the most part, the courts have been protective of their right to set support awards on a case-by-case basis and have rejected the notion of adherence to uniform standards for child support. While this may be reasonable in a society in which few divorces occur and children are seldom born out of wedlock, the actual incidence of these phenomena has led to a situation that is inequitable in its consequences and probably counterproductive as well. As Garfinkel et al. have pointed out, virtually any divorced person can point to another whose circumstances are similar but who got a better (or worse) settlement at the hands of the courts.[9] Such inequity is bound to lead to disrespect for the legal-judicial system at best and, at worst, noncompliance with support orders by those who feel that they were the victims of an unfair and arbitrary process. One cannot help but wonder what our record of voluntary compliance with income-tax laws would look like if tax liability were established on a case-by-case basis, as is the child-support obligation.

Although there is growing interest in the development and voluntary adoption of uniform standards for child-support payments, I, for one, have expressed concern with the notion that such standards be developed within a minimal framework. That is, some proponents, in an attempt to ensure that child-support payments meet minimal standards of adequacy, have developed formulas and schedules in such a way as to meet the minimal economic needs of a child but leave the door open for adjudication of additional support when the income and means of the obligor so warrants. Although this may be a necessary preliminary step toward fostering equity between families, such an approach is implicitly based upon a cost-sharing rather than a resource-sharing approach. In addition to possessing the disadvantages of the cost-sharing approach, minimum standards for child-support payments, if widely adopted, may lead to institutionalization of the notion that these amounts are all that are necessary, fair, and reasonable. Thus, minimum standards would become accepted as the norm, while anything in excess of these would come to be viewed as excessive. Although some children and custodial parents whose current support payments are nonexistent or less than these proposed standards may benefit from their adoption, those whose support payments are based upon a resource-sharing approach, which implies no attempt to measure the (elusive) cost of a child, may be disadvantaged by the adoption of such standards.

Liability for Child Support

The issue of who should be liable for the payment of child support has begun to attract the attention of scholars and, more recently, journalists.[10] It is probably no small coincidence that the development of sophisticated genetic tests that can be used to facilitate successful organ transplantation as well as to ascertain the actual biological parentage of a child has given rise to novel arguments in favor of limited child-support liability on the part of fathers of children conceived outside of marriage.

Previously it was possible for the respondent in a paternity suit to limit his child-support liability by securing the testimony of other men who had sexual access to the mother of the child in question because the blood-typing techniques that were formerly employed were of limited value in excluding the range of possible fathers. Such practices quite naturally had the effect of reducing the number of such cases that were filed, brought to trial, or resolved with much satisfaction of certainty.

Technological advances that now allow for parental identification that approaches the 100 percent certainty level, together with technological and legal developments that give women greater control over conception and its outcome, have been followed by the advent of claims of sexual trickery and denial of the principle that men and women should share equally in the risks of pregnancy entailed in consensual intercourse.[11]

It would be easy to conclude that the debate on this issue is divided along political (for example, feminist versus sexist) or gender lines. Clearly this is not the case, however. One theme does appear to divide the debaters, however: those who would expect each party to sexual intercourse to take responsibility for her or his own conceptive risk rather than relying upon the sexual partner to protect her or him, appear to place their focus of concern more upon the fundamental right of the child to be supported by both parents than upon the rights of the parents to escape support liability.

A similar analysis may be applied to the question of a biological mother's right to deny unilaterally the rights of her child to the knowledge of, support by, and personal relationship with the child's father. While some would grant a woman the right to use a man's body (sperm) for the purpose of conceiving a child whom she wishes to bear and raise for her own gratification, others view this as a fundamental denial of the child's basic right to the benefits of dual parentage. The many facets of this issue make it an enormously complex one, but at its heart lies the issue of whether a child's right to a claim on the personal and economic resources of both parents is superior to the right of either or both parents to deny that claim by anonymity, misrepresentation, or convoluted rationale, or even with the sanction of the courts. It is fair to say, however, that no matter how appealing is the rhetoric of the superiority of children's rights in this matter, the reality is that it is adults, not children, who control the sources of political and economic power and that between men and women, the former possess by far the greater share. Given this, it is only reasonable to expect the continuation of adversarial exercise between parents, frequently resulting in outcomes that favor men to the disadvantage of women and children.

A second major area of concern related to the question of who should be liable for the support of a child involves the responsibilities and obligations of adults other than the natural or adoptive parents of a child. These may include blood relatives or nonrelatives, and the issues are as varied as the imagination may allow, including such extreme cases as the extent of liability of a physician or pharmaceutical company for failure of a birth-control device or surgical procedure. Without clouding the basic issue with these more esoteric situations—situations for which there are civil remedies—the more-common and troublesome dilemmas involve the parental child-support liability of minors who become parents, stepparents, and what has been termed recently in the literature the psychological parent.

While the courts and public child-support enforcement officials have apparently shown no reluctance toward establishing a support obligation on the part of minors who become parents of children born outside of marriage, there is no empirical evidence as to the frequency with which these cases are actually brought to court, what the outcomes are, or what the long-term effects are in terms of the relative shares of support borne by each parent and other relatives. Although factual evidence is growing insofar as the relative shares of support borne by divorced and separated parents and never-married women who head households, especially those who receive AFDC are concerned, the special problem of support for children of minors has not been addressed. A chief reason for neglect of this area of inquiry, neglect that persists in the face of evidence of an epidemic of teenage births that do not result in adoption, is the lack of visibility of this population. Many of these young mothers may continue to reside in the homes of their parents for several years. Unless the larger family unit requires public assistance, it is unlikely that this subfamily will come to the attention of public officials who would be instrumental in establishing and enforcing a child-support obligation. Anecdotal evidence suggests that embarrassment and widespread acceptance of the notion that the pregnancy was the primary fault of the young woman and her parents may result in an even more inequitable outcome for this population than for the older divorced, separated, and never-married population of women and their children. Thus, parents' attempts to protect themselves and their young daughters from embarrassment and blame may have more serious long-range consequences in terms of a child's right to parental acknowledgment, care, and support and may actually serve to perpetuate the norm of unilateral (female) responsibility for contraception and child rearing. Ultimately, these young women will move out of their parents' homes, often with their children. Because many states still have limited statutes of limitations on paternity litigation, the young mothers of these children may find themselves with no legal recourse for establishing paternity or a support obligation. Even in the absence of such statutes of limitations, the passage of time may have eroded much of the evidence of paternity, including knowledge of the father's whereabouts. With the discontinuance of support from their own parents, these young mothers will face being the sole legal parent, with all of the obligations that this implies, for the duration of the child's minority. The child will thus be permanently deprived of her or his claim on the real and personal resources of a father. It remains for policymakers and lawmakers, and professionals such as social workers, to enlarge their view of the long-term consequences of this problem and to take the necessary steps toward the prevention of its occurrence.

The issue of liability for child support on the part of the psychological parent is a bit less straightforward. Although it is an undeniable fact that grandparents and stepparents often shoulder a disproportionate share of the economic and personal responsibility for children not born to them, whether this should be the case is a normative and political question.

Much of this nonparental child support is attributable to the personal preferences of the adults involved, but evidence from empirical studies, legal case materials, and anecdotal sources suggests that there are at least two other major reasons for the shifting of economic responsibility to persons other than the natural and adoptive parents: necessity—that is, lack of adequate support from parents who do not live with their children—and the lack of normative standards to guide the determination of child-support contributions that are independent of consideration of the resources available to the children within the home in which they reside. In regard to this latter point, it is virtually impossible to avoid shifting a disproportionate share of the economic responsibility for a child to the adults in the child's household when child-support awards are based upon an ex post facto calculation of need. To paraphrase Sawhill, it is difficult to base a determination of support liability upon a standard of living for a child independent of the standard of living enjoyed by the other members of the child's household.[12] This has implications for the single-parent family, especially those headed by low-income women, and the future prospects of the children in these families, but it also has implications for the relative share of the burden of support that is implicitly shifted to stepparents. In the event that a woman remarries a man with earnings higher than hers, for instance—an outcome that can be expected to occur across the income spectrum—it is even more likely that her husband will assume a greater share of the burden of support for the children from her previous marriage. This responsibility may be genuinely welcomed by some stepparents, but many are likely to perceive this outcome as inequitable.

This type of problem has caused many who have struggled with it to propose standards that are primarily based upon considerations of the ability to pay that is evidenced by the absent parent, with little or no consideration given to the resources available in the home of the child. However, one can expect a high level of resistance to be manifest by parents who are expected to contribute support to children who reside in households with standards of living that are higher than their own standard of living. This problem may be more acute in situations in which the absent parent has taken on additional family responsibilities. The stepparent of the child in question, then, is in a position of subsidizing a standard of living for a child at a level above that to which the parent living elsewhere is willing or able to contribute a proportionate share. An analogy can also be drawn to cases involving grandparents, though the courts appear to be more reluctant to allow for this kind of shift in responsibility. One reason given for the differing view as to the liability of stepparents versus grandparents is that there are really two households residing in the same unit in the latter instance. Another is that grandparents are grandparents—not psychological or surrogate parents, as stepparents are often presumed to be. Although many states exempt them from liability, some states' family codes extend parental child-support liability to stepparents, especially if the children in question are welfare recipients or applicants.[13] By so doing, we tend to institutionalize the expectation that some stepparents (especially stepfathers) will assume a share of the economic responsibility for their spouse's children. As Carol Bruch has suggested, such a notion of nonparental liability for support, implicit or explicit—may be seen as a remnant of a patriarchal and sexist view whereby women and their children become the property (responsibility) of any man whom they marry.[14]

Recently it has been suggested that if stepparent liability were to become the general rule, such liability may extend even beyond the termination of marriage.[15] The pragmatic and practical dilemma faced by the courts, policy-makers, and others whose primary stated objective is to promote the well-being of children is whether it is of greater benefit to the child to promote the parental responsibilities of these psychological parents, including both economic support and visitation, when the alternative may leave the child without the contributions of a second parent altogether. This kind of dilemma gives rise to concern that paternity-determination efforts in the public sector may lead to practices that do not provide sufficient protection for men who voluntarily admit paternity when, in fact, they may not be the biological fathers of the children in question.[16] After all, perhaps it is better for a child to have a father—any father—with all of the psychological and financial benefits that this relationship entails, than none at all.

The normative dividing point on this issue appears to involve a choice as to whose rights and needs are paramount: those of the adults or those of the child. Although many may approach these as mutually exclusive, in fact, there is no necessary reason why the rights and needs of children cannot be made the dominant factor in shaping public policy while safeguards are built in for the protection of the basic rights of adults. This approach may be more costly and involve greater personal and professional effort, but it may have greater social value as well.

The Role of the Public Sector

Since 1950, with the passage of NOLEO, ("notice to law enforcement officials" of the deprivation of parental support due to the abandonment or desertion of a child), an amendment to the Social Security Act, public involvement in the enforcement of state laws requiring parents to support their children has grown, and several themes have emerged, themes that have become clearer as a consequence of the establishment of the federal Office of Child Support late in 1974.[17]

Although the argument as to whether the public sector should be involved at all in the area of child support is probably moot, the question of the extent and philosophy of involvement in this heretofore private area of family life, is unresolved.[18] In spite of current political deliberations that have created uncertainties as to future prospects for the funding and administration of the AFDC program, including child-support enforcement services (Title IV-D of the Social Security Act amendments of 1974), there is little doubt that financial assistance for children in low-income, female-headed families will continue, as will public efforts to place some portion of the burden of support for these children upon their fathers. Whether publicly supported child-support enforcement services should be restricted to welfare recipients or continue to be extended to nonrecipients, and under what conditions, is one of the major policy issues in this area.

The rationale for publicly supported enforcement of the parental child-support obligation was never before as clear as it became at the time of the passage of the amendment to the Social Security Act that established the federal Office of Child Support Enforcement. The expressed purpose of this endeavor was the reduction in the cost of AFDC and, after an initial grace period in which a small portion of child-support collections was disregarded for the purpose of establishing the grant level, child-support collections were effectively taxed at a 100 percent rate, reducing AFDC grants on a dollar-for-dollar basis.[19] In lieu of the economic incentives for cooperation on the part of AFDC mothers, which would have been provided by establishing a lower benefit reduction rate, policymakers chose to adopt mandatory administrative requirements for mothers' cooperation in the identification and location of the fathers of their children. The justification for this was based upon the belief that this latter approach would lead to greater AFDC cost reductions than would the former approach. In other words, federal officials were convinced that mandatory cooperation requirements, rather than built-in economic incentives for cooperation, would lead to greater AFDC cost reductions and that this, in turn, would better serve to justify the program. Whether this choice is justifiable on empirical grounds has never been either addressed or established, to my knowledge. What is true, however, is that the AFDC cost-reduction rationale has persisted as the primary justification for enforcement activities, and is likely to continue. Whether it should continue is another issue.

Since the establishment of the Office of Child Support Enforcement, provision of child-support enforcement services to non-AFDC recipients has been alternately a temporary and a permanent feature of the program. The original justification for the extension of enforcement services to this population was based upon an AFDC cost-avoidance rationale, which has haunted IV-D administrators who have been unable to establish a reliable and politically acceptable means of estimating the magnitude of these avoided costs. Without a means of measuring these avoided costs, estimates of the overall cost-effectiveness of the IV-D programs must rely upon collections and costs for AFDC recipients only. This problem has led to a de-emphasis of the non-AFDC portion of the program and extensive efforts to improve the cost-effectiveness of the AFDC portion of the program, which has failed to show substantial improvement in its efficiency over time. These efforts have included the development and implementation of strategies for "prioritizing" AFDC child-support cases in ways that may lead to improved cost-effectiveness.[20] Such case priority systems usually involve "creaming" or "filtering" cases that have socioeconomic, legal, and demographic characteristics that are associated with more successful enforcement outcomes. It is reasonable to expect, however, that these case-priority systems will be more successful in states with very high AFDC need standards and benefit levels due to the larger pool of AFDC clients with higher socioeconomic status in these states. The higher socioeconomic status of these families suggests that the fathers of the AFDC-dependent children also have higher socioeconomic status. Thus, one can expect higher child-support collections, yet because of higher ceilings on welfare eligibility, cost-effectiveness figures will improve because recipients will continue to remain on the welfare rolls. States with low ceilings on welfare eligibility, however, are not likely to benefit very much from such priority setting strategies due to the highly restricted pool from which to draw cases and the fact that very small child-support awards will render families ineligible for welfare. Once off the welfare rolls, these cases will no longer appear in the cost-effectiveness figures for the state.

In sum, there are numerous reasons for poor collection and cost performance by states, many of which have more to do with the legal, economic, and demographic characteristics of the states than they do with the administration and management of the states' IV-D programs. This, however, is not the more-relevant issue. The point is that the original and persistent rationale for the public investment in child-support enforcement activities— that of reducing direct AFDC expenditures—has created a situation in which the IV-D program is politically vulnerable. If AFDC cost-reduction is its primary reason for existing, then failure to demonstrate AFDC cost-reduction becomes its undoing.

In the meantime, state IV-D administrators report rapid increases in requests for child-support enforcement services from non-AFDC recipients and growing anger at the program's failure to act on these requests. While these services are often provided on a fee-for-service basis, sometimes according to a sliding-fee scale, administrators admit to placing low priority on these cases because, unlike the AFDC cases, non-AFDC child-support services do not have the potential for making money with which to offset AFDC costs and, at best, they can only break even.

As divorce rates increase and child-support-payment performance continues to be a problem throughout the population, awareness of the larger problem has created a climate in which the AFDC cost-reduction rationale of public child-support enforcement services is being challenged. As knowledge increases as to the importance of economic support for children across the income spectrum and the disproportionate share of this support that is being borne by the single parent, stepparents, and more-distant relatives, commitment is growing in the direction of publicly subsidized enforcement services based upon reasons other than protection of the public purse. Among these reasons are included the belief that all children have a basic right to be supported by both parents, to the best of their economic and personal abilities, and a recognition that society has a vested interest in enforcing this right for the purpose of encouraging respect for the law and a sense of personal responsibility and promoting parental equity in the sharing of economic responsibility for children.

In keeping with the public-service rationale for child-support enforcement efforts, state and local governments are adopting, expanding, and funding family-court referee and legal services and automated collection and disbursement systems, for example. While improvement in child-support payment performance is certainly a major objective of these efforts, the reduction in welfare dependence is not, though it is a likely consequence. Because they focus upon fostering the general welfare of children who do not benefit from the personal and economic resources of both parents in an intact family, these services often include divorce mediation, family counseling, and visitation enforcement services as well. The expansion of these types of services represents a concrete public response to the growing recognition of the problem of nonsupport and undersupport of children by parents with whom they do not live. By providing these services on the basis of promoting the best interests of children—rather than reducing welfare outlays—we may expect that these services will contribute to the institutionalization of the notion that adequate and equitable parental child support is the right of all children and the responsibility of all parents.

Summary

The myriad dilemmas that are associated with the issue of the parental child-support obligation are often complicated and are certainly laden with emotion. The social and personal values underlying our legal, administrative, and private practices in this area have led to inconsistencies and inequities of considerable measure. While simple, ameliorative solutions to the problems and dilemmas identified in this and subsequent chapters are unlikely, it is our intention to provide readers with as full an exploration of these as possible, together with some suggestions for change—change that we hope will lead to more dialogue, experimentation, and improvement in our public posture with respect to the parental child-support obligation.

Notes

1. U.S. Department of Health and Human Services, Office of Child Support Enforcement, *Child Support Report*, OCSE Publication No. 003, vol. 4, no. 2 (February 1982, p. 7).

2. See chapters 4, 7, and 18; C. Jones et al. "Child Support Payments in the United States," working paper 992-03 (Washington, D.C.: Urban Institute, 1976), pp. 90-109; J. Cassetty, *Child Support and Public Policy* (Lexington, Mass.: Lexington Books, D.C. Heath and Co., 1978), pp. 47-61.

3. Ibid.

4. Canadian Institute for Law Research and Reform, *Matrimonial Support Failures: Reasons, Profiles, and Perceptions of Individuals Involved, Technical Report* (Edmonton, Alberta: University of Alberta, March 1981), vol. 2.

5. H. Ross and I. Sawhill, *Time of Transition: The Growth of Families Headed by Women* (Washington, D.C.: Urban Institute, 1975), pp. 133-153.

6. D. Greenberg and D. Wolf, "The Economic Consequences of Experiencing Parental Marital Disruption," *Children and Youth Services Review* (Spring 1982); T. Espanshade, "The Economic Consequences of Divorce," *Journal of Marriage and Family* (August 1979).

7. Chapter 10.

8. Chapter 8.

9. Chapter 18.

10. Chapters 5 and 6.

11. P. Terasaki, "Resolution by HLA Testing of 1000 Paternity Cases Not Excluded by ABO Testing," *Journal of Family Law* 16, no. 3 (1978): 543.

12. Chapter 7.

13. H. Krause, *Family Law in a Nutshell* (St. Paul, Minn.: West Publishing Co., 1977), pp. 217-219.

14. Chapter 9.

15. Krause, *Family Law*, pp. 217-219.
16. Chapter 16.
17. Cassetty, *Child Support*, pp. 7-10.
18. Chapter 16.
19. Ibid.
20. D. Mastran, D. Rogers, and J. Moffett, *Overview of the Case Handling and Statistical Evaluation (CHASE) System* (McLean, Va.: Maximus, Inc., August 1980).

2 A Historical Perspective on Child-Support Laws in the United States

Sanford N. Katz

Historically, the state has been concerned with the welfare of children and has recognized a responsibility for the care and protection of children who are left alone, either by death or desertion.[1] It was a concern for parentless children that led the state to assume financial responsibility for these children earlier in this century. Benefits were originally intended for the children of deceased parents. Today a majority of the beneficiaries of AFDC programs are recipients because a parent fails to pay support. It is, however, in the interests of the state to prevent an abandoned child from becoming a public burden, and child-support enforcement has evolved within that context. The primary focus of welfare-reform efforts has been to place the financial responsibilities of child support on the birth parents.

As early as 1935, the Congress, with the passage of the Social Security Act, endorsed the thrust for public relief programs to be developed within each state.[2] Although the states have always been responsible for child-support enforcement, public income-support programs such as AFDC have been initiated at the federal level. The language establishing the AFDC benefits program states that it is "for the purpose of encouraging the care of dependent children in their own homes or in the homes of relatives by enabling each state to furnish financial assistance and rehabilitation . . . to needy dependent children . . . to help maintain and strengthen family life."[3] AFDC benefits are for needy dependent children.

But what of the financial-support obligation of the parent who is absent from the AFDC home? A large number of parents who default on their support orders are in a position to pay. Many believe that parents flee from the jurisdiction where the support order was made to avoid payment. In 1941 a bill to make it a federal crime to avoid child-support payments by leaving the state was introduced in three successive sessions of Congress and failed each time.[4] A bill to impose civil remedies for desertion and nonsupport was introduced in 1947, to make it possible for a dependent to obtain an authorized registration order from his state, which would be enforceable in the state to which a parent had moved.[5] The Fugitive Felon Act was passed in 1948, making it a federal offense for one who traveled in interstate commerce to avoid prosecution for a felony under state law. But this act did not achieve much in terms of providing for support, for two reasons. First, it made prosecuting cases difficult because of the requirement that prosecution must take place in the district in which the felony was committed (the dependent's state), and a petitioner must be approved by the U.S. attorney general or an assistant attorney general; second, even when the defendent was found guilty, incarceration made it difficult for the parent to meet the child-support obligation.[6]

New York was the first state to pass the Uniform Support of Dependent's Law in 1949.[7] Within the year, ten other states passed similar laws.[8] The law permitted a suit to be initiated in one state and terminated in another. This new concept of a two-state suit made it possible for a dependent family to file a petition in its own local court and have the petition sent by mail to the state where the nonsupporting parent resided.[9] Under this law, the state court that received the petition from the initiating court could hold a hearing to determine whether the parent was liable for support. Once the extent of liability had been determined, the court could send the money to the dependents.[10]

Following the passage of the New York law, the National Conference of Commissioners on Uniform State Laws met and approved the Uniform Reciprocal Enforcement of Support Act (URSEA) of 1950,[11] which has gradually been adopted by every state (in different versions) and has been amended from time to time. It is clear that the act's intent was to provide for reciprocity where states have similar laws, making it possible to alleviate some of the financial burden that would otherwise rest with the state welfare system.

Although the act was a positive step forward, it did not solve the problem, for a number of reasons. Two reasons for its failure are readily apparent: the process is time-consuming, and it costs money. Under the act, at the request of the court or the welfare department, a prosecuting attorney was obligated to represent a petitioner.[12] A large number of those who filed petitions for enforcement under this act did so with the assistance of the local district attorney's office. Because of the increasing case loads in county prosecutors' offices, these attorneys did not place a high priority on URESA cases. According to Nelson in his 1970 article in *Prospectus*,[13] 40 percent of the cases filed in Michigan were never pursued.[14] The act relied on the responding state's liability to locate the parent being sought and to bring the parent into its court and make sufficient inquiries, leading to an appropriate determination of support. But there have continued to be problems in dealing with different judges in different states. It is unlikely that a judge in a responding case is sufficiently informed as to the circumstances of the petitioner in the other state. The fact that the dependents are not likely to appear in court makes it more difficult for judges to render an informed decision. They cannot be aware, in making decisions, or environmental factors that would influence the judge in the dependent's own jurisdiction. Furthermore, for the act to be enforceable, it was necessary for the dependents to know the nonsupporting parent's residence so they could contact him or her. It is not uncommon for a parent who has been assessed child-support payments to depart with no forwarding address.

A 1967 change in the Social Security Act encouraged states to obtain contributions from parents who were financially able to pay support. In addition, it made available various means through which absent parents could be located and requested to make contributions. The problems with this act and the reasons why we are not able to determine the effectiveness of its amendments stem from the nature of the Department of Health, Education and Welfare (HEW). Child-support enforcement was not a high priority in the HEW welfare program at that time. A second reason for our inability to gauge the level of success is the failure of HEW to require state cooperation in enforcing child-support laws. In 1974, the Senate Finance Committee found it necessary to pass "new and stronger legislation in this area" because of noncompliance with the provisions of the 1967 act.

The House of Representatives responded to the need in 1974, when it added Title XX to the Social Security Act. Under this provision, HEW was mandated to organize a separate unit to oversee the operation of state child-support programs.[15] Additionally a federal parent locater service was made available to states.[16] This service made some federal records available to states to assist them in tracing parents who have deserted.

The response by the Congress in 1974 involved the federal government to a far greater extent than ever before. The reasons for this federal response may be attributed to the ever-increasing number of individuals who qualify for AFDC benefits because of a parent's failure to meet the support obligation. The 1974 amendment was a direct response to the public's dissatisfaction with rising welfare payments to so-called welfare cheating, cheating by desertion. Senator Long of Louisiana said it best:

> Should our welfare system be made to support the children whose father cavalierly abandons them—or chooses not to marry the mother in the first place? Is it fair to ask the American taxpayer—who works hard to support his own family and to carry his own burden—to carry the burden of the deserting father as well? Perhaps we cannot stop the father from abandoning his children, but we can certainly improve the system by obtaining child support from him and thereby place the burden of caring for his children on his own shoulders where it belongs. We can—and we must— take the financial reward out of desertions.[17]

The need for reform from within the act and the welfare system was made clear to the Senate by a Rand report.[18] It indicated that (1) costs of legal process prohibited actions by any but the rich and welfare recipients; (2) judges and lawyers found support cases boring and in some instances were hostile to the idea that fathers are responsible for their children; and (3) in California, where the study was conducted, even the state welfare agencies seemed uninterested in enforcing child-support obligations.[19] Additionally, the study destroyed some of the myths about the socioeconomic background of many deserting fathers. The report found that many parents who failed to pay support were in a position to pay (with incomes of $25,000 to $30,000 a year), and many were self-employed professionals who falsified their incomes so that the amount of support that was ordered would be lower.[20] After the House of Representatives acted, the Senate responded. The Child Support and Establishment of Paternity provisions of Title IV-D of the Social Security Act were part of a package of amendments enacted by both houses of Congress on December 20, 1974, and signed by President Ford on January 4, 1975.[21]

A number of excellent provisions in this act merit attention. First, the states are reimbursed for 75 percent of their administrative costs of enforcement. With the expectation of reimbursement, there is an incentive to implement the program and enforce it. Second, the provision of the act establishing the parent locater service (a specific function of IV-D) also makes the duty of determining paternity part of the state's function under IV-D. The facilities available for such determinations are to be made to all applicants; therefore nonwelfare applicants may have equal access, subject to a reasonable application fee in some states.[22] This is a significant provision because it serves as a form of preventive welfare reform. It is important to provide the resources to keep potential welfare recipients out of the welfare system.

This act is by no means the perfect solution. Questions of law remain as to access to federal courts under Article III of the Constitution. While the federal court is now authorized to enforce child-support orders that arise under state law,[23] access to the federal courts is subject to the discretion of the secretary of health and human services.[24]

There has been a consistent pattern in child-support law-reform efforts. The laws have attempted to emphasize enforcement of support orders, in which the key to success lies in the actual collection mechanisms. The increase in divorce has left more children in need of support than ever before. With the rise in divorce and the number of parents under court orders to pay support, the focus should be on feasible alternatives of collecting support when parents fail to meet their obligations.

The statistics point to the inability of state courts to enforce child-support orders: "Seventy-five percent of all divorced or separated women with minor children in their custody receive *no child support at all*. Less than three percent of these custodial parents receive more than $250 per month. These figures represent more than 10 million children."[25] Obviously the support order itself is meaningless if the courts have no effective method to ensure that it is obeyed. The process of income withholding, as a remedy for nonsupport, is rapidly "becoming the single most effective tool for enforcing support obligations."[26]

By this method, earned income is withheld and paid to a party who has support rights. Withholding may be authorized by court or by statute and may be accomplished by "an employer, government agency, public trust or corporation, pension or retirement fund, workers' compensation fund, death or disability fund, or annuity."[27] Thus, the broader term *income* is used as opposed to *wage*, since the withholding affects sources of income including and in addition to wages.[28]

Federal Income Withholding

State income withholding laws are an effective remedy for nonsupport. In fact, most of the states have at least some type of statutory scheme to allow a court to order mandatory wage withholding.[29] There are, however, many variations among the jurisdictions, ranging from voluntary wage assignments to set-offs of tax refunds. Unfortunately, most of the state statutes deal with wages instead of income. To reap the benefits of income withholding and still overcome the variations and limitations among state laws, Carrad and Chambers have each proposed that a uniform federal system of income withholding be established.[30] Carrad suggests a floating federal wage-attachment statute that would provide a uniform national remedy for support orders issued by state courts.[31] Chambers prefers federal wage-withholding laws to tap the absent parents' major source of wealth at its origin.[32] Both of these theorists have turned to a federal system because the sundry state systems do not function effectively.

Under the Carrad and Chambers proposals, the federal income-withholding system would apply each time a state court orders child-support payments. Chambers suggests that a master computer file, based on the parent's social security number, could be used to keep track of both job-related information and the amount of the support obligation. He would place the onus on employers to check with the Social Security Administration (SSA) to determine whether they are required to withhold support payments from a new employee.[33] Carrad, on the other hand, would impose an affirmative duty on obligors to inform employers of the support obligation: "Failure to do so might make it mandatory for the employer to discharge the obligor, or, more effectively, impose a ten percent civil penalty (to be paid to the child) on the amount due during the unreported period."[34] Like Chambers, Carrad envisions a centralized computer system to organize and implement the new process. Both proposals recognize the paramount importance of having the system function effectively and efficiently so that the support obligation travels with the parent from job to job.

Three problems with these proposed federal withholding systems are apparent. First, neither the self-employed nor the unemployed would be affected by the system. Second, only those obligors who have been ordered by a court to pay support would be registered with the SSA. Third, a federal withholding system necessarily contemplates the creation of an administrative body to implement, oversee, and, most importantly, distribute the payments to the children.[35]

Chambers raises several other areas of concern: "He points out that there is resentment about involuntary income assignment by the population in general."[36] Indeed control over disposition of income and prevention of federal intrusion into private business relationships are two of the most fundamental underpinnings of our democratic society. Furthermore, Chambers's system presupposes the willingness of employers to make SSA checks on all employees. And Carrad's proposal relies on parents who were formerly unwilling to make payments, despite the obvious threat of court sanctions, to register with their employers.

Despite these drawbacks, both Carrad and Chambers are convinced that a federal income-withholding law would be an important advance in child-support enforcement. Major disadvantages are that payments would be deducted as regularly as pension contributions from workers' paychecks, and the speed and simplicity of a computer-based system would make the cost of locating delinquent obligors less expensive than repeated court costs.[37]

State Income Withholding

Income- and wage-withholding laws have been implemented in various ways among the states. The two most common forms include assignment of income, which may be either voluntary or involuntary, and court orders requiring the withholding of income. Other civil remedies include lien-effective judgments, bond-guaranteed payments, and set-off tax refunds. Inherent civil contempt powers of the courts to jail a person for failure to comply with a court support order is another method of civil enforcement. Almost all states have enacted criminal laws to enforce child-support orders.

Voluntary Assignments

Under this system, obligors agree to assign a portion of their income to be withheld by their employer and paid to the proper person. Although "one of the most effective techniques for obtaining regular payment of child support obligations . . . relatively few states have statutes which authorize the use of wage assignments and require the employer to honor them."[38] Voluntary assignment programs are most effective when state child-support personnel encourage their use. In Virginia, for example, where the benefits of voluntary assignments are stressed, an average of one-third of all new support orders are assigned.[39]

The most obvious benefit of a voluntary wage assignment is that regular payments are made to the children, and the employee-obligor does not fall behind in the obligation. Families receive support regularly, and taxpayers' money is saved when welfare costs are recovered.[40] Public-assistance rolls diminish. Like its federal counterpart, however, this method of enforcement presupposes a willingness among employers to accept the program. Some states allow the employer to deduct a reasonable service charge to offset the expense of the assignment.[41]

Wage assignments are less effective than income-withholding procedures because they require an additional step before they can become operable. Income-withholding statutes are directed specifically to the obligor's employer. Voluntary wage assignments, on the other hand, are addressed to the delinquent parent. Unfortunately they entail "an additional legal step that is unnecessary by requiring the parent to appear to execute the assignment."[42]

Involuntary Assignments

Enforcement of support orders by voluntary assignments is dependent upon the obligor's willingness to make payments. Most states give their courts the discretion to impose involuntary assignments on parents who fail to make their payments.[43] Typically the court will reduce past support payments owed to a judgment and will then direct an income-withholding order to the obligor's employer; however, this is a discretionary remedy, and many courts fail to exercise the option. Consequently several states have passed mandatory assignment laws, indicating that conditions under which courts must order an assignment. These mandatory laws fall into two major categories: (1) those that require that an assignment be part of every order for support at the time it is established, to go into effect immediately or at the time a specified default in payment occurs; and (2) those in which application is made to the court after a specified default has occurred to which the court must respond by ordering the obligor to assign income or the employer to withhold income.[44]

Additionally, some states have combined garnishment action with a voluntary assignment,[45] and many states have statutes requiring that every support order contain an automatic assignment provision.[46] These become effective after a default in payment. New York implemented an assignment-in-every-order statute in 1979.[47] "In New York City alone there is an 80 percent payment rate on those orders which include the withholding provision, which may or may not be in effect, versus a 40 percent payment rate on orders which do not include the withholding provisions."[48]

California law requires that the parent to whom payment is due petition the court, under penalty of perjury, to order an assignment when the obligor has fallen behind in payments.[49] This assignment, established at the time of the delinquency, is issued without notice to the obligor. Since this statute was enacted only in January 1981, no statistics are available regarding the efficiency and performance of this system; however, this new process eliminates preorder hearing requirements, which were mandated under prior California law. Consequently, a decrease can be expected in both the expense and delay involved in obtaining an involuntary assignment order.

Lien-Effective Judgments, Bond Guarantees, and Tax Set-Offs

Another means of ensuring payment, which has met with some success, is the establishment of a lien on real property when the support order is issued.[50] A lien has the effect of making it impossible for the obligor to sell the land without paying past-due support. A court can order that a lien be foreclosed to satisfy the absent parent's arrears. An obvious advantage of a lien-effective judgment is that child-support payments are, in effect, secured. The success of this strategy, however, depends upon the obligor's owning real property upon which a lien can be executed. Further, an obligor who is not yet in arrears may sell the property, thereby avoiding this method of enforcement. Nebraska has resolved this problem by making the child-support order have the effect of a lien that is not dependent on the obligor's delinquency. In Nebraska, the lien remains in effect throughout the child's minority.[51]

Requiring that a bond be posted to guarantee support payments is yet another attempt to ensure that the absent parent fulfills court-imposed duties. This type of enforcement process is discretionary, and most states allow the court to vary the amount of security demanded, depending on how much it deems necessary to ensure payment. This statute applies to bond for orders in marriage-dissolution cases only.[52] The evident advantage of this method is that the court may declare the bond forfeited in addition to invoking other enforcement measures in the event the obligor fails to make payments. The security can then be forwarded to the dependenet family as a hedge against past-due support. Conversely, bond guarantees presuppose the ability of an absent parent to provide a substantial bond upon court order. If an obligor cannot afford the bond, the system fails.

Still another method that can be used to ensure payment of child support is the seizure of the obligated parent's tax refund. Set-off tax refunds have been implemented in most states to apply in situations where a debt is owed to the state. That is, "In those cases where public assistance is being paid to dependents, the support rights and rights to collect support under any order are assigned to the state. Any arrearages under those support orders constitute a debt owed to the state, and are subject to set-off."[53] Iowa laws of 1980 allow set-off tax refunds in non-AFDC cases as well.[54] The biggest advantage of tax set-offs is that the cost to the state is relatively minimal. In fact, "Oregon finds it cost-effective to set-off $25 tax refunds."[55] Obligors can be located easily and rapidly through the use of the tax set-off system. States that do not yet have income tax systems are, obviously, not able to utilize this approach.

Criminal Enforcement

"All 54 states and jurisdictions have passed statutes making nonsupport a crime."[56] One of the most important applications of criminal nonsupport laws is the use of arrest warrants to aid in locating an obligor in another state. When nonsupport is a felony,[57] the National Crime Information Center computer network may be used.[58] This interstate communication system makes it relatively easy to locate an obligor. When a crime is the equivalent of a felony or provides for a jail sentence in excess of one year, extradition across state lines is possible. Wisconsin is an example of a state with a statute carrying such a penalty. Another advantage of criminal nonsupport laws is their apparent deterrent value. Fear of imprisonment can be an effective enough incentive to cajole payment from a reluctant obligor. Unfortunately, the converse may also be true in certain situations. Some absent parents may be willing to take their chances of being caught, or even going to jail, rather than pay child support. Therefore the most effective use of criminal nonsupport laws must be in conjunction with other civil remedies to ensure the operation of an efficacious system of child-support enforcement.

Discussion and Summary

Each method of child support has distinct advantages. Regrettably, each has drawbacks as well. Consequently, a state or federal legislature must engage in a balancing act, weighing all the pluses and minuses inherent in each system to arrive at an effective method that is paramountly concerned with the protection of children's interests.

Several key elements can be gleaned from the evaluation of the different systems. First, the term *income* must be broadly defined so that sources of capital other than wages alone can be reached by the courts. Second, the system must be flexible enough to follow the obligor from job to job with relative ease. Third, employers, rather than employee-obligors, must be charged with the burden of registering the absent parent with the enforcement system. This should promote cooperation with the enforcement process.

Legislators must demonstrate a serious commitment to child-support enforcement. The task of altering child-support enforcement programs in a responsible manner, while incorporating these ideals into reality, is the first step toward an intelligent formulation of that program for America.

Notes

1. *See generally* 4 C. Venier, *American Family Laws* 56 (1936).

2. Act of August 24, 1935, ch. 531, § 1, 49 Stat. 620, as amended, 42 U.S.C. § 301 (1976 & Supp. III 1979).

3. 42 U.S.C. § 601 (1976).

4. S. 1265, 77th Cong., 1st Sess. (1941); S. 761, 78th Cong., 1st Sess. (1943); S. 453, 79th Cong., 1st Sess. (1945).

5. H.R. 4580, 81st Cong., 1st Sess. (1949); Locker, *Enforcement of Child Support Obligations of Absent Parents—Social Security Amendments of 1974*, 30 S. L.J. 631 (1976).

6. Locker, *supra* note 5 at 631.

7. N.Y. Dom. Rel. Law art. 3-A (McKinney 1964).

8. W.J. Brockelbank & F. Infausto, Interstate Enforcement of Child Support 4 (1971).

9. *Id.*

10. *Id.*

11. *Id.*

12. Uniform Reciprocal Enforcement of Support Act § 11.

13. Nelson, *Family Support from Fugitive Fathers: A Proposed Amendment to Michigan's Long-Arm Statute*, 3 Prospectus 399 (1970).

14. Locker, *supra* note 5, at 630.

15. *Id.* at 634. The House and Senate passed an amended version.

16. 42 *U.S.C.* §§ 653, 653(b)(1) (1976).

17. 118 Cong. Rec. 8291 (1972).

18. M. Winston & T. Forsher, *Nonsupport of Legitimate Children by Affluent Fathers as a Cause of Poverty and Welfare Dependence* v, vii (1971).

19. Stonder, *Child Support Enforcement and Establishment of Paternity as Tools of Welfare Reform—Social Services Amendments of 1974*, 52 *Wash. L. Rev.* 169, 171 (1976).

20. *Id.* at 172.

21. 42 U.S.C. § § 651-60 (1976 & Supp. IV 1980).

22. *Id.* at § 654 (6).

23. See note 19 *supra* at 186.

24. 42 *U.S.C.* § 660 (1976).

25. Carrad, *A Modest Proposal to End Our National Disgrace,* 2 *Fam. Advoc.* Fall 1979, at 31.

26. National Conference of State Legislatures, Information Release #2, at 1 (Spring 1981).

27. *Id.* at 2.

28. *Id.* Regarding garnishment of wages, *see* Comment, *Wage Garnishment: Still Driving the Wage-Earning Family to the Wall,* 17 *Santa Clara L. Rev.* 631 (1977).

29. National Conference of State Legislatures, *Comments of Beneficial Laws Final Report,* 9, 10 (Spring 1981).

30. See note 25 *supra*; D. Chambers, *Making Fathers Pay: The Enforcement of Child Support* 5 (1979).

31. See note 25 *supra* at 33.

32. Chambers, *supra* note 30, at 261.

33. See note 26 *supra* at 4.

34. See note 25 *supra* at 43.

35. See note 26 *supra* at 5.

36. *Id.*

37. See note 25 *supra* at 43.

38. See note 29 *supra* at 3.

39. See note 26 *supra* at 7.

40. *Id.*

41. *See, e.g., Va. Ann. Code,* § 631-272 (1980).

42. See note 29 *supra* at 7.

43. *See, e.g., Md. Ann. Code,* art. 16, § 5B (1981).

44. See note 26 *supra* at 7.

45. *See, e.g., Utah Code Ann.,* § 78-45b-13 (1953).

46. *See, e.g., R.I. Gen. Law Ann.* §§ 15-5-16 & 15-5-28 (1981); *Wis. Stat. Ann.* § 767.265 (West 1981).

47. *N.Y. Pers. Prop* §496 (McKinney 1976).

48. See note 26 *supra* at 8, 9.

49. *Cal. Civ. Code* § 4700 (West 1982).

50. *R.I. Gen. Law Ann.* § 15-5-28 (1981).

51. *Neb. Rev. Stat.* § 42-371 (1978).

52. *Ind. Code Ann.* § 31-1-11.5-15 (West 1980).

53. See note 29 *supra* at 20.

54. 1980 Iowa Acts ch. 1069.

55. See note 29 *supra* at 20, 21.

56. *Id.* at 33.
57. *Wis. Stat. Ann.* § 52.05 (West 1981).
58. See note 29 *supra* at 33.

3 The Sexual Politics of Current Child Support

Isabel Marcus

In many Third World societies, the colonial power utilized and developed the apparatus of the state for the purpose of imposing commercial practices and codes to prepare traditional society for penetration by capitalism. However uneven the impact of these practices and codes may have been, the crucial point is that the colonial authority was prepared to act as a matter of public policy to encourage, facilitate, and protect certain interactions and transactions.

Other traditional societal practices were left largely untouched or at least were not subject to rapid transformation by the apparatus of the state. These spheres of activity remained under the control of those native authorities recognized by their colonial masters. Activities connected with religion and family life were administered with relatively little intervention from colonial authorities unless some outrageous (by Western standards) custom (such as *suttee*) was involved. One can draw upon this historical pattern to ask questions about the operation of the family-law system in the United States.

Perhaps the most obvious parallel is that in the United States, there have been major efforts to develop uniform commercial practices essential to the development of an industrial economy. Far less attention has been turned to the development of uniformity in family law. Despite recent efforts to develop a uniform marital property act, we exist in a system with fifty separate family-law codes and no measure of scholarly agreement about an appropriate classification category scheme for them.[1]

The conventional explanation for this situation relies on the pattern of colonization and territorial expansion of the United States and the choices made in a federal structure regarding the allocation of power. But while sufficing to explain the past, it does not address the threshold question of why the national government did not attempt to ensure uniformity in family-law practice as a condition of statehood. While reasonable people may agree to disagree about the particular advantages and/or disadvantages or cost and benefits of allocating the major responsibility for the development and implementation of an area of public policy to a particular level of government, surely there is nothing intrinsic in family law that precludes the national authority from exercising substantial power in this issue area. In fact, the federal government has insisted that a particular marital practice—polygamous marriage among Mormons—be outlawed as a condition of the entry of the territory of Utah into the Union. This position is open to the not-unjustifiable claim that the states have been the laboratory for social experimentation in many public-policy issues areas and that a federal structure of government can benefit from the infusion of ideas and programs tested in local jurisdictions. Such smaller-scale programs are useful for many reasons: they may not be subject to the immense conflicting pressures operative on the national government, their scale may permit more imagination, their failure may not damage the lives of as many citizens.

But there is a darker side to this matter. Consider the states as analogues to native authorities in the colonial administrative scheme—likely to be responsive to tradition and custom as well. Family law with its ties to tradition is an appropriate sphere for those native (read "state") authorities. Like other native authorities, these authorities may demonstrate by their actions a commitment to a family structure endorsed and upheld by tradition. Like other authorities concerned with equity and justice, these native authorities may proclaim a concern for, and a benevolent attitude toward, dependent persons. But persons classified as dependent may not necessarily fare well.

One crucial difference between the fifty state jurisdictions and societies subjected to colonial rule is that mobility among tribal societies was far more limited than mobility among the fifty jurisdictions. Reliance upon native authorities within a highly mobile society such as ours may increase the likelihood of undesirable or arbitrary family-law outcomes in the parties' eyes. In fact, the contemporary condition of a high degree of mobility for both sexes and various age groups serves to emphasize the problem of lawmaking and interpreting under the aegis of traditional authorities. In effect, there is a strong rationale for a strategic preference for uniformity in public policy developed and implemented at the national level over the tactical desirability of a few progressive jurisdictions along with the likelihood of a number of traditional ones in the family-law area.

Some scholars would rely upon constitutional interpretation to justify the premise that an inequality of support apportionment between old and new dependents in favor of the new is allowable if not desirable. According to this argument, it is that under the rubric of the state's compelling interest in ensuring the economic and social survival of the present conventional nuclear family unit, the parent deemed able to pay child support and liable for it is given a constitutional underpinning for a unilateral choice to discriminate economically. This reasoning sets aside the long, arduous struggle to extend protection to claims of persons who are dependent and may be systematically disadvantaged by virtue of age (as are children) or sex (as are women). There is a risk involved for each new unit able to benefit in such a manner with the state's blessing. It, too, may become an old, or prior, dependent unit, with the attendant deprivation consequent upon its shift in status. If this is the case, it may be that in the guise of a seemingly important public-policy desideratum—preservation of the existing nuclear family—there lurks the specter of unilateral choice, which accommodates varying degrees of irresponsibility on the part of a parent with the ability to pay child support. Such unilateral reprioritization of one's family-support obligation is currently backed by the state.

Justice would be better served by strict enforcement of the requirement that the new unit take the parent with existing support obligations to the old unit, with a lien against his or her income that is not subject to unilateral reprioritization. Remarriage is not the basis for a change in debt-discharge obligation for any other purposes.

Another issue raised frequently in the more recent literature appears to be harmless but the implications are far more profound and revealing than the authors may have intended. It has been suggested that in default proceedings, the courts forgive arrears as an incentive for the regular payment of future support obligations. The behavioral assumption underpinning this proposal is that the accumulation of unpaid prior obligations is a motivating force in the defaulting parent's unwillingness to pay current child-support obligations. The basic problem with this assumption is that no behavioral evidence supports it.

Lawyers, law professors, and judges often operate on behavioral assumptions that are untested, at best and fly in the face of a nonlegal reality at worst. For example, in the initial cases alleging sexual harassment in employment as a cause of action under Title VII, some judges opined that a rash of litigation, including frivolous claims, might arise if the cause of action were to be allowed. This floodgate theory assumes that most people are litigators. Moreover, it demeans the legitimacy of the valid claims by focusing on the likelihood of false claims.

Of more immediate relevance here is the prevailing belief that judgments are largely self-executing. The behavioral assumption underlying this belief is that people respect courts and are law abiding, therefore by and large, they will obey a court order. From a functional perspective this belief is sensible, for at the heart of any inquiry that attempts to understand the relationship between the governors and the governed is the decision of the latter to obey the dictates of the former. Without a significant measure of voluntary compliance, no system could long survive.

Studies on attitudes toward compliance with the law among children reveal that children, especially younger ones, tend to believe laws are objective, timeless, and unchanging. As children mature, their attitudes toward law may become more subjective, but on the whole a general commitment to law-abidingness, as a norm, remains. Individual adults may profess an abstract commitment to the norm, but they may behave quite differently or engage in noncompliant behavior in specific situations. In recent literature, two types of noncompliant behavior have been identified: rule rejection and rule exception.[2] Rule rejection arises in that situation in which an individual disagrees with or questions the right of the government to make such a law. Rule exception arises in that situation in which the citizen supports many laws that he or she does not obey.

Into which category falls the failure to make court-ordered or voluntarily agreed upon child-support payments? Do defaulting parents challenge the prerogative of the courts to order such support? What are the grounds of that challenge? Or do defaulting parents acknowledge the court's prerogative in this issue area while convincing themselves that they are exempt from compliance with the order? We do not know. But there are sound public-policy reasons for entertaining the hope that child-support failures are an instance of rule exception. Responses to rule-exception-type noncompliance would appear to be modest, manageable, or less overwhelming. Whereas rule rejection conjures up images of widespread noncompliance against which the law seems relatively helpless, rule exception points to upgraded enforcement to minimize slippage.

If child-support failures are viewed as instances of rule exception, it is said that noncompliance is the consequence of unreasonable support awards. On this line of reasoning, reasonable child-support awards would ensure compliance. This alleged unreasonableness-of-support-orders rationale is suspect, however. Or, perhaps more accurately, I suspect it to be the surface rationale and not the underlying justification for noncompliance.

There are many other less attractive but equally compeling and realistic explanations for an individual's adoption of the rule-exception posture: failure to separate hostility toward the former spouse from court-ordered obligations to the children; loss of interest in the old unit; and reinforcement of traditional gender-stereotyped roles in which males maintain a power relationship over females through dollar dispensing and in which women need to seek an outside protector (the courts).

Whatever the rationale regarding rule-exception behavior, there is a cost-benefit calculus involved. In other words, the utility of compliance outweighs the utility of noncompliance. Individuals making this calculation may not operate with full information, but we assume that they are not without information.

It follows that we must ask what information is available to the actors, especially the child-support defaulters. No doubt such persons know that there are widely differing responses and attitudes on the part of courts to the enforcement of the order. Judicial discretion may well be a fairly constant force in their favor in many jurisdictions. Also persons who should be receiving child support know from contact with the legal profession that lawyers are not enthusiastic about child-support enforcement cases. In effect, noncompliance may be abetted by the legal system itself, an unappealing prospect.

Child-support failure is widespread; it is not limited to the fathers of AFDC children.[3] In fact, it seems not unreasonable to claim that child-support failure probably is one of the most massive instances of lawlessness in this country. When one compares it with other instances of possible widespread rule-exception behavior such as failing to declare all items subject to duty brought back to the United States from a trip to a foreign country, one is struck by a significant difference. In these other instances, there is an obligation to obey law that is presumed to be known to all. In the instance of child support, there is something more direct and immediate than general knowledge of the law: either a voluntary agreement negotiated by the parties incorporated into the court order or a court order without a negotiated settlement. In either instance the immediate involvement of the legal system should not be minimized.

The incidence of lawlessness is shocking, and the absence of data dismaying. It is cold comfort to rationalize these deficiencies by saying that when dollars, dependency, and disruption of family stability are at issue, the least-attractive aspects of human behavior are more likely to surface, if not prevail.

Notes

1. See Mary Ann Glendon, Property Rights upon Dissolution of Marriages and Informal Unions (unpublished manuscript, July 31, 1981), for a discussion of the problems of a classification system.

2. R. Harrell Rodgers, Jr., & Charles S. Bullock III, *Coercion to Compliance* (Lexington, Mass: Lexington Books, D.C. Heath and Company, 1976). p. 13.

3. Robert Mnookin, *Review: Using Jail for Child Support Enforcement,"* 48 *U. Chi. L. Rev.* :338 (1981).

4

An Analysis of Child-Support Transfers

Annemette Sørenson
and *Maurice MacDonald*

Perspective on Information Needs

Is Child Support a Social Problem?

Child support from absent parents may be judged a social problem if there are children whose support is deemed inadequate or if it seems that the distribution of child-support income among recipients is inequitable. Although equity and income adequacy are inherently subjective concepts, there is some general agreement about how to define them for child-support income.

The official poverty lines frequently serve as a gauge for determining whether a household has an adequate income. Thus it seems sensible to consider how well child-support payments contribute to reductions in the incidence of poverty among children eligible for support. If the data indicate many eligible children remain needy, this might be taken as important evidence of widespread lack of support. Yet this may be only circumstantial evidence because the absent parent's ability to pay must also be accounted for. For instance, if most officially poor, support-eligible children remain poor although they receive payments from absent parents that constitute high proportions of those parents' ability to pay, then there would be an income-adequacy problem but not necessarily a child-support problem. Hence it seems clear that the adequacy of child-support payments ought to be assessed with respect to both recipients' needs and absent parents' ability to pay. Unfortunately, there are very few data on absent parents. The Michigan Panel Study is the only nationally representative data set currently available that has information on the income of absent fathers, and even this is restricted to a subsample of all absent fathers. For about three-quarters of the approximately six hundred who were eligible for child support, current information was available for only the mother and her children. Cassetty and Jones et al. had to rely on predivorce income for many absent parents' actual ability to pay.[1] And the relatively small

This research was supported by the Institute for Research on Poverty with the Division of Economic Assistance of the Department of Health and Social Services, State of Wisconsin, and by the Graduate School of the University of Wisconsin.

Michigan Panel sample of support-eligible households also restricts our ability to analyze important differences in support income that are associated with variation in state child-support enforcement.

There is less consensus about equity. What constitutes evidence that child-support incomes are fairly distributed? Two ideas about child-support equity often appear in the literature. Perhaps the more-prevalent one is that similarly situated children ought to receive about the same amount of support from absent parents, the ability to pay permitting. Another common idea, concerning vertical equity, is that insofar as possible, the children's standard of living should be maintained at the level they experienced before becoming eligible for child support. The first idea is much easier to assess with available data, since it requires only information on the characteristics of support-eligible children and the amounts of support they receive. Our review of the empirical knowledge provides this type of assessment. Evaluating how well children are able to maintain their living standard after they become eligible for support payments requires an analysis of panel data that has not been conducted. The Panel Study of Income Dynamics would permit these comparisons of children's well-being before and after support eligibility. Saul Hoffman has analyzed relationships between changes in marital status and the economic status of women and children, but he did not specifically examine the influence of child support on children's economic status after marital disruption.[2]

Policy Issues and Analysis of the Support Process

It is widely believed that child support is a serious social problem, despite the increased efforts of state IV-D agencies and the 1975 expansion of federal powers to assist the states under Public Law 93-647. Policy analysts have proposed various mechanisms to improve child-support collection, but these differ substantially, so it is difficult to use them as guides for collecting specific information. To limit our scope and yet remain policy relevant, we focus primarily on two general aspects of the current support process that are seen as the logical opportunities for policy intervention: the processes that establish a child-support award, and payment performance once an award status is established. If the policy concern is to remedy inequities in child support, then these can be viewed as originating in an inequitable awards process and/or in an unfair or haphazard enforcement process. If the policy is mainly concerned with the adequacy of child support for the needy, it is likely that an increase in award amounts will be advocated; however, such a policy must be concerned with enforcement since better awards are ineffective without it. Therefore it seems generally worthwhile to have some fairly accurate knowledge of the relative importance of award status and of the enforcement process in determining child-support income.

Later in the chapter we provide the kind of multivariate analysis that is needed to separate the influences of the award process and award status from those of payment enforcement. In that analysis we find it useful to think of award status as having two important antecedents: demographic eligibility (that is, the characteristics that describe an eligible child-support recipient unit) and legal marital status (divorced, separated, and so forth). These variables may condition the likelihood and amount of the support award and also have their own effects on child-support income. To illustrate, children of never-married mothers must have paternity established to obtain support. Once such an order is established, it may also be more difficult to enforce.

Descriptive Knowledge

Data on Child Support

The data come from three recent studies—the 1975 Survey of Income and Education (SIE), the March 1979 supplement to the Current Population Survey (CPS), and the 1977 AFDC survey—each of which provides data on a national sample of households. All women in the SIE and CPS sample households who were living with one or more children whose father was absent from home were interviewed about the support the absent father provided his children. The SIE, conducted in 1976, provides data on child-support payments during 1975 for about five thousand women. The CPS, conducted in 1979, provides data on child-support payments for seven thousand women during 1978; it also notes whether the woman has been awarded child support. Supplementing the data from these two surveys are data on women receiving AFDC in 1977. The AFDC survey consists of a sample of case histories reported by social workers. For this study we selected women who received AFDC in March 1977 and who had at least one child living at home whose father was absent because the marriage had dissolved or because he had never been married to the mother. The AFDC survey provides data on child-support award status—and about the amount awarded—and on payments of child support during the survey month, either directly to the family or to the IV-D agency. The payment figures used in this study are obtained by summing these two figures. Similar information was collected in the CPS study, but no published data were available on support awards at the time of writing. Therefore the AFDC survey in one respect was the most complete data source at our disposal. Its drawback, clearly, is that women on AFDC are a special subsample of the population of women who are potentially eligible for child support.

It is characteristic of all three data sources that little or no information on the absent parent is collected. The CPS study did ask the woman about the absent parent's income during 1978; no tabulation based on these questions has been published, perhaps the quality of data may be problematic. In the AFDC survey, the case worker was asked to supply some information about the absent parent, but the proportion of unknowns on these questions is high and reduces the usefulness of such items. It is fair to say that these recent studies of child support provide a reasonably good basis for describing and evaluating the child-support situation for the custodial mother; that is, they provide sufficient data to evaluate the need for child support and analyze the role of child support in the economic well-being of children living away from their father. But these data provide only indirect information on the absent parent's situation, on his reasons for not agreeing to a child-support award or not complying with one, and on the effect of child-support payments on his economic well-being. In other words, these data sources allow us to study and gain an understanding of the child-support payment process only indirectly—by relying on the assumption that the mother's characteristics and current situation will tell something about the absent father's ability and willingness to pay child support. This may be an unfortunate result because in light of the previous findings of Jones et al. and Cassetty, the absent father's ability to pay is the most important determinant of the likelihood that a woman will ever receive any child-support payments.[3] The Panel Study of Income Dynamics data used by Jones et al. and by Cassetty are in many ways inferior to the recently collected CPS data, but this study is still the best available source of information about the absent parent. It is ironic that none of the recent surveys have focused on the party who is to pay child support; after all, if this problem is to be remedied, it is most likely not sufficient to show the consequences of nonpayment; its causes also must be assessed. We approach this problem here by assuming that the mother's characteristics, at least to some extent, reflect the absent parent's ability and willingness to pay child support. We have no way of assessing the validity of such an assumption with the available evidence.

Who Is Getting Child Support?

Previous research has demonstrated that a large proprotion of women living alone with children never receive any support from the child's absent father, and that the women who do receive child support often receive this in insufficient amounts and at irregular intervals.[4] This conclusion is not contradicted by more-recent data on national samples of women living with children whose father is absent from home. Table 4-1 gives the percentage

Table 4-1

Child-Support Recipiency Rates for Women Living with Children Eligible for Child Support

Characteristics of Mother	Percentage Receiving Some Child-Support Payments		
	1975 SIE	1977 AFDC	1979 CPS
All women	25.3	10.5	34.6
Race or origin			
Black	10.7	5.4	13.7
White	31.2	15.3	42.6
Spanish origin	16.5	8.2[a]	24.0
Marital Status			
Divorced	42.0	23.3	51.9
Separated	18.1	21.9	26.7
Never married	4.0	4.8	6.3
Remarried	26.2	—	39.0
Nonlegal separation	—	7.7	—
Education			
Less than 12 years	14.6	9.5	22.6
High school	29.2	13.1	38.1
12 years or more	38.4	14.8	45.6
Number of children			
1 child	23.1	—	30.2
2 children	27.8	—	41.9
3 children or more	25.9	—	35.0

Sources: Current Population Reports, *Divorce, Child Custody, and Child Support,* Special Studies Series, No. 84 (Bureau of the Census, U.S. Dept. of Commerce, 1979), table 8; Current Population Reports, *Child Support and Alimony,* Special Studies Series, No. 106 (Bureau of the Census, U.S. Dept. of Commerce, 1980), table 1; "1977 AFDC Survey Data."

[a]Includes a small number of cases classified as American Indian or other.

of women, living with children eligible for child support, who actually received some child-support payment during a specified time period.

It is evident from table 4-1 that only a minority of demographically eligible women receive any child-support payments. One in four of the women surveyed by SIE reported that they received some child-support payments during 1975; in the CPS data, close to 35 percent of the women had received some child-support payments during 1978. While the recipiency rates for women in the SIE and CPS surveys are not impressive, they certainly are much better than that reported for mothers on AFDC in 1977. This, of course is no surprise, since one of the main reasons that women receive AFDC is that there is no support from the children's father. On the other hand, AFDC rules require efforts on the part of both the mother and the child-support enforcement agency to collect support from the absent father. In only one of ten cases did the absent parent actually pay child support, either directly to the mother or to the IV-D agency. (The tax rate on child-support payments is 100 percent for many AFDC recipients. It is therefore likely that AFDC recipients would underreport child support, either because the recipients never see the money being paid to the IV-D agency or because private payments would be kept private. Since the AFDC survey relies on caseworker reports, only the second possibility presents a problem for this analysis.

Table 4-1 also describes sociodemographic differentials in recipiency rates. In all three data sources, white women are at least twice as likely to receive child support as are black women. Divorced women are more likely to receive child support, and women who have never married their child's father rarely receive any payments. The education differentials in all three data sets show that women with the fewest years of schooling also are least likely to receive child support. In the 1979 CPS data, the recipiency rate for women with more than a high school diploma is twice that for women with fewer than twelve years of schooling.

Although caution is needed, it seems that there may have been some increase in the percentages of women receiving child support. The SIE data report that 25 percent received some support payments in 1975, while the CPS data estimate the percentage to be close to 35 percent. No similar improvement seems to have taken place for women who receive AFDC. Both the 1973 and the 1975 AFDC survey estimate that about 10 percent received child-support payments during the survey month.[5] To the extent that women who receive child support can get off AFDC or avoid becoming dependent on the program, the lack of change in recipiency rates for the AFDC population is not inconsistent with an improvement in rates for the population in general.

The data reported in table 4-1 demonstrate that (1) only a minority of women demographically eligible for child support receive any such payments; (2) there is a great deal of variation in recipiency rates for sociodemographic groups of women; and (3) the child-support situation may have improved somewhat durng the latter part of the 1970s in the general population, though no improvement was observed for the AFDC population.

Child-Support Awards and Payments

Data on recipency rates tell little about the process of collecting child support. The first step toward collecting such support is to obtain a child-support agreement with the child's father. Many women living with children whose father is absent from home are not legally eligible for child support because they have never obtained any award or an agreement from the child's father to contribute to the support of the child. Table 4-2 shows who, among potentially eligible women, actually have child-support awards and who among legally eligible women receive payments.

Table 4-2
Child Support: Award Status and Recipiency

Mother's Characteristics	1979 CPS: Total Sample		1979 CPS: Poor Women[b]		1977 AFDC	
	% with Award	% Received Payment[a]	% with Award	% Received Payment[a]	% with Award	% Received Payment[a]
All	59.1	71.7	38.1	58.9	37.4	38.6
Race or origin						
Black	28.8	63.0	22.4	61.4	15.4	39.9
White	70.7	72.9	53.1	58.3	37.4	38.2
Spanish	43.8	65.4	28.2	59.2	20.5	31.0
Marital Status						
Divorced	79.8	73.3	70.2	55.1	67.8	34.7
Separated	45.1	72.6	38.0	62.8	47.0	47.7
Nonlegally separated	—	—	—	—	17.0	47.7
Never married	10.6	81.3	8.3	74.4	12.7	42.6
Remarried	77.1	68.3	54.9	55.0	NA	NA
Education						
Less than 12 years	46.3	61.4	31.1	51.1	27.4	36.1
High school	63.7	72.9	48.0	64.1	32.2	40.3
12 years or more	69.3	79.4	43.3	69.7	34.0	41.0

Sources: "1977 AFDC Survey Data", table B; CPR, *Child Support and Alimony,* table 1.
[a]Percentages of all those with child-support awards who actually received payments.
[b]Women with incomes below the poverty line in 1978.

Three of five women have a legally binding child-support agreement. If every liable absent parent paid child support, then only 60 percent of mothers living with children who have an absent father would have received any such payments during 1978. Furthermore, award status varies dramatically among subgroups of women. Poor women are much less likely to have such an award: only 38 percent of mothers on AFDC and of poor women in the 1979 CPS sample report that they do. The legal status of the mother vis-à-vis the child's father is another important determinant of award status. Black women and women with fewer than twelve years of schooling are much less likely than other women to have a child-support award, to a large extent, they are more likely to have children out of wedlock and to be poor. The importance of marital status is well illustrated in table 4-3, which shows the proportion of black and white women with a child-support award, by marital status. There are still race differentials within marital-status groups, but they are much smaller than the difference between all white and all black women.

The data presented in tables 4-2 and 4-3 show that there are great differences in child-support award status among sociodemographic subgroups of women. Legal status is important, but the mother's resources and the ab-

Table 4-3
Child-Support Award Status, by Mother's Race and Marital Status

Marital Status	Black Women	White Women
Divorced	50.0	73.4
Separated	34.1	57.1
Nonlegally separated	18.3	33.0
Never married	14.1	17.4

Source: Tabulation from "1977 AFDC Survey Data"

sent parent's ability to pay are factors that determine whether a woman has a child-support award.

Given that a woman has a child-support award, what is the likelihood that she will receive payments? As table 4-2 shows, almost three out of four women with an award surveyed in 1979 reported that they had received some child-support payments during 1978. Poor women in the CPS sample were less successful: only 59 percent received payments during 1978, and among women receiving AFDC in 1977, only 39 percent reported any child-support payments, either directly to the family or to the IV-D agency. The recipiency rate for women with a child-support award varies very little with other characteristics of the mother. Black women in the CPS sample are slightly less likely to receive payments than are white women, but in both samples of poor women there are no differences between white and black women. Interestingly enough, never-married women who have a child-support award are more successful at collecting this award than are other women. Women with many years of schooling also are more likely to receive payments, maybe because the absent parent's ability to pay is greater.

Most striking about these results is the small variation in recipiency rates among subgroups of women. No characteristic of the custodial parent, except economic standing, is strongly related to whether she receives any child-support payments. This is, of course, in sharp contrast to the results for award status, which was found to vary greatly among subgroups of women. These findings suggest that obtaining the child-support award is not only a necessary first step but is also a relatively effective way to obtain support from the absent parent. There is room for a great deal of change at that stage of the process. Once child support is awarded, the likelihood of collecting at least some of the award is relatively similar for women whose resources may differ with their race, education, and marital status. The fact that poor women are less likely to collect does suggest that the absent father's ability to pay is an important factor, but none of the available data sources allow us to show directly how that ability influences payment performance.

The Economic Importance of Child Support

The average amount received during 1978 by CPS respondents who received any support was $1,800 per year, or $150 per month (table 4-4). The support increases with the number of children, from an average of $1,288 for women with one child to $2,752 for women with four or more children. The support per child is lower the more children there are to support. Divorced and separated women receive somewhat more child support than women who have remarried. Whether this reflects a decline in the need for support or other characteristics of women who remarry, we cannot tell from the data in table 4-4. Cassetty also found that the custodial parent's remarriage had a negative effect on the amount of support received.[6] Never-married women receive an average of only $976 per year. There may be different reasons for this low level of support; these women and their partners tend to

Table 4-4
Mean Money Income of Custodial Parents, by Child-Support Award and Recipiency Status

	Mean Money Income				
		Support Award			
			Payments Received		
Mother's Characteristics	No Award	No Payment	Own Income	Support Income	Payments as % Total Income
All	$4,841	$6,126	$7,145	$1,799	20.1
Marital status					
Divorced	7,500	7,837	8,631	1,951	18.4
Separated	4,815	5,425	6,271	1,906	23.3
Never married	3,915	a	3,546	976	21.6
Remarried	4,372	4,587	5,585	1,602	22.3
Race					
Black	4,444	6,872	5,977	1,294	17.8
White	5,154	6,140	7,322	1,861	20.3
Spanish	4,555	a	5,604	1,318	19.0
Educational attainment					
Less than 12 years	3,497	4,507	5,108	1,503	22.7
High school	5,252	6,149	6,273	1,664	21.0
College	6,078	8,777	8,306	2,089	20.1
4 years or more	10,949	a	13,865	2,576	29.7
Number of children					
1	5,077	7,047	7,219	1,288	15.1
2	4,584	5,720	7,173	1,995	21.8
3	4,605	5,230	7,182	2,528	26.0
4 or more	4,311	a	6,500	2,752	29.7
Poverty status	2,742	3,003	2,317	1,219	34.5

Source: From 1979 Current Population Survey. See *Child Support and Alimony,* table 1.
[a]Population base is less than 75,000.

be very young and thus to have low income, often there is only one child involved, and the support may be lower for children born out of wedlock than for other children. The absent parent's ability to pay may be the reason for the relatively high support paid to older women (whose partners would have been older men with higher incomes) and to women with many years of schooling, and for the relatively low child support received by poor women.

Although the average child-support payment is relatively low, it constitutes a significant part of the family income for many custodial parents. In table 4-4, the mean money income for women with no child-support award is lower than for women with an award, whether they received payments or not.

Money income varies, of course, by the mother's characteristics, but in most subgroups of women those who receive child-support payments are much better off economically than are other women. This is not, however, solely due to the fact that they are awarded and receive child support. The women who get child support also tend to have higher incomes before child support than other women. There are some interesting exceptions to this pattern that suggest that women who live at the margin of poverty and who receive child support do not have incomes of their own higher than other poor women. Women whose total income was below the poverty line and who did receive child support had, for example, a mean income of their own of only $2,317—$400 less than women who had no award and $700 less than women with an award who did not receive any payments. This pattern is also reflected in the figures for black women and for never-married women, a large proportion of whom have incomes below the poverty line. This may simply mean that poor women who do not receive child-support income are eligible for a larger AFDC grant than are women in similar circumstances who do get child support.

Child support constitutes an important part of the custodial parent's income, especially if there are many children in the family or if the mother's income is low. For a woman with one child getting child support, the payments constitute 15 percent of total money income; if the woman has four or more children, child-support payments constitute almost a third of income. For women with incomes below the poverty line, child-support payments constitute 34 percent ot total money income.

Another way of measuring the economic importance of child support for the custodial parent is to study the relationship between child support and poverty rates. Table 4-5 presents data on the percentage of women with incomes below the poverty level, by child-support status. In 1975, a third of the women who did not receive child support had incomes below the poverty line, but only 12 percent of those who did receive support were poor. This does not imply that the payment of child support brought these women out of poverty; in fact, if this group of women had not received any child support at all during 1975, the poverty rate would have gone up to only 19 percent.

Table 4-5
Poverty Rates, by Child-Support Recipiency Rates

Support Status	Percentage with Income below Poverty Level
SIE 1975	
No support payments in 1975	32.3%
Received support payments in 1975	12.4
If no support had been received in 1975	18.9
CPS 1979	
No support payments in 1978	37.9
No award	42.1
Did have award	25.3
Received support payments in 1978	14.3
If those with award had received full payment in 1978	14.0

Source: CPR, *Divorce, Child Custody, and Child Support,* table 7; CPR, *Child Support and Alimony,* table 1, 2.

Again we see that women who in other ways are not well off also tend not to get child support. These findings are supported by the 1979 CPS data. Of those women who did not receive child support in 1978, 38 percent had incomes below the poverty line, compared to only 14 percent of the women who had child support. Women who had an award but received no payments were better off than women with no award, suggesting that although child-support payments are important for the family economy, much of the association between child support and the custodial parent's total money income is because the better off economically the custodial parent is, the more likely she is to have an award and to collect it.

Equity of Support

The results reported here, as well as those previously reported, make it clear that the current child-support system results in gross inequities, both horizontally and vertically.[7] The horizontal inequities are strongly reflected in the fact that only 60 percent of demographically eligible mothers have been awarded child support and in the great variation in award status among subgroups of women. Vertical inequity arises if the support a child receives from a father he or she lives with is different from the support he or she

receives from an absent father. Clearly, the many instances where no support award exists means that children in those families are much worse off
economically after a marital dissolution than before. In cases where child
support is awarded, the lack of payments by many absent fathers also results in vertical inequities. Where payment is forthcoming, it is more difficult to assess the degree to which the child is worse off after the father has
left the household. The relatively low level of support reported in the CPS
survey suggests that many children who receive child support do not receive
a fair share of their absent father's income. The data presented here, however, allow no satisfactory assessment of the degree to which there is an
equity problem in cases where child support is being paid.

The tables presented so far provide a fairly good description of which
demographically and legally eligible women are receiving child support and
how much they receive. They further demonstrate the gross inequities and
the inadequacies existing under the current child-support system, although
the lack of data on the absent parent's ability to pay does limit our knowledge of whether the absent father supports his children to his full ability. To
gain a better understanding of the process by which a custodial parent ob-
tains child-support income, we need to analyze the different stages of the
child-support collection process in a multivariate context.

The Process of Collecting Child-Support Income

The first step in collecting child support is to obtain a child-support award;
then the problem becomes one of enforcing the support order. Here we analyze the support-collecting process in four steps. First, we estimate a model
for award status—what determines the likelihood that a woman has a child-
support award. Next we look at the determinants of the level of child-support awarded, given that there is an award. This is followed by a model for
recipiency status—that is, whether a woman who has an award receives any
payments. The fourth model estimates the amount of child support paid,
given that there is an award and that some payment was made. Each of
these four models is estimated by ordinary least-squares regression.

To estimate these four models, we need data on child-support awards
and payments. The CPS data would be well suited for this analysis, but the
public-use version of the data did not become available in time. The analysis
we present here therefore makes use of the 1977 AFDC data, which provide
sufficient information about child-support awards and payments. The limitations entailed by using a sample of women who receive AFDC does present
a problem if we want to make inferences from the results obtained for this
population to all women eligible for child support. We address this issue in
the concluding remarks but note here that the data presented so far do suggest

that the process of child-support collection is quite similar for poor women and all women in general. The likelihood of having a child-support award and of collecting the award was lower for poor women; however, socio-economic differentials in both award and recipiency status were quite similar in the two population groups.

Although there may be problems in generalizing from results based on the AFDC survey, these data in one sense are more appropriate for the analysis of the child-support collections process. Policies of public intervention are aimed primarily at securing child support for women who, in lieu of child-support income, must depend on AFDC. From a public-policy point of view, a study of the child-support collection process among AFDC mothers may be more informative than one based on data for the general population of women eligible for child support.

Variables Used in the Analysis

The research of Cassetty and Jones et al. suggests that four sets of factors explain variations in award status and child-support income: the absent father's ability and willingness to pay, the custodial parent's need for support, and the enforcement of child-support awards.[8] In their studies, and in the one reported here, it is necessary to rely on indirect measures of these factors since no data set provides any direct measures. In each of the four models we estimate, we use the following variables as indicators of one or more of these factors.

Marital Status. The mother's legal status vis-à-vis her youngest child's father is used to construct four dummy variables for marital status. Women who are divorced from the absent father are the reference groups, and legally separated women, nonlegally separated (deserted) women, and never-married women make up the three categories included in the regression equation. The mother's marital status is primarily used as an indicator of the ease with which a child-support award may be made. A woman who has never married the child's father not only has to obtain a child-support award but also must establish paternity for the child, something that often proves difficult. In addition, it may be reasonable to see marital status as an indicator of the absent father's willingness to pay child support. A father who has lived for some time with his children may be presumed to take more interest in their well-being than a father who never married the mother and never lived with the child.

Schooling. The number of years the mother has attended school is used as an indicator of the mother's resources for obtaining and collecting child support and of the absent parent's need for support. The education variable is constructed as three dummy variables: fewer than twelve years of schooling, more than twelve years, and education unknown. The left-out category is women with twelve years of school.

Race. Race, like schooling, is seen as an indicator of the mother's resources or need for support and of the absent father's ability to pay. Black women and women of Spanish origin are compared to white women in all of the regression models.

Age of Youngest Eligible Child. The age of the youngest eligible child is introduced as a proxy for the duration of time since the marital dissolution. It may be seen as an indicator of the absent parent's willingness to pay, which declines with time, and of the time available to the custodial parent to obtain a child-support award.

Number of Children Eligible for Support. This variable is seen as an indicator of the custodial parent's need for support. Since we here measure both support awards and actual payments per child, we expect this variable to have a negative effect on both awards and payments. This does not mean that women with more children get less support, only that the average payment per child is lower the more children there are. The number of children eligible for support may also be an indicator of the absent father's previous commitment to the family. If that is the case, we may expect this variable to have a positive effect on the probability of having a child-support award and perhaps on payment of support as well.

Location of Absent Parent Unknown. This dummy variable tells whether the whereabouts of the absent father is known. It is seen as an indicator of the absent father's willingness to pay child support.

A Model for Child-Support Award Status

The dependent variable in this model is a dummy variable, taking the value of 1 if one or more of the mother's eligible children has been awarded child support. If none of the children has a child-support award, the variable takes on the value of 0. The ordinary least-squares estimates of the model for child-support-award status are given in the first two columns of table 4-6.

Divorced women are much more likely to have an award than are other women. The effect of the dummy variable for marital status is -0.22 for legal separation and -0.48 for nonlegal separation and never married. Since the range of the dependent variable is from 0 to 1, these differences between marital-status groups are quite large. Clearly the problems of establishing paternity and of locating a spouse who has deserted have substantial effects on the likelihood that the mother will have a child-support award.

The mother's race has a significant effect on award status, but her educational attainment does not. Nonwhite women are less likely to have a child-support award than white women, even after controlling for marital status and the other variables in the model. This may mean that nonwhite women have more difficulty obtaining a child-support award, either because it is too costly for them or because they consider the absent father's ability to pay so low that the payoff is not worth the trouble.

The positive effect of age of youngest child means that the older the child, the more likely the mother is to have an award; this presumably just means that it takes time to get an award. The positive effect of the number of eligible children we interpret as reflecting greater commitment to the children on the part of fathers with many children. Both of these effects are small in magnitude, but knowledge of the absent father's whereabouts is strongly related to the probability that the mother has an award. If the location of the absent parent is unknown, the mother's probability of having an award is reduced by 0.13.

In addition to the variables characterizing the mother, we introduced a series of dummy variables for states in order to assess whether the likelihood of having a child-support award varies significantly among states, after controlling for compositional differences in the AFDC population. Because Michigan can be identified as a state with one of the most-effective child-support collections systems, it was used as a reference category in the equation for award status.[9] The fifty-one dummy variables for other jurisdictions (Puerto Rico is included) add a significant 2.6 percent to the explained variation in award status. Eleven states are similar to Michigan, and one is better; fewer percentages of women in the remaining thirty-nine states have a child-support award. The mean difference between this group of states and Michigan is 16 percent, with a range of 7 percent to 25 percent. These differences are relatively large in light of the fact that the range of variation in the dependent variable is between 0 and 1. In the state with the lowest proportion of women with a child-support award, the percentage of women with an award is fully 25 percent below the Michigan level.

Amount of Child Support Awarded

The child-support award per child per month is the dependent variable in the second model estimated in table 4-6. The model is estimated for women who have been awarded child support. We expect the father's ability to pay to be an important factor in the determination of child-support awards, but

Table 4-6
Regression Models of the Child-Support Collection Process

Independent Variables	Award Status		Support Award per Child		Recipiency Status		Payments per Child	
	Unstandardized Regression Coefficients	Standard Error	Unstandardized Regression Coefficients	Standard Error	Unstandardized Regression Coefficients	Standard Error	Unstandardized Regression Coefficients	Standard Error
Support award per child	—	—	—	—	0.0002	0.0002	0.69*	0.02
Legal separation	-0.22*	0.02	6.21	2.63	0.04	0.03	12.00*	3.69
Nonlegal separation	-0.48*	0.01	1.00	1.80	0.02	0.02	-1.26	3.03
Never married	-0.48*	0.01	-9.30*	1.57	0.07*	0.02	-2.04	2.67
Less than 12 years schooling	-0.01	0.01	-4.51*	1.42	-0.02	0.02	-4.67	2.41
More than 12 years	0.02	0.01	-2.50	2.57	0.02	0.03	-1.87	4.14
Education unknown	-0.03*	0.01	-3.01*	1.46	0.001	0.02	0.86	2.39
Black	-0.05*	0.01	-5.52*	1.64	-0.04	0.02	1.08	2.91
Other nonwhite	-0.10*	0.01	-8.33*	3.25	-0.07	0.04	-4.00	6.18
Age of youngest child	0.002*	0.001	-0.86*	0.12	0.00	0.001	-0.14	0.21
Number of children	0.04*	0.002	-9.13*	0.41	0.02*	0.005	-3.80*	0.70
Location of absent parent unknown	-0.13*	0.01	1.63	1.22	-0.20*	0.01	2.09	2.60
Constant	0.23*	0.02	99.95*	3.30	0.50*	0.04	35.41	5.25
State dummies (Michigan reference category):								
Number of states similar to Michigan	11		44		17		44	
Number of states worse off than Michigan	39		7		34		6	

Mean b	−0.16	−21.35	−0.24	−23.55
Range of b	−0.07 to −0.25	−14.96 to −40.38	−0.11 to −0.44	−18.12 to −33.62
Number of states better off than Michigan	1	0	0	1
Mean b	0.21	—	—	36.00
Range of b	—	—	—	—
Adjusted R^2	0.37	0.14	0.08	0.45
F for regression	173.51 (62, 18339)	15.87 (62, 5537)	8.57 (63, 5536)	25.48 (63, 1825)
F for state dummies	14.83 (51, 18339)	3.20 (51, 5537)	5.29 (51, 5536)	2.64 (51, 1825)
Mean	0.3043	62.23	0.3373	59.76
Standard deviation	0.4601	41.87	4728	50.50

Source: AFDC 1977 Survey Data.
*Significant at 0.01 level.

the custodial parent's need for support should also be expected to have an influence. The estimates reported in table 4-6 lend some support to these hypotheses. Black women and women with fewer than twelve years of schooling are awarded less child support than are other women, and women who never married the child's father also have lower awards. It is reasonable to view these results as evidence of their importance to awards. On the average, women with little schooling, black women, and never-married women would be expected to have partners with lower income than other groups of women. At the same time, these groups of women are those for which the need for support may be greater; if that is the case, the ability to pay dominates the need for support when child support is awarded.

The negative effect of the number of children on child-support awards reflects the well-known fact that the award per child decreases with the number of children. This partly reflects the assumption that the cost of the first child is higher than costs of subsequent children, but it presumably also is a function of the absent parent's ability to pay.

The negative effect that the age of the youngest child exercises on awards probably reflects just the fact that many awards are not indexed. The older the youngest child, the lower the average award. This effect is small though—only $0.86 per year. In other words, a woman with a child of twelve would get about $8 less per child per month than a woman with a child two years old.

In this equation we again introduce a set of dummy variables for states after all the variables characterizing the custodial parent have been introduced. The reference category is Michigan. The addition of the fifty-one state dummies to the model increases the explained variation by 2.5 percent, an increase that is significantly different from zero. In contrast to the model for award status, we find that the vast majority of states are similar to Michigan; that is, the amount of child support awarded per child does not vary among these states after controlling for the custodial parent's characteristics. In seven states, however, the average award is significantly lower; there, the mean is $21 below that for Michigan. In the worst state, it is $40 per child per month below Michigan and most other states. These differences are net of any compositional differences in the population of custodial parents.

A Model for Recipiency Status

Once a woman has been awarded child support, the question becomes whether she collects any of the money awarded. In the third model, we predict whether a woman with a child-support award receives any payments under it. The dependent variable is a dummy variable taking the value of 1 if the woman or the IV-D agency received some payments during the survey month. The most remarkable feature of this model is that it is not very successful at predicting who, among women with child-support awards, actually will receive payments. This is consistent with the small variation in the recipiency status of subgroups of women that we observed in table 4-2. Somewhat surprisingly, never-married women with a child-support award are more likely to collect payments than other women. The more children a woman has, the more likely she is to collect, and if the absent parent's location is unknown, the likelihood of collecting is dramatically lower. None of the other variables in the model has any effect on recipiency status. There are no racial differences in recipiency rates, net of the other variables in the model, and the amount of support awarded does not affect the probability of receiving payments.

The positive effect of never married is difficult to interpret without additional data. It may mean that once the hurdle of obtaining an award is surpassed for the never-married mother, collecting it does not present a big problem. Or perhaps the few never-married mothers who do get an award constitute a select group of people whose partners, for one reason or another, are willing and able to pay child support. This may also explain the positive effect of number of children. A possible interpretation is that the custodial parent's need for support does prompt absent fathers who have agreed to pay child support actually to do so. The fact that women who do not know where the absent parent is are much less likely to receive payments shows that disappearance is one way to get out of paying child support.

Although these effects are significant, the variables characterizing the custodial parent together explain only 3.6 percent of the variation in recipiency status—less than the set of dummy variables for states, which add 4.4 percent to the explained variance. Seventeen of the states are similar to the reference category, Michigan, but in thirty-four states, women with a child-support award are less likely to receive payments than Michigan women are. On average, women who live in these states are 34 percent less likely to receive payments that women who live in Michigan. Given that we have controlled for the support award amount and the custodial parent's characteristics, this seems to suggest that some states are more effective than others in enforcing child-support awards and that better state-enforcement efforts may improve the situation of custodial parents considerably.

Determinants of Child-Support Income

The last step in modeling the child-support collection process is to look at the determinants of the actual payments received by the custodial parent or by the IV-D agency on her behalf. In this model, the payment received per child during the survey is the dependent variable. The model is estimated for women who have child-support awards and who received some payment during the survey month. If child-support awards were paid as stipulated, the only variable should be the amount of child support awarded; however, there are reasons to suspect that the world is not perfect, so we estimate the model by including all of the independent variables used in the previous models. The results are given in the last two columns of table 4-6.

The most important variable in the model is, not unexpectedly, the amount of child support awarded, which explains 41 percent of the variation in payments. For every dollar awarded, the payoff is $0.69. After controlling for amount of support awarded, the characteristics of the custodial parents do not tell us much about how much they receive in child support. Legally separated women tend to get higher payments than other women, presumably because the award has not been in effect for a long period of time. Women with many children tend to get less of their child-support award, maybe because the total support obligation increases with the number of children, putting more of these fathers in a situation where they feel they cannot pay the full amount. It is noteworthy that neither race nor education of the custodial parent has any effect on the payments received.

In this model there are significant differences between states; the fifty-one dummy variables add 2.2 percent to the explained variation. Forty-four states are similar to Michigan. In six states, women who collect child support are paid less per dollar awarded than are women living in the rest of the country. The difference is not trivial; in the worst state, women with the same child-support award and the same individual characteristics received almost $34 less per child per month than women in Michigan and similar states.

Summary and Discussion of Results

The results of the multivariate analysis have provided further support for many of the findings reported in earlier studies. The analysis has extended our understanding of the process of collecting child support by showing how important it is to distinguish between the two stages of that process—obtaining an award and enforcing it—and by suggesting that state enforcement efforts may well be significantly improved over present levels.

Characteristics of the Parents

Previous studies of child-support collection by Jones et al. and Cassetty have shown that child-support income varies greatly with the custodial mother's characteristics and with indicators of the absent father's ability and willingness to pay child support.[10] Jones et al. did attempt to distinguish between the process of obtaining and of enforcing an award, but they had to rely on a crude indicator of award status: whether the mother had ever received child support. We had data that allowed us to distinguish clearly between the two. As suggested by Jones et al.'s tentative results, this turned out to be an important distinction.

The analysis clearly shows that it is at the stage of awarding child support that the inequities of the current system are the greatest. Women who either had to locate the father or to establish paternity for the child were at a clear disadvantage in getting a child-support award. This is not surprising but it does point out that the women who most need the support of child-support enforcement agencies are the never married and those who have been deserted by their husbands. It was also evident from the analysis that there are nontrivial race differentials in award status and that these cannot be explained by the fact that a larger proportion of nonwhite women are never married. The most straightforward interpretation of this effect is that nonwhite women not only have fewer resources of their own, and maybe less support by institutions such as child-support collection agencies and the courts in getting a child-support award, they are also more likely to have former husbands or partners who are unable to provide any support for the child, a fact that may discourage attempts to get a support order or may make judges hesitant to impose one.

The analysis also showed that the custodial parent's characteristics are of some importance for the amount of support awarded. Awards made by the courts or by voluntary agreement are determined by the absent father's ability to pay and by the custodial parent's need for support.[11] The fact that women with few years of schooling, nonwhite women, and women who never married the child's father have lower child-support awards lends support to the hypothesis that the absent father's ability to pay is an important determinant of how much he is legally obliged to pay. The data do not provide any support for the contention that the custodial parent's need also enters into the setting of child-support levels. This is probably because we have to rely on very crude and indirect indicators of both the absent father's ability to pay and the custodial parent's need for support.

Recipiency status and actual child-support income are virtually independent of the custodial parent's characteristics. The model for whether women with a child-support award receive any payments explains a very low proportion of the variance, and only two of the variables characterizing the mother have significant and positive effects: number of children and being a never-married woman with a support award.

The actual child-support income obtained by women who do receive some payments is determined primarily by the amount of support awarded, and there are few and small differences among the returns to subgroups of women.

There are no race differentials in recipiency status or in the amount of child support actually collected for each dollar awarded. Nonwhite women are less likely to have a child-support award and they are awarded less child support per child, but once they have an award, they receive payments as frequently as white women do, and they collect the same proportion of each dollar awarded.

This finding has clear implications for the issue of child-support reform. Improving procedures for collecting child support clearly is of importance. In the present system only seventy cents of each awarded dollar is actually paid, but the success of child-support reform will, to a large extent, depend on its capacity to solve the problem of securing child-support awards to all eligible children.

Differences between States

In addition to variables characterizing the parents of the child eligible for child support, we also introduced a series of dummy variables for states in the regression analysis that allowed us to compare Michigan (the left-out category) to the fifty-one other states and jurisdictions in the sample. We ascertained that there are differences among states, net of compositional differences in the AFDC population, though we have no information about the sources of these differences. It is fairly well established that some states put more effort into the child-support collection process than others, so this finding of differences among states supports the hypothesis that public-policy interventions may be successful.[12]

There are significant differences among states at each stage of the collection process; some states are always significantly worse off than Michigan. In thirty-nine of fifty-one states, women demographically eligible for child support were less likely to have been awarded support than women in Michigan and the remaining twelve states. For those women who did have a support award, the state in which they lived did not make much difference in setting the amount of support, since only seven set lower awards than Michigan. This may suggest that the courts, despite the lack of common rules, set child support in similar ways.

Once child support had been awarded, the probability of collecting any of the award varied significantly by state. The difference was quite large; it is clearly possible to improve collection of awarded child support. Once some payment is received, however, the payment on each dollar awarded does not differ much from state to state, except for six states where, on the average, women receive $24 less per month per child than women living in other states who have been awarded the same amount of child support.

This simple analysis of state differences in the child-support collection process has convinced us that state policies of public intervention have an impact on the child-support income received by custodial mothers and that these policies matter most at the stages of helping women obtain a child-support award and of locating the absent father. We have no direct evidence that differences observed among states actually reflect differences in state policies, but we believe that our interpretation is reasonable.

The multivariate anlaysis is based on data for women receiving AFDC. We suspect that the pattern of effects will be quite similar for the general population of women, given the similarities in simple tabulations based on the CPS and AFDC data (see table 4-2). The fact that our results based on AFDC data are consistent with those based on the Panel Survey of Income Dynamics data lends some support to this expectation.[13]

Future Studies of Child Support

Our analysis of child support in the United States in the 1970s used data on AFDC mothers and a national sample of mothers, demographically eligible for child support, to attempt to answer the question, Who pays what to whom?

We can give only a partial answer to that question because none of the recently collected data on child support allow us to say much about the absent father who is supposed to pay child support. We know much more about who, among potentially eligible women, has child-support income. This chapter has therefore been limited almost exclusively to analyses of the situation faced by the mother with custody of the child, insufficient for a clear understanding of the processes of child-support collection. The almost total lack of knowledge about the absent father's ability to pay and his reasons for not paying makes it difficult, if not impossible, to assess whether the current child-support system is equitable once a child-support award has been made. It is clear that a great many inequities arise because so many women never become legally eligible for child support. We can say next to nothing about the extent to which the inequities would continue should this problem be solved.

Future studies of the child-support problem should be concerned with this problem. There is very little else to be learned from additional studies of the custodial mother's situation unless it can be seen in the context of the absent father's ability and willingness to provide support for his children.

Notes

1. J. Cassetty, *Child Support and Public Policy* (Lexington, Mass.: Lexington Books, D.C. Heath and Company, 1978); C.A. Jones, N.M. Gordon, and I.V. Sawhill, "Child Support Payments in the United States," Working Paper 992-03 (Washington, D.C.: Urban Institute, 1976).

2. S. Hoffman, "Marital Stability and the Economic Status of Women," *Demography* 14 (1977):67-76.

3. Jones, Gordon, and Sawhill, "Child Support Payments"; Cassetty, *Child Support*.

4. Jones, Gordon, and Sawhill, "Child Support Payments"; Cassetty, *Child Support*.

5. Jones, Gordon, and Sawhill, "Child Support Payments"; M. Mac-Donald, "Collecting Child Support for AFDC Mothers," Institute for Research on Poverty Discussion Paper (1979), pp. 564-579.

6. Cassetty, *Child Support*.

7. Jones, Gordon, and Sawhill, "Child Support Payments"; Cassetty, *Child Support*; Current Population Reports, *Divorce, Child Custody, and Child Support*, U.S. Census Bureau, Special Studies Series (Washington, D.C.: GPO, 1979), p. 23, No. 84; Current Population Reports, *Child Support and Alimony, 1978, Advance Report*, U.S. Census Bureau, Special Studies Series (Washington, D.C.: GPO, 1980), p. 23, No. 106.

8. Cassetty, *Child Support*; Jones, Gordon, and Sawhill, "Child Support Payments."

9. D. Chambers, *Making Fathers Pay* (Chicago: University of Chicago Press, 1979); U.S. Department of Health and Human Services, *Child Support Enforcement Statistics: Fiscal 1979* (Rockville, Md.: U.S. DHHS, 1980).

10. Jones, Gordon, and Sawhill, "Child Support Payments"; Cassetty, *Child Support*.

11. Chambers, *Making Fathers Pay*.

12. Department of Health and Human Services, *Child Support Enforcement Statistics*.

13. Jones, Gordon, and Sawhill, "Child Support Payments"; Cassetty, *Child Support*.

**Part II
The Parental Duty to Support:
Establishing Standards for
Child-Support Liability**

5

Threshold Issues Associated with the Parental Obligation of Child Support

Edward M. Young

Who should support a child? The obvious answer—the child's parents—may appear self-evident, but this has not always been so. The child born outside of the legal bonds of marriage was once commonly considered "no-one's child," the illegal or "illegitimate" offspring of an "unlawful" union.[1] A more enlightened society, motivated at least in part by the financial burden that a growing number of out-of-wedlock children has placed on that society, has taken steps to ensure that both parents are legally required to contribute to their child's support, whether those parents are married or not. All that is required to trigger this support responsibility is a legal adjudication of paternity, a task made more feasible by developments in immuno-hematology (blood testing) and other scientific fields that can establish the genetic linkages between parent and offspring with acceptable reliability.

Other recent developments—legal and social, as well as scientific—have begun to make this issue more complex. Where, in the past, sexual activity outside of marriage was generally condemned, in some circles, it is now not only accepted but also condoned and even encouraged. Where unmarried women who had children were once ostracized, some single women are now consciously choosing to have children and raise them without being married. Newspapers and magazines contain scores of articles on the rise in teenage sexuality, the growth of illegitimacy, the problems of single-parent families, and the rights of divorced fathers. All of these issues, and more, stem from changing attitudes toward sexuality and parenthood. And they all have a common factor: the increase in the number of children who are not living in a traditional family situation and for whom the question, Who should support a child? is very important.

This chapter addresses that question in light of two key developments in which science and law interact to create and attempt to sort out problems. These issues—the implications of the Supreme Court's *Roe* v. *Wade* decision in 1973 and the role of contraceptive technology in the sexual relationship—are presented here as representative of the issues that legislators, courts, and policymakers will have to address if the determination of child support is to be equitable for all parties. And since recipients of the AFDC program include many of those children who are born out of wedlock, these issues should be of concern to the nation as a whole.

The thrust of these two issues is to consider whether there are circumstances that mitigate or abrogate the responsibility of a parent to support a child. The answers are ambiguous, based on numerous, and sometimes conflicting, legal and social considerations. The situations also raise a host of complex problems regarding how decisions will be made.

Legalized Abortion

Currently conservative political and religious groups are confronting the nation's Congress with their demand that the 1973 *Roe* v. *Wade* decision be countermanded by legislation, or even a constitutional amendment, that would outlaw abortion. They claim that when the Supreme Court determined that a woman in the first trimester of pregnancy had the unilateral right to decide whether to seek an abortion, an event applauded by women's rights groups, immoral and socially destructive behavior was condoned.

Regardless of the morality issue, others have seen different implications in *Roe* v. *Wade*.[2] Relevant to our question, it has been claimed that since the male partner in conception has no voice in the decision of whether to abort, a decision that may be seen as constituting proximal, if not a necessary, cause of birth, his liability for support of the child should be limited, if not totally removed. The problem arises when the man and woman disagree over the decision, and while circumstances may vary, there are two basic situations.

In the first situation, the man wishes the woman to have an abortion, a type of belated birth control, and the woman chooses not to and brings the child to term. The traditional causal chain—intercourse, conception, birth— is seen to have a new link: the conscious decision of whether to abort, inserted between conception and birth. The conscious decision in the former chain, the assumed mutual decision of whether to have intercourse, and the risk of the consequences of conception and birth, are now superseded by a unilateral decision on the part of the mother. The man may publicly state his wishes that the woman abort and may even offer to pay for the procedure, but the decision is solely the woman's. Under current law, if that decision is negative, the man is liable to support the child under the same conditions that any other child-support determination is made. Is this a fair and equitable situation for the man?

The second situation is one in which the man does wish the child to be born and tries to keep the woman from having an abortion. A number of court cases have decided that the man is not a party to the woman's decision and, should she choose to abort, has no further recourse.[3] Thus, even if the man offers to take custody and completely support the child, he cannot legally influence the mother's decision.

By so unequivocally removing the man from the supposed causal relationship between the decision to abort and the birth of the child, it may be argued that his liability to support should take that fact into consideration. Specifically, the woman's decision not to abort when the man wishes otherwise should place the burden of support on the woman. The scientific possibility, medical safety, and legal permissibility of abortion make this a tenable argument, assuming, of course, that the woman is free to choose because there are no medical, religious, or other uncontrollable obstacles to that choice. A number of issues make that argument less than compelling, however.

The legal issues surrounding this discussion have been raised by Swan and assessed by Levy and Duncan.[4] The latter conclude that "upon examining the nexus between conception and birth from a tort, contract and criminal law analogy, it becomes clear that the nexus is not broken by the impact of *Roe* v. *Wade*"[5] They further state, "The mother's decision to bear does not refute the rational basis for holding fathers at least equally liable with mothers for the support of children resulting from the parents' sexual union."[6]

These issues are supplemented by other considerations that increase the unlikelihood that the courts will consider eliminating a father's liability to support based on a mother's decision with regard to abortion. One of these is the inequality of economic conditions that currently exists between men and women. While some women's rights advocates may support a position that a woman who decides to have a child should bear the responsibility for that decision, and while women have made considerable progress in creating conditions that allow them to generate income and be less dependent on husbands or other men for support, the fact that women do not yet earn as much as men, either because of different job classifications or through inequitable compensation for similar jobs, perpetuates a situation where absent fathers must continue to contribute to the support of children if those children are to have benefits comparable to their counterparts in families with both parents present.

Another consideration is the fact that many children of single-parent families, especially children born out of wedlock, are supported by the public through the AFDC program. The spiraling costs of this program led to the creation, in 1975, of the federal Child Support Enforcement Program, requiring states to pursue actively the establishment of paternity and legally enforceable support obligations against absent parents and to enforce those obligations. It is highly unlikely that public policy would support a reduction in paternal liability. In a sense, that argument would attempt to deny a known causal linkage and its ensuing responsibility and place the responsibility on the public, for whom the only causal linkage is a commitment to those unable to provide for their own needs.

Implications of Advances in Contraceptive Technology

Science has succeeded in producing a variety of relatively safe, reliable methods that make it possible to engage in sexual intercourse with a significantly reduced risk of conception. One of the characteristics of the newest methods is that they are designed to work within a woman's body, either by controlling egg production or by attacking sperm before they can fertilize the egg. Another characteristic is that, in many cases, the woman has virtually unsupervised control over the use of the technology. For example, in the case of oral contraceptives, effectiveness is not only dependent upon timely use (proximity to time of intercourse) but on the regularity of use (throughout the course of the menstrual cycle).

At first glance, the introduction of these technologies would appear to have the simple effect of reducing the number of unwanted children, those whose conception was not an intended or desired outcome of intercourse. Of course there is still some risk since no technology (surgical sterilization excepted) is certain of blocking conception. A further examination reveals that there are implications of these developments that bear directly on our question of who should support a child.

The issue concerns the possibility that one party may unilaterally and intentionally subvert the effectiveness of the method. The means of so doing range from not using the method at all (such as when the woman does not take the birth-control pills) to not using the method correctly (such as not using adequate concentrations of contraceptive foams or jellies). For the purpose of our discussion, it is necessary to consider circumstances under which the duty of child support can be mitigated as a result of the intentional misuse of contraceptive technology.

There are, of course, situations in which the man may perpetrate an intentional misuse of contraception, by puncturing a condom before use or by misrepresenting himself as having been effectively sterilized. However, even when the man desires conception, he can do nothing to ensure that the woman will not choose to abort. The possibility of a woman's having to bear the long-term economic effects of the man's action is limited. More likely it will be the man who is placed in a position of having to support a child he was deceived into believing was not desired by either party.

At issue here is whether individuals have a right to sexual intercourse free of possibility of risk and whether that right can be violated by the action of the other party. Until recently, courts have held that the issue of deception and contraceptive use is irrelevant in considering the father's duty to support his offspring.[7] In essence, they have ascertained that the man's responsibility to support and maintain a child is not relieved by his belief, based on whatever assurances the woman offered, that she had taken adequate measures against conception.

A recent decision by a New York City family court, however, has opened the possibility that a man's claim that he was deceived into being an unwilling sperm donor in a consciously procreative act on the part of the woman can in fact reduce, if not totally eliminate, his child-support liability.[8] In that case the woman was known to have told others that she was not using birth-control pills in order to have a child out of wedlock by a particular man. Intercourse occurred, the man later claimed, under false pretenses that the woman had taken precautions against conception. Based on scientific evidence (the human leukocyte-antigen or HL-A test), the man was adjudged to be the biological father of the child, and the mother sued for support. The court ruled in favor of the father, and, while his obligation to support was not completely voided, placed severe limitations on the extent of that liability. Thus, while not removing a man's liability for support even when he is the victim of a wrong on the part of the woman, the court refused to place a liability of the extent that would normally be entailed in a more mutually generated mistake.

The impact of this decision, should it be upheld, is unclear. On the one hand, it could open the door to a host of such cases with claims that have been raised since the earliest paternity cases.[9] The courts may be placed in the difficult position of having to decide on the facts in implied contracts between parties in sexual intercourse, ranging from whether the woman was appropriately using a contraceptive method, to the man's understanding of the woman's contraceptive preparedness. As Levy and Kingsley have suggested, a formula might be devised whereby a number of factors, including the statistical probability of conception entailed in the supposedly employed method and the possibility that deception might have been detected, would be considered to determine the extent of the man's liability.[10] Such approaches, based on the introduction of a contract philosophy into the sexual relationship—a concept not foreign to recent developments in family law—would require a considerable increase in responsibility on the part of the courts.

Irrespective of the contractual issue, other considerations include whether the man's responsibility should be limited in cases in which the outcome, vis-à-vis conception, can never be certain. Even if he believes he is relatively safe from the possibility of conception, it may be argued that he voluntarily enters into a situation with known possible consequences. Furthermore, it is also possible for the man to take contraceptive precautions regardless of his understanding of the woman's action. Given these factors, it is questionable whether the man's freedom of choice with regard to parenthood is as limited by the woman's claims as was argued in the New York case.

Another factor is the viability of placing the entire burden of personal and economic support on the woman. Since many cases of out-of-wedlock birth require public support, the issue of limiting paternal liability becomes academic, as the public is not likely to subsidize the right of fathers who allege deception to avoid all responsibility for child support. To the extent possible, the responsibility for support will be placed on the father when a known causal linkage exists, irrespective of his intent to procreate, before it is placed on the public. Even when public support is not an issue, the persistence of inequalities between men and women may preclude the political feasibility of exempting men from child-support responsibility for such a reason.

Discussion

The situations described represent a linkage between social, scientific, and legal issues with regard to the threshold issues of the child-support obligation. Sexual intercourse, the potential biological consequences of which include the conception and birth of a child, has attained new status in all of those areas. This status has had numerous outcomes, among which is a suggested reconsideration of the issue of who should support a child that is unintended. Men and women, both of whom are presumed to be rational and responsible, may now, to a greater extent than ever before, engage in sexual activity. Sexual relations are no longer restricted to marital relationships in which the parties intend conception and birth to be an outcome of their union. Were such an outcome to result among the unmarried, it is viewed as a mistake.

Society accepts such an understanding, but it also has affirmed that the parties who made the mistake accept the consequences: the financial support of the child. This situation, which has always been the case when the parents were legally married, has been extended to parents of children born outside those bounds. Thus, the status of biological parenthood, the facts of which can now be fairly accurately ascertained, is still seen as the governing factor in determining who is to support a child.

It is this status view of child-support liability assignment that has recently come under question. The possibility of two biologically capable individuals engaging in sexual intercourse with a substantially reduced risk of conception, by virtue of technological developments in contraception, or birth, by virtue of the legal availability of medically safe abortions, has produced a situation in which people feel they have a right to engage in sex without fear of the biological consequences. Under this view, sex that is engaged in for purposes other than procreation may be viewed from the standpoint of a contract between the parties. That contract, stated or implied, entails the acceptance of responsibility for the consequences should they ensue accidentally, either through the failure of the contraceptive method or because an abortion is not possible. It is this contract view that some believe should supplant the status view of the liability for the support of a child.

If there is to be an effective contract, each part must act in good faith. When one party intentionally fails to uphold his or her end of the contract, the other party may arguably be held blameless. While the application of this principle is fairly obvious in the second situation, it also applies to the first. In what has sometimes been termed recreational sex, there is an implicit assumption that neither party intends pregnancy to result. When contraception has not been used, a medically safe and legally permissible abortion in the first trimester of pregnancy is a possibility. Should the woman (since the Supreme Court has decided that the decision is solely hers) decide not to have an abortion, it may be argued that she has violated her end of the contract, thereby relieving the man of his responsibility.

The introduction of a contract analogy into the consideration of liability for support of an unintended child raises an interesting possibility, primarily for men: that a father may not be automatically assumed to be financially liable for the support of his child, whether married to the child's mother or not. There is no logical reason why a married man should not be extended the same privilege of worry-free, recreational sex as an unmarried man. Although this situation stems equitably from a variety of social, legal, and scientific developments, the advisability of carrying those arguments to their logical extreme is questionable.

As most observers would readily agree, trends in births among unmarried women, especially teenagers, make it unlikely that the need for support for these children at a level that is greater than their mothers alone can provide will evaporate. The sources that may be legally required to provide such assistance include the biological father and the public. In light of this choice, as was demonstrated in the New York family court decision, the father will be held liable, regardless of the merits of the contract determination, before the public is required to contribute. The capitulation of the court in this matter can be viewed as deference to political realities or evidence of insecurity as to the fairness and objectivity of the basic decision. Perhaps more important than the issue of parental rights and responsibilities is the consideration of the child's welfare. Programs such as Planned Parenthood have long emphasized the benefit of the intention of procreation in two persons producing a child. Nevertheless, it is a fact that many children, born both within and outside marriage, are not intended at the time of intercourse. Such laws as the Uniform Parentage Act are designed to protect the rights and responsibilities of all children and parents, regardless of the latter's marital status or procreative intent. These laws seek to reinforce the linkages between parents and children in terms of support, inheritance, and access to custody and visitation.

The heart of such linkage is the verifiable biological association between intercourse and birth. Other means of insemination aside, the primary cause of conception is sexual intercourse. In the normal biological course of events, sexual intercourse is a necessary, though not a sufficient, condition to conception. Furthermore, it is arguable that few men (since men are the major focus of the deception and abortion arguments) can be forced to engage in intercourse without taking appropriate precautions. Therefore, a responsible man who willingly engages in an act with known possible consequences may be fairly held responsible for those consequences. If he is not willing to be held responsible, he should not commit the act in question.

These considerations suggest that the status view should still govern the answer to the question of who should support a child. The principal focus of a contract concept should not rest upon a man's liability for support but upon highlighting his responsibility for ensuring that conception not occur, either by abstaining from intercourse or by taking necessary contraceptive precautions for his own protection.

Notes

1. Harry Krause, *Illegitimacy: Law and Social Policy* (Indianapolis: Bobbs-Merrill, 1971), pp. 1-5.

2. George Swan, "Abortion on Maternal Demand: Paternal Support Liability Implications," *Valparaiso University Law Review* 9 (1975): 243-246.

3. Martin Levy and Elaine Duncan, "The Impact of *Roe vs. Wade* on Paternal Support: A Constitutional Analysis," *Family Law Quarterly* 10 (Fall 1976):185-189.

4. Swan, "Abortion"; Levy and Duncan, "Impact," pp. 193-194.

5. Levy and Duncan, "Impact," p. 200.

6. Ibid., p. 201.

7. "Misrepresentation of Birth Control Use Not Actionable Tort," *Family Law Reporter*, June 3, 1980, p. 2525.

8. "Man Deceived into Fathering Child Has Only Qualified Duty to Support," *Family Law Reporter*, October 27, 1981, pp. 2884-2885.

9. Ellen Goodman, "Reluctant Paternity—A Case Waiting to Happen Happens," *Los Angeles Times*, November 13, 1981, sec. II, p. 7.

10. Martin Levy and Jessica Kingsley, "Fundamental Issues of Child Support" (Paper presented to the Wisconsin Workshop on Child Support Enforcement, University of Wisconsin, Madison, April 1981).

6

Reconsidering the Basic Premises of Child Support: A Comment on *In Re Pamela P.*

John J. Sampson

The Decision

On October 8, 1981, one of the better-known family-court trial judges in the country, Judge Nanette Dembitz, handed down a decision of the New York family court, *In re Pamela P.*[1] The question presented was the responsibility for child support of a father tricked into siring an out-of-wedlock child. This case was of first impression in New York, and apparently the issue had been raised only once before in a reported decision.[2] The father's assertion was accorded more than a modicum of respect; perhaps this was partially accounted for by the fact that he is the famous hero figure, Frank Serpico of book and movie fame.[3] The trial court determined that the mother's deception had been fully proved. The father had requested contraception information from her prior to engaging in sexual intercourse. The mother conceded that she had not employed birth-control methods but denied that she had so represented herself. A "completely credible" witness testified that the mother had told him two months earlier that she intended to have Serpico father her child, knowingly or not. The court found that fraud and deceit was convincingly established by the mother's premeditated, deliberate, and intentional misrepresentation. It also recognized that the father was something of a willing victim and not a helpless dupe. For example, he knew that birth-control pills could be ineffective. Moreover, there was no certainty he would have refrained from sexual intercourse had he known the full extent of the risk. But the court stated that "the requirement of proximate causation is inapposite in considering the relevance question here; the law has accepted standards for right conduct between individuals."[4] The mother's intentional deceit barred her from receiving financial benefit at the expense of the father except in exigent circumstances involving extreme hardship to the child (not present in the facts shown).

Judge Dembitz then embarked upon an extraordinary constitutional adventure. *Eisenstadt* v. *Baird*[5] and *Carey* v. *Population Services*[6] were cited as guarantees for all men and women to choose contraception and to avoid procreation. Next, *Shelley* v. *Kramer,* a 1948 case refusing court enforcement for racially discriminatory restrictive covenants in housing, was cited for the proposition that a state court may not sanction the private act of an individual if an official action with similar impact would be unconstitutional.[7] Therefore, so the logic went, because the state could not prevent the use of contraceptive methods by the parties, the mother's deceptive act was analogous in effect. The father was deprived of full and true freedom of choice by her deceit. According to Judge Dembitz, child support ordered under these circumstances would condone and encourage such conduct and place the "imprimatur of the state" on private interference with reproductive choice. "Since a support order . . . would raise constitutional doubt under the Fourteenth Amendment, it should be denied."[8]

Reevaluating Basic Premises

The connection between the birth-control issues of *Pamela P.* and the post-hoc determination fixing the exact obligation of child support is not readily apparent. Combining these issues seems to require a series of logical connections of highly dubious validity. Except for this case, existing law throughout the nation provides a ready answer regarding the extent of support liability of parents: both biological parents are, or can be adjudicated to be, liable for child support. The use of, or failure to use, birth-control methods is irrelevant. Until the 1980s the question had never been asked. In today's world, no traditional belief is immune from challenge.

What Interest Does the Child Have in the Litigation?

The most pernicious aspect of *Pamela P.* is its implicit assumption that a battle over child support is litigation purely between the parents. Although obligatory deference was allegedly given to the best interests of the child, examination of the decision reveals that this was little more than lip-service. As is almost universally true in the United States in cases of this nature, the child was not a party. A party to a lawsuit must receive notice and be given an opportunity to be heard. A custody battle often might be viewed as a version of a contest over "title" much as litigants contest title to real property or personalty. The passive object of this lawsuit often has little or nothing to say about his fate. Absent independent representation for the child by an attorney *ad litem*, it is likely that in most analogous situations, the child's interests will be subverted and his claims, apart from the claim of the mother, will be ignored.[9] How else can the result be explained? Here there were three individuals involved in the lawsuit; two wrongdoers and an innocent person who had claims against both wrongdoers. The traditional notions of common sense and justice must be turned inside out for the degree of wrongdoing between the two guilty individuals to effect the claims of the innocent victim. Nonetheless, this is the result.

In sum, the first and most important lesson of the *Pamela P.* decision is oblique but compelling: the basic premises that the child's interest will be served by the adversarial clash of his parents is fundamentally defective. Only through independent representation can the child be fully protected from conflicts of interests with both parents.

What Are the Duties of Child Support?

Traditionally, the primary obligation of child support was placed squarely on the father: "The primary obligation of maintenance of the children was on the husband and father . . . [who is] most capable of discharging it."[10] Although this sexist anachronism persists to this day in the laws in some states, a mutual duty has become the norm.[11] As a Texas court noted several years ago:

> The duty of the spouse[s] to support their minor children is equal. This does not mean, however, that the court must divide the burden of support of the minor children equally between the parties. The court's order . . . should reflect a due consideration of the respective abilities of the spouses to contribute . . . . [Texas law] does not require that the parents make mathematically equal contributions for the support of their children. It only provides that each parent has the equal obligation, in accordance with his or her ability, to contribute money or services which are necessary to the support of his or her children.[12]

It seems to be a basic premise of courts ordering periodic child-support payments that the obligation will be fulfilled. Support obligors, however, do not always dutifully and diligently make their payments; quite the converse is true.[13] This assumption was present in *Pamela P.*; the validity of the premise in the particular case is no more or less predictable than in any other case. The only real distinction between this case and more conventional litigation is that the father advanced a new and novel excuse for not wanting to pay. His rationalization, if not his attitude, differed, but the root issue in *Pamela P.* was only a minor variation on an all-too-familiar theme: The father did not want to pay child support because he would rather keep the money and spend it on himself.

The *Pamela P.* court did recognize a limited duty of paternal support under the circumstances. First, the opinion constructed an elaborate, albeit absurd, rationale supposedly based on the U.S. Constitution, which relieved the father of his support obligation. Such an absolutist position could result in politically unfortunate consequences: the child could become a public charge while the father escaped all financial liability. To avoid this, it was necessary to build in an escape clause to offset, at least partially, the newly created excuse for nonsupport. The court accomplished this by creating yet another constitutional right. Candidly admitting that "research reveals no prior consideration of parental obligation from a constitutional standpoint," the court created such a right.[14] That is, the duty of parental support was found to be but a "reciprocal of the fundamental constitutional right to beget and raise children. . . . Accordingly . . . enforcement of the parental support duty is a compelling state interest that justifies diminution of the right to free procreative choice."[15]

Thus did the court find two constitutional rights where none had existed before. The most newsworthy aspect of the decision is the new grounds for escaping support. Of far more significance is the finding that parents have a constitutional duty to support their children. Thus *Pamela P.* could well stand as an important first step in reversing an unduly narrow view of the duties of citizens. Perhaps demanding individual responsibility from parents will lead ultimately to an acceptance of societal responsibility for the well-being of our children in a natural progression. This latter will require a thoroughgoing revision of the *parens patriae* doctrine. To date the state has merely claimed the right to intervene in the family unit when necessary to protect children from harm.[16] Future generations may rightly view this narrow commitment as barbaric.

In sum, this second aspect of *Pamela P.* holds promise for future development. Unfortunately, the actual result of the decision belies the promise. In fact, the court's acceptance of the father's excuse to avoid his support duty overshadows any value the opinion might otherwise have. The challenge to the basic premise that the state has a compelling interest in parental support gets lost in the shuffle.

Does Child Support Support the Child?

As is usually the case, *Pamela P.* assumes that the child-support order will have a meaningful impact on the child. Actually, even if the obligor faithfully obeys the order, the average paying obligor does not come close to supporting the child with the periodic payments made. The most cursory research into the cost of raising a child leads to the conclusion that typical support payments fall far below the total amount needed for a reasonable level of support in modern America. For example, the well-publicized Bureau of Labor Statistics budget for a typical family of four discloses substantial costs of child rearing. In 1979, a four-person family lower-budget level was $12,500, the intermediate-budget level was $20,500, and the higher-budget level was $30,300. Although a fully proportionate share might not be allocated to the support of the two children in the model family, at least a 25 percent to 33 ⅓ percent share should be assigned as costs of the children. Typical child-support orders for two children, then, would average $3,000 to $10,000 as projected by the various budget levels.[17] Further, even the Internal Revenue Code considers that a noncustodial parent paying $1,200 per child, per year is presumptively paying only one-half of the total cost of support. Apparently Congress determined that, as of 1976, an average of approximately $2,400 would be a fair estimate of the yearly cost to raise a child in the United States.[18] This estimate may still be in the ballpark, but only at the lower-income levels.[19] Typical support orders in the nation do not approach this level on average,[20] and the actual payment experience is much more dismal.[21]

Is There a Constitutional Right to Recreational Sex?

Although not well articulated, the *Pamela P.* decision seems to segregate sexual conduct into two separate and distinct categories: deliberately procreative and recreational. Seemingly, both classes are entitled to separate, independent, constitutional protection. The mental intent of the actor, perhaps secretly held, may well determine the responsibility for the consequences of the act. The basic premise is that intercourse for the purpose of procreation is entirely different from intercourse purely for the purpose of pleasure. And the intended results of this recreational sex should be risk free to an innocent participant. Such a conclusion follows if no distinctions are recognized by the law or by society between spouses, live-in lovers, parties to an affair, or those engaged in a series of one-night stands.

Previously the law has made distinctions on such traditional bases. Apparently Judge Dembitz regards such views as stereotypical and old-fashioned. If recreational sex is to be risk free, it is only a small jump to an action in tort if an innocent receives a communicable disease. The risk free atmosphere of the brave new world proposed will certainly keep the courts busy.

Is Any Remedy Appropriate in Cases of Procreative Deceit?

Perhaps in a perfect world, society would choose to resolve all conflicting claims to establish the comparative rectitude of multiple wrongdoers. But even then, given the hypothetical concept of perfection, such dispute resolution should be determined in an independent action severed from the claim of an innocent victim. In the present context, if the father can prove fraud against the mother, his claim could serve as an offset against her claim for her own support. Because the child-support claim is not for the mother, who acts only as a conduit for the receipt of support payments for the child, that aspect of the litigation will be unaffected. In the event of a public outcry demanding a legal remedy to the conception by deceit and fraud problem, resort to tort law can be made available.

The choice must be made by judges or legislators to protect fathers who claim they are defrauded. There is even a possibility that day may almost be upon us. For example, even before *Pamela P.,* a California intermediate appellate court was presented with this same argument and rejected it by the closest of margins. In *Stephen K.* v. *Roni L.,* the court accepted, *arguendo,* the assertion that the mother had tricked the father into siring the child.[22] The court found no cause of action by a divided vote of three to two. Incidentally, the alleged mother-tortfeasor against whom damages was sought was represented by a legal services office. Given that fact, obviously the claim for damages was only intended to be an offset against the father's obligation to pay child support. The court further acknowledged that a tort had been committed, at least in the sense that a civil wrong had occurred between the parties. But the court then went on to state:

> It does not lie within the power of the judicial system, however to remedy all human wrongs. . . . Although [the mother] may have lied and betrayed the personal confidence reposed in her by [the father], the circumstances and the highly intimate nature of the relationship wherein the false representation may have occurred, are such that a court should not define any standard of conduct therefore.[23]

Notes

1. 7 Fam. L. Rep. (BNA) 2784 (N.Y. City. Fam. Ct. 1981).

2. Stephen K. v. Roni L., 105 Cal. App. 3d 640, 164 Cal. Rptr. 618 (Dist. Ct. App. 1980).

3. Detective Serpico was the subject of a well-known biography: P. Maas, Frank Serpico (1973), and a film, *Serpico* (Paramount, 1974).

4. 7 Fam. L. Rep. (BNA) at 2784.

5. 405 U.S. 438 (1972).

6. 431 U.S. 678 (1977).

7. 334 U.S. 1, 18 (1948).

8. 7 Fam. L. Rep. (BNA) at 2784.

9. *See* A.B.A. National Institute, Advocating for Children in the Courts (1979); Ardagh, *California Code Section 4606: Separate Representation in Dissolution Custody Proceedings,* 14 U.S.F.L. Rev. 571 (1980); Redeker, *Right of an Abused Child to Independent Counsel in the Role of Child Advocate in Child Abuse Cases,* 23 Vill. L. Rev. 521 (1978); Speca,

Representation for Children in Custody Disputes: Its Time Has Come, 48 U. Mo. K.C. L. Rev. 328 (1980); *cf.* Berdon, *A Child's Right to Counsel in a Contested Custody Proceeding Resulting from a Termination of the Marriage,* 50 Conn. B.J. 150 (1976); C. Bryant, *Advocating for Children in Emergency Removal Proceedings,* in Protecting Children Through the Legal System 3 (1981).

10. Fulton v. Fulton, 52 Ohio St. 229, 39 N.E. 729, (1895).

11. H. Krause, Child Support in America 4 (1981).

12. Friedman v. Friedman, 521 S.W. 2d 111, 115 (Tex. Civ. App.—Houston (14th Dist.) 1975) (citing as support, J. Sampson, *The Texas Equal Rights Amendment and the Family Code: Litigation Ahead,* 5 Tex. Tech. L. Rev. 631, 636-637 (1974)).

13. D. Chambers, Making Fathers Pay: The Enforcement of Child Support (1979); D. Chambers, *Men Who Know They are Being Watched: Some Benefits and Costs of Jailing for Nonpayment of Support,* 75 Mich. L. Rev. 900 (1977).

14. 7 Fam. L. Rep. (BNA), 2875.

15. *Id.*

16. H. Clark, Law of Domestic Relations 572 (1968).

17. "Autumn 1979 Urban Family Budgets," in U.S. Dept. of Labor, Bureau of Labor Statistics, News (Apr. 30, 1980).

18. 3 I.R.C. §152(e)(2)(B).

19. Edwards, *Users Guide to U.S.D.A. Estimates of the Cost of Raising a Child,* Family Economics Review (Winter 1979).

20. H. Krause, Child Support in America 10-18 (1981).

21. *Id. passim.*

22. 105 Cal. App. 3d 640, 164 Cal. Rptr. 618 (1980).

23. *Id.* at 643, 164 Cal. Rptr. at 620.

**Part III
The Parental Duty to Support:
Establishing Standards for
Child-Support Payments**

7 Developing Normative Standards for Child-Support Payments

Isabel V. Sawhill

As rising marital instability and out-of-wedlock childbearing put an increasing proportion of children at risk of living in a single-parent family, the question of financial responsibility for children takes on new urgency.[1] Analyses of the living arrangements of children suggest that if current trends continue, by 1990 about one-third of all children will live with a divorced parent before they reach age eighteen.[2] Support may be provided by the custodial parent (in the form of earned or unearned income), by the absent parent (in the form of child support), or by the state (in the form of public assistance). Presumably public assistance is a last resort, to be used only when private resources are insufficient. But at what point does this occur? What are the joint and separate responsibility of parents for their children's economic welfare?

Several studies have now documented the extent to which absent parents support their children.[3] In an early study done at the Urban Institute, we examined data for a nationally representative sample of about five hundred eligible female-headed families.[4] We found that about 60 percent of absent fathers contributed to the support of their children and that the average amount paid, among those who paid any, was around $2,000 per family (in 1973 dollars).[5] Support payments represented 12 percent of a father's predivorce earnings across a broad range of the income spectrum.[6] In another study, based on data collected by the Census Bureau in the spring of 1976, it was found that about one-fourth of divorced, separated, remarried, or never-married women with children received child-support payments, and the mean amount received was $2,430 per family.[7] Still another study, based on a supplement to the April 1979 Current Population Survey (CPS), found that about 35 percent of such women received payments and that the mean amount received was $1,800.[8] What can we conclude from these data? Are fathers paying a fair share of the costs of raising their children? And what is the mother's financial obligation?

The answers to these questions can come only from looking at the facts in a broader, more explicitly normative, context. The purpose of this chapter is to provide that context by examining the adequacy and equity of

Funding for this study was provided by the U.S. Department of Health, Education and Welfare and by the Ford Foundation.

79

child-support payments. It attempts to develop a set of standards against which actual performance can be evaluated. Ultimately all standards must be based on value judgments. The primary objective of the current effort is to make these judgments and their implications clear, thus providing a framework for a more-intelligent debate on these matters. A subsidiary, and admittedly more controversial, objective is to move toward some substitution of administrative rules for judicial discretion in establishing support obligations. There will always be individual circumstances and disagreements that will need to be adjudicated, but there should also be some general principles that might be applied, at least initially, in a more-routine fashion. In many cases, administrative determination of support obligations might be acceptable to all parties concerned. Moreover, such a procedure would probably be cheaper, potentially more equitable, and less damaging emotionally than the current case-by-case, court-based review of parental responsibilities. Thus, this chapter attempts to specify a set of rules that might be used in establishing child-support obligations. No claim is made that these formulas can entirely replace individual judgments. At a minimum, they could prove to be useful to the judicial decision-making process within which there currently appears to be no consistency.[9]

I start with a simple model of parental responsibility for child support derived from a set of explicit normative premises. This model is gradually refined as the discussion proceeds and some formulas for determining child support and alimony obligations are developed.

Then I apply alternative child-support formulas to data for a small sample of divorced and separated couples. This exercise makes it possible to compare the actual support being received by children to what one would expect them to receive on the basis of the set of standards previously developed. The purpose is to show how sensitive support payments are to different normative assumptions and to indicate, in a rough way, the possible improvements in the income position of female-headed families that might result from a more generous flow of private transfers. In addition, these improvements are shown to have important implications for the needed level of public transfers.

The Conceptual and Normative Basis for Child Support and Alimony

The Basic Model

The basic model is premised on two principles:

1. After a divorce, children should be supported at a level commensurate with their standard of living before divorce, if this is consistent with principle 2.

2. Where a reduction in standards of living is required because two households must now be supported instead of one, there should be equal sharing of available resources between the two households after adjustments for differences in family size.

Both of these basic principles are debatable. The first principle assumes that it is desirable to maintain as much stability as possible in a child's life—that deprivation is better defined in relative than in absolute terms. It is consistent with the prevailing view of experts in the fields of law, economics, and psychology. Although these experts agree that it is important to protect a child's relative standard of living, it could be argued that it is some minimum standard of need that should be met. According to this view, the primary obligation of the absent parent is to keep the children out of poverty or to provide them with certain essentials commonly found in family budgets. Beyond this, any allocation of resources to a former family would be at the discretion of the absent parent.

Many discussions of support obligations are not explicit on the issue of whether absolute or relative needs should be the guiding principle. For example, the regulations issued in connection with Title IV-D of the Social Security Act (creating new incentives for the states to obtain child support from the absent parents of children on welfare) are quite vague on this question. The regulations read as follows:

a. There shall be a formula to be utilized by the IV-D agency in determining the amount of the support obligation pursuant to 302.50 when there is no court order covering the obligation. Such a formula must take into consideration the following criteria:

1) All earnings, income and resources of the absent parent including real and personal property;
2) The earnings potential of the absent parent;
3) The reasonable necessities of the absent parent;
4) The ability of the absent parent to borrow;
5) The needs of the child for whom the support is sought;
6) The amount of assistance which would be paid to the child under the full standard of need of the State's IV-A plan;
7) The existence of other dependents; and
8) Other reasonable criteria which the State may choose to incorporate.[10]

The welfare savings associated with the application of a relative-needs standard are significantly greater than those associated with the application of an absolute needs standard.

The second principle recognizes that parents have rights, which must be balanced against the rights of the children. Equity in this situation is defined generally as a proportionate sharing of available resources between a supporting parent and his or her children in cases where they are no longer living together.

To these two normative principles we add a fundamental assumption: it is difficult to provide one standard of living for the children and another for the custodial parent if they are all sharing the same household. It is assumed, in other words, that children must have an adult caretaker who shares with them food, living space, and certain other amenities and that the welfare of the children is not entirely independent of the welfare of the custodial parent. Although certain types of expenditures might be specifically targeted to meet the children's needs (such as clothes, education, or health care), and other types of expenditures that could be excluded as being purely adult oriented, such distinctions are probably not very feasible or sensible in the typical case.

The difficulties of coming up with a direct estimate of the costs of children are laid out in a recent article by Jacques van der Gaag. The estimates of the percentage increases in income needed to support a first child and still maintain the same level of economic well-being vary from 6 percent to 35 percent.[11] Where individual circumstances dictate, however, some modification of the formulas developed below might be called for. If one accepts this assumption, one must also face the possibility of windfall gains for the custodial parent.

The next step is to embed these two basic principles (the relative-needs principle and the equal-sharing principle) in a series of formulas. For the moment, it is assumed that there is no income other than earned income, that there is no asset accumulation, no child care expenses for employed parents, no income taxes, and no economies of scale in family living.

If Y_{nc} = earnings of the custodial parent, Y_c = earnings of the custodial parent, N = number of children, and T_{cs} = transfer of income from noncustodial to custodial parent, then

$$T_{cs} = Y_{nc} - \frac{Y_{nc} + Y_c}{N + 2}. \tag{7-1}$$

The first term on the right-hand side of the equation indicates how much income the noncustodial parent has, and the second term indicates how much he or she is entitled to keep for his or her own support. For example, if a couple has two children and each parent has $10,000 in income, this formula implies that the custodial parent should receive $5,000 from the noncustodial parent. T_{cs} is not allowed to take on negative values; that is, transfers from the custodial parent to the noncustodial parent for child support do not make sense. After the transfer, each household would have equal per capita income.

Adjustments for Economies of Scale

An immediate objection to formula 7-1 will be its failure to take into account economies of scale in family living. It represents the extreme position of assuming no economies of scale. At the other extreme, one could assume full economies of scale—that is, that all costs of maintaining a household are fixed and none vary with the number of people to be supported, in which case there would be zero transfers in the example. Intermediate between these two extremes is a range of assumptions about the nature and magnitude of economies of scale that need to be explored.

There is no simple way to measure precisely how economic needs vary with family size. Undoubtedly there are some efficiencies from sharing resources within a single household. Although expenditures on food, clothing, education, and medical care are likely to vary substantially with family size, the cost of consumer durables and even housing is much more invariant. Economic need may also be related to the age and sex of household members. Past attempts to measure these differences have produced what are usually called *equivalence scales,* an index showing how income would need to vary in order to provide similar standards of living for families of different sizes and types. One technique used in deriving equivalence scales is to assume that families spending the same proportion of their income on some basic commodity, such as food, have equivalent living standards since it had been observed that increases in real income generally lead to a reduction in the fraction of income spent on food or other necessities. This standard, however, has been criticized as being arbitrary and overly sensitive to the basic commodity chosen for deriving the scale. A second technique, and one that is used in constructing the official poverty lines, is to calculate the food needs of different types of families (based on nutritional requirements) and to apply a multiplier to account for nonfood needs. The equivalence scale derived from this procedure is reproduced in table 7-1. This scale is also somewhat unsatisfactory since nutritional standards are not well understood and since there is no reason why nonfood needs should vary with family size in the same way as food needs. In fact, since expenditures on food probably increase more with family size than do other types of expenditures, it is likely that this scale underestimates economies of scale or the cost savings experienced by larger households. In the absence of any better empirical evidence on economies of scale, the index in table 7-1 will be used as a basis for calculation, but its possible biases should be kept in mind, as should those of the similar equivalence scale used later in this chapter in table 7-5.

The importance of the assumptions made about economies of scale is demonstrated in table 7-2, where three different child-support formulas have been developed around three different assumptions. Each formula has

Table 7-1
Equivalence Scale Derived from Official Poverty Indexes

Female Head of a Nonfarm Family with:	Needs Relative to a Single-Person, Male-headed Nonfarm Family (P)
1 child under 18	1.26
2 children under 18	1.49
3 children under 18	1.89
4 children under 18	2.19
5 children under 18	2.43
6 or more children under 18	2.96

Source: U.S. Department of Health, Education and Welfare, *The Measure of Poverty* (Washington, D.C.: Government Printing Office, 1976), p. 80.

then been used to calculate the financial liability of the noncustodial spouse in the fictional example where there are two children and each spouse has earnings of $10,000 per year. The results are quite sensitive to the assumptions made.

We can generalize the results thus far by stating that

$$T_{cs} = Y_{nc} - \frac{Y_{nc} + Y_c}{k} \qquad (7.2)$$

where assumptions about economies of scale are embedded in the factor k. Then for convenience, we can rewrite formula 7.2 in the form:

$$T_{cs} = (1 - 1/k)\, Y_{nc} - (1/k)\, Y_c. \qquad (7.3)$$

Adjustments for Child-Care Expenses

In the example where both parents were assumed to have $10,000 of income, no adjustment was made for the fact that the mother is likely to have child-care expenses if she is working and earning this much income. These expenses will vary with the number and ages of the children and other factors. Whatever the case, it seems appropriate to deduct such expenses, if any, from the custodial parent's income and to enter only the net income figure in the child-support formula since this type of work-related expenditure falls on only one parent and may be sizable. Moreover, without such

Table 7-2
Implications of Different Assumptions about Economies of Scale

Formula	No Economies of Scale	Full Economies of Scale	Using Equivalence Scale from Table 7-1
	$T_{ca} = Y_{nc} - \dfrac{Y_{nc} + Y_c}{N+2}$ (1)	$T_{ca} = Y_{nc} - \dfrac{Y_{nc} + Y_c}{2}$ (2)	$T_{ca} = Y_{nc} - \dfrac{Y_{nc} + Y_c}{1+P}$ (3)
Child-support liability (T_{ca})[a]	$5,000	$0	$1,968
Resulting income position of custodial spouse	15,000	10,000	11,968
Resulting income position of noncustodial spouse	5,000	10,000	8,032

Note: T_{ca} = transfer of income from noncustodial to custodial parent; Y_{nc} = income of noncustodial spouse; Y_c = income of custodial spouse; N = number of children; P = equivalence scale (estimated needs of a female-headed family with N children relative to a male living alone).

[a] Y_{nc} = $10,000; Y_c = $10,000; N = 2. The value of P comes from the equivalence scale in table 7-1 and equals the estimated needs of a female-headed family with N children relative to a male living alone. We could also calculate the estimated needs of a male-headed family with N children relative to a female living alone, which would make both P and T slightly higher (since men are presumed to need more food).

a deduction, mothers would be encouraged to choose unpaid (and untaxed) work in the home over paid (and taxed) work in the market. Thus, we now have

$$T_{cs} = (1 - 1/k) Y_{nc} - (1/k) (Y_c - C). \qquad (7.4)$$

This provision will have the effect of increasing the support payment by some fraction (equal to $1/k$) of total child-care expenses. If, in the example, the mother spends \$2,000 per year on child care, then she would receive a support payment of \$1,000 in the full-economies-of-scale model (formula 7-2 in table 7-2). Both parents would end up with \$9,000 in income after deducting both child-support and child-care expenses.

Adjustments for Income Taxes

Currently, child-support payments are not deductible for the payor or considered taxable income to the recipient (although alimony is), giving rise to a tax-induced substitution of alimony for child support. Moreover, this probably leads to a lower level of overall support than would otherwise prevail since every dollar of child support costs $1/(1 - t)$ dollars in before-tax income (where t is the tax rate). The apparent justification for current practice is that parents are not permitted a deduction for the full costs of supporting their children in an ongoing marriage and therefore should not be permitted one after a divorce. Parents are, of course, permitted a personal exemption for each child, but this rarely, if ever, equals the full cost of support. This ignores the advantages of income splitting to married couples, however.

Under current income-tax laws, married couples are permitted to split their income and use the split half as a basis for selecting the tax rate to apply to their total income. The tax rates used in this calculation will be lower than what they would have been in the absence of splitting because of the progressivity of the rate structure.

Without delving into the merits of this system, a somewhat separate issue, it is worth pointing out that a decision to use postsupport instead of presupport income as a basis for taxation would be consistent with the current tax treatment of family income. Support payments would be deducted from the payor's income and added to the recipient's income in calculating each household's taxable income. Thus, postsupport income would continue to be more or less equally split between the two households, depending on the equivalence scale used. Assuming, equally divided income, however, total tax liability would decline somewhat since the noncustodial parent would now be eligible for the lower rates applicable to single individuals and the custodial parent or the still-more-favorable rates applicable to heads of households. Given the decline in ability to pay that maintaining two households usually entails, some might consider this an equitable outcome.

To summarize, then, support payments probably should be based on the before-tax income of each parent, but taxable income should be defined as income net of any support paid or received.

Preserving Incentives to Work

The amount of earned income available to either spouse will depend on work effort of each. But the necessity of providing child support, or the expectation of receiving it, may remove incentives for one or both parents to maximize their earnings. To the extent that a father must share any increase in his income with his former family, his incentive to improve his economic status will be diminished. Similarly, a mother who knows that her support payment will be reduced as her own work effort increases may also have little incentive to contribute to her own or her children's support.

In the formula developed thus far, the incentives for both spouses to work are positive, but there is some tax on earned income. Note that by using equation 7.4 we can derive the support tax rate (that is, the rate at which support payments change as the income of each spouse changes) as follows:

$$\Delta T_{cs}/\Delta Y_{nc} = 1\ 1/k$$
$$\Delta T_{cs}/\Delta Y_{c} = -1/k.$$

Since k is always greater than one, $1/k$ is always less than one, and the support tax rate on both incomes is less than 100 percent. However, the larger k is, the higher the tax rate on the father's relative to the mother's income, and only in the extreme case of the full-economies-of-scale model does the mother's tax rate rise to the level of the father's tax rate (at which point both equal 50 percent). Thus, work incentives for the father are more likely to be preserved where substantial household economies are built into the payments formula. If, on the other hand, female labor supply is more wage elastic than male labor supply, keeping a low tax rate on female earnings could be considered desirable.

Adjustments for Postdivorce Changes in Economic Status

The discussion thus far implies that child-support payments are to be adjusted to reflect any change in income that may occur after a divorce. This principle is embedded in current law. Moreover, in an ongoing marriage, children share in whatever shifts in economic well-being their parents experience. The question is whether these changes should similarly affect their standard of living after a divorce. In other words, should current values of Y_c and Y_{nc} be used in calculating T_{cs} in equation 7.4? (In the case of decreases in income, the question is moot; current values will have to be used.)

In the usual case, where the mother has custody, improvements in her economic status will automatically improve the standard of living of the children in her care. An increase in the mother's income will not lead to a dollar-for-dollar increase in the children's standard of living, however, since there would be some downward adjustment in the support obligations of the father. Increases in the father's income, on the other hand, might be treated somewhat differently for a number of reasons. First, the principle that children be supported at a level commensurate with their standard of living before the divorce, so as not to disrupt their lives, implies that downward adjustments in support payments are to be avoided but that, by the same token, upward adjustments are not required. Second, unlike parents in an ongoing marriage, divorced spouses have no opportunity to enjoy the full benefits of family life unless they remarry. Fathers, especially, are denied these benefits since they do not live with their children. This argument assumes that children bring pleasure to both parents and that this pleasure varies directly with opportunities for child-parent interaction, leading to clear-cut benefits for the parent with custody. However, if the satisfactions of spending time with children are positive but eventually diminish with increased interaction, then it is not necessarily true that mothers gain more enjoyment than fathers from traditional custody arrangements, especially if the father has generous visitation rights. Moreover, the presence of children in the household may reduce the mother's chances of ever remarrying. Third, there are joint consumption benefits associated with spending income on other family members, but they are only available to individuals who share the same household. Trips to Disneyland or steak dinners may be as enjoyable for a mother as they are for her children. These three considerations may argue for using income at the time of divorce rather than current income as a measure of the absent parent's ability to pay.

Finally, it could be argued that neither current income nor income at the time of divorce or separation adequately captures ability to pay. Some attention may also need to be given to potential income or to an expected career path. There is evidence, for example, that consumption patterns are geared more closely to permanent or lifetime expected income than to current income. This might be accomplished by allowing upward (downward) adjustments in income as long as the absent parent's current income was below (above) expected income for an individual with his age, education, and occupation.

As a general principle, we are left with three alternatives. The first is using the noncustodial parent's current income as a measure of ability to pay. The second is using income (or full-time earnings) at the time of divorce as a standard. (In this case, some adjustment for inflation in the years following divorce would be needed to preserve the children's real standard of living.) The third alternative is more complicated but not unfeasible. It would require developing tables of expected earnings by age, education, and occupation to use as guidelines for whether a postdivorce adjustment in ability to pay was called for.[12] Before adopting any of these alternatives, several additional issues need to be discussed.

Adjustments for the Economic Needs of a New Family

The formulas developed thus far have implicitly given priority to the absent parent's first family. Although some people will view this as appropriate, others will consider it to be inequitable. The regulations issued in connection with the new federal legislation on child support, for example, specify that all legal children should be treated equally in deciding how to distribute parental resources.[13] Figure 7-1 suggests how such a principle might be implemented. Basically the adjustment involves redefining k as the needs ratio between the custodial and noncustodial households after adjusting for the presence of any new children in both households. The income of a new spouse enters into the formula indirectly by determining what proportion of the support of any new children can be borne by their other parent (the new spouse). For example, if a man remarries a woman whose income is equal to his and they have one child, he is considered responsible for one-half of the support of the new child, and this increases the family size used in the calculation of a needs standard by one-half of a person (see figure 7-1).

Thus far, the discussion has centered around meeting the needs of children and ensuring that the costs of meeting these needs are equitably shared between both parents. It has been suggested that the special benefits that may be enjoyed by the mother as a custodial parent argue for some modification of the payments formula in the direction of a reduced burden for the father. This reduction in the father's support rate could come either from an increase in his own earnings with no change in his support obligations or from a dollar-for-dollar reduction in his support obligations as the mother's income position improves. However, a dollar-for-dollar reduction in his payments with increases in her income, although it would maintain the children's standard of living, would also remove all incentives for the mother to work or to maximize her earnings. It is especially important to preserve work incentives for the mother, given the possibility that she may remarry and stop working altogether. It has also been suggested that all

A. Schematic representation of separation and remarriage

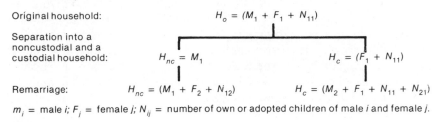

m_i = male i; F_j = female j; N_{ij} = number of own or adopted children of male i and female j.

B. Alternative child-support formulas

(1) Priority to first family

$$T_{cs} = (1 - 1/k)\, Y_{nc} - (1/k)\,(Y_c - C)$$

where $k = 1 +$ $\dfrac{\text{needs standard for } F_1 + N_{11}}{\text{needs standard for } M_1}$

(2) Equal treatment for all children

$$T_{cs} = (1 - 1/k)\, Y_{nc} - (1/k)\,(Y_c - C)$$

where $k = 1 +$ $\dfrac{\text{needs standard for custodial household of size } m}{\text{needs standard for noncustodial household of size } n}$

where $m = F_1 + N_{11} + r_c N_{21}$

where $n = M_1 + r_{nc} N_{12}$

where r_c = the proportion of the custodial household's income contributed
by the custodial spouse (F_1)

where r_{nc} = the proportion of the noncustodial household's income contributed
by the noncustodial spouse (M_1)

Figure 7-1. Adjusting for the Economic Needs of a New Family

children should have equal claim on parental income, necessitating an adjustment (in k) for children born in subsequent marriages. If we incorporate these two modifications into equation 7.4, we then have

$$T_{cs} = (1 - /k)\, Y_{nc} - 1/k\,(Y_c - C) \tag{7.5}$$

where Y_{nc} = noncustodial parent's income at time of divorce and $k = 1 +$ adjusted needs standard of custodial household/adjusted needs standard of noncustodial household. Note that support obligations do not vary with remarriage unless remarriage indirectly affects one or both spouse's work behavior or childbearing. As we have already seen, incentives to work are built into the formula, and although disincentives to further childbearing might be considered desirable, such disincentives usually penalize children as well as their parents. Use of formula 7.5 would also provide incentives for the noncustodial parent to reduce artificially his or her income in the year prior to divorce. To avoid this problem and to attempt to get a measure of normal income, it might be appropriate to use earnings averaged over the past three (or more) years. Also, to the extent that both parents have children in their care, either because there is a shared custody arrangement or because one or both spouses has a new set of children, then some (weighted) average of Y_c and $\overline{Y}_c$ or of Y_{nc} and $\overline{Y}_{nc}$ might be used as measures of ability to pay.

We now need to consider the case of a mother who devotes, or has devoted, some significant proportion of her time to homemaking and child care. Just as there are indirect consumption benefits associated with being the children's caretaker, so too there are indirect costs if this necessitates being out of the labor force or constantly juggling career and family responsibilities. These costs are, or should be, the basis for what is usually called alimony or spousal maintenance. Unlike child support, alimony is not intended to protect the standard of living of children but to compensate an ex-wife for her prior investment in child care and homemaking. However, it is not always possible to separate them into two discrete or unrelated payments.

A Digression on the Rationale for Alimony

In an ongoing marriage, both husband and wife share the costs of a decision to allocate some or all of the wife's time to nonmarket work. Their joint money income is reduced by both the immediate loss of the wife's salary (current opportunity costs) and the impairment of her later career prospects (long-term opportunity costs). In a utility-maximizing framework, such a decision may be entirely rational; that is, both parents may believe that the value of time devoted to children or homemaking compensates for the opportunity costs. In the case of a divorce, however, the wife may end up paying a disproportionate share of these costs unless some further allowance is made to compensate her for an earlier (and in some cases continuing) investment of this sort.

Whether such compensation is due the wife depends on one's view of marriage. One view is that marriage is a partnership with a lifelong commitment to another individual and a complete sharing of economic costs and rewards. Implicit in the lifelong-partnership view is the idea that the risk of divorce is small and that alimony provides a kind of insurance against this risk. Without alimony, there is no protection of the wife's homemaking investments.

A second view of marriage is that it is a limited partnership in which husbands share their incomes with their wives, but only for as long as their marriage is intact. According to this view, there is no need for alimony because women who enter a traditional marriage do so knowing that there are financial risks for them personally, and they have the choice of accepting or rejecting these risks after comparing them to the potential rewards.

In a world in which only limited-partnership marriages (without alimony) existed, the number of women willing to marry and/or devote themselves to homemaking activities might be lower than in a world where the lifelong-partnership model (with alimony) prevailed, and these women might be able to use their scarcer numbers to exact more-favorable terms from their potential spouses. The real problem arises when women agree to marry and be homemakers under the terms of the lifelong-partnership model and later discover that the limited-partnership model is in effect. The long-run solution to this problem requires that young people marry with an explicit understanding, and perhaps even a written agreement, about these matters.

Adjustments for the Long-Term Opportunity Costs of
Marriage and Child Care (Alimony)

One of the costs of raising children and of providing other unpaid services within the home is that it reduces an individual's long-run earnings potential. Since the benefits of marriage and children accrue equally to both spouses, it can be argued that these costs should also be shared on a fifty-fifty basis.

An example may help to clarify the issues in this area. Assume a marriage takes place between two people whose abilities, work experience, and educational backgrounds are identical at the time of marriage. The wife drops out of the labor force to become a full-time homemaker or mother and remains out of the labor force until the time of the divorce. The general situation is diagrammed in figure 7-2, which incorporates the following simplifying assumptions:

1. Both spouses have equal ability and human capital (such as education) at the beginning of working life.
2. Earnings increase by a fixed percentage amount for each year that an individual is in the labor force.
3. There is no depreciation or appreciation in earning ability during the years when one is out of the labor force. Ability or skills may depreciate from nonuse or from obsolescence. They may appreciate due to greater maturity or the transferability of what is learned in a nonmarket environment to a paid job, but on net balance, we assume no change.

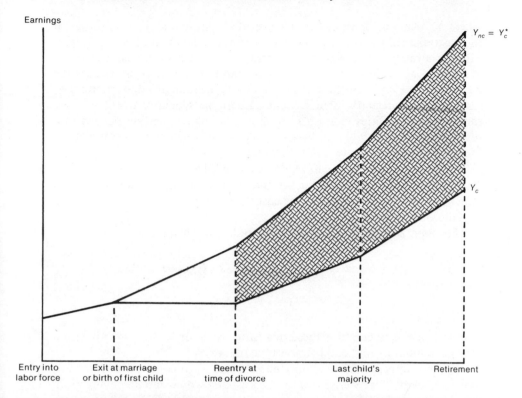

Notes: Y_{nc} = earnings of noncustodial spouse; Y_c = earnings of custodial spouse; Y_c^* = earnings of custodial spouse if she or he worked continuously. Assumes both spouses have equal ability and human capital at the beginning of working life.

Figure 7-2. Postdivorce, Long-Term Opportunity Costs Faced by Married Women

4. There is no catching-up process once one reenters the labor force, just a resumption of normal growth in one's earnings.

Modification of any of these assumptions is, of course, possible but not likely to alter substantially the nature of the argument being made here.

Based on these assumptions, the postdivorce, long-term opportunity costs faced by women are equal to the shaded area in figure 7-2. It is these costs that should be shared by their ex-husbands. (Note that there is a growing absolute gap between the earnings of the two spouses due to the cumulative effects of the husband's greater earnings and experience at the time of divorce on his subsequent income.) Specifically, annual alimony payments should be equal to:

$$T_a = 1/2 \, (Y_c^* - Y_c) \qquad (7.6)$$

where Y_c = annual earnings of the custodial spouse and Y_c^* = earnings of the custodial spouse if she or he had continuous labor-market experience. More accurately, Y_c^* represents the earnings of the custodial spouse in the absence of any role specialization within the family that compromises the labor-market success of the custodial vis-à-vis the noncustodial spouse. For example, if a husband's job determines the couple's location or if the wife's family responsibilities cause her to choose a less-demanding occupation, these choices could reduce Y_c below Y_c^*. Also the homemaking spouse might be the noncustodial spouse, in which case $T_a = 1/2\,(Y_{nc}^* - Y_{nc})$.

In the example here, we have also assumed, for convenience, that $Y_c^* = Y_{nc}$ (both spouses had equal talents and training at the beginning of their marriage). In this rather specialized case, both spouses end up with identical postalimony incomes.

To summarize the discussion to this point, we now have:

$$T_{cs} = (1 - 1/k)\,\overline{Y}_{nc} - 1/k\,(Y_c - C)$$

$$T_a = 1/2\,(Y_c^* - Y_c).$$

The next task is to combine these two formulas in order to come up with a combined alimony and child-support payment.

It is not appropriate to simply add T_{cs} and T_a to come up with a combined payment. If we were to do so, the husband would end up paying more than his share of the long-term opportunity costs of marriage and children. The reason for this is that the lower the wife's current income as a result of forgone opportunities, the higher his expected child-support payment. (In other words, $\Delta T_{cs}/\Delta T_c$ is negative and equal to $1/k$ in formula 7.5). In an analogy to the situation in an ongoing marriage, he implicitly shares these opportunity costs because they affect his liability for child support. To avoid this problem of double liability, we now need to modify the child-support formula by substituting each spouse's postalimony incomes for their actual incomes as measures of their respective abilities to contribute to the support of the children. That is:

$$T_{cs} = (1 - 1/k)\,(\overline{Y}_{nc} - T_a) - 1/k\,(Y_c + T_a - C).$$

Once this substitution is made, it is then possible to add T_a (as a measure of the husband's share of the opportunity costs represented by the difference between Y_c^* and Y_c) to T_{cs} (as a measure of how much each spouse should contribute to the support of the children). The resulting formula is:

$$T = T_{cs} + T_a = (1 - 1/k)\,\overline{Y}_{nc} - T_a) - 1/k\,(Y_c + T_a - C) + T_a,$$

which simplifies to:

$$T = (1 - 1/k)\,\overline{Y}_{nc} - 1/k\,(Y_c - C). \qquad (7.7)$$

Equation 7.7 is identical to equation 7.5. In other words, the payment of alimony is implicit in the payment of child support as long as child-support obligations are based on a proportionate sharing of the total income of both spouses. If the husband provides a dollar in alimony payments to the wife, this is exactly offset by a dollar's reduction in his child support obligations.

Once all of the children have reached majority, no more child support would be required, but the husband would continue to be liable for the alimony portion of the formula, or $T_a = 1/2\,(Y_c^* - Y_c)$ until his wife's retirement. Out of this income she might purchase her own retirement insurance or social security benefits. The husband should be required to carry sufficient life insurance to enable his alimony payment—or its lump-sum equivalent—to be paid up until his wife's retirement in case he should die before that time.

Treatment of Wealth

Thus far, it has been assumed that no property and no assets exist to be divided at the time of divorce. In reality, most couples will have some assets (in the form of both tangible property and financial wealth), as well as some liabilities. The difference between the value of their assets and their liabilities determines their net worth, which may be either positive or negative.

If each partner starts marriage with a zero net-worth position and with equal amounts of human capital, then one might argue that any net-wealth accumulation during the marriage ought to be equally divided between the two at the time of divorce. If they begin marriage with unequal endowments of physical, financial, or human capital, then some adjustment might be made for these initial differences.

Finally, in some cases, a lump-sum settlement or division of property may be based not only on past contributions to marital wealth but also on the capitalization of some or all of the expected future liabilities for child support or alimony. The only difficulty encountered here will be projecting the future values of the variables in equation 7.7 for each year and calculating their present value using some reasonable rate of interest. In theory, however, all future payments could be reduced to a single sum and this amount paid at the time of divorce if the spouse liable for such payments had sufficient liquid assets after an equitable division of existing property had been made.

Deriving Empirical Estimates of the Homemaking Spouse's
Potential Earnings (Y_c^*)

With the exception of k and Y_c^*, the values of all of the variables in equations 7.6 and 7.7 are directly observable. If the homemaking spouse is not currently employed, it may also be difficult to estimate Y_c. In this case, some measure of current opportunity cost or of last-earned income corrected for both inflation and economy-wide increases in productivity might be used. We have already discussed the estimation of k and have provided some illustrative values in table 7-1. In this section, the estimation of Y_c^* will be discussed.

Reasonable estimates of Y_c^* might be obtained by observing how long a woman has been out of the labor force (n), the rate at which earnings increase with each year of experience (r), and what the woman's current earnings are (Y_c). We can then calculate:

$$Y_c^* = Y_c (1 + r)^n. \tag{7.8}$$

For example, if a woman's current earnings are \$8,000 per year, and if she has been out of the labor force for ten years, and if earnings increase by 2 percent with each additional year of experience (other things equal), then:

$$Y_c^* = \$8,000 \, (1.02)^{10} = \$9,760 \text{ and}$$
$$Y_c^* - Y_c = \$1,760 \text{ and } T_a = \$880.$$

The value of r will tend to vary with the woman's characteristics, especially her education and age. Individuals with high levels of education tend to work in occupations that provide more on-the-job training than those with lower levels of education, and thus their earnings increase more rapidly with years of experience. (This implies more alimony for better-educated women.) In addition, there is a tendency for earnings to increase most rapidly in the early years of an individual's career and more slowly thereafter. Some empirical evidence suggests that the average value of r is about 1 or 2 percent per year.[14] It also appears that women do not receive as high a rate of return on years of experience as similarly educated men. Or to put it another way, even after adjusting for differences in experience and education, it has been variously estimated that women still earn anywhere from 20 to 40 percent less than men. This residual differential has been attributed to labor-market discrimination.[15]

The possible existence of labor-market discrimination introduces a new complication in estimating Y_c^*. In the absence of discrimination and assuming no home investments on the part of wives, men and women with the same age and education would have the same earnings, on the average. For example, to estimate potential earnings (Y_c^*) for women in the ith age and education category, all we would need to do is to look at the mean full-time earnings of men in the same age and education category. If there is discrimination, however, we would not get the same answer as if we had applied formula 7-10 to a woman's current earnings. Specifically, using the male-earnings-as-a-proxy method will always yield a higher estimate of Y_c^* than using formula 7-8 if there is any labor-market discrimination. Thus, using the male-earnings-as-a-proxy method will yield a higher alimony figure in formula 7-7 and involves "taxing" individual husbands for systemic causes of women's lower earnings. If one believes that systemic causes require systemic solutions, then this would argue for using formula 7-8 to calculate an individual husband's liability. One would have to rely on equal opportunity or other antidiscrimination laws to eliminate labor-market inequities. As long as such inequities exist, women (and children) will tend to bear a disproportionate share of the costs of divorce.

If formula 7-8 were to be widely used as a guideline for calculating alimony payments, more refined estimates of r would need to be developed. We would need to know how r varies with education, age, and other characteristics. With an increasing amount of longitudinal and retrospective data now becoming available on labor-force experience, such research should be quite feasible.

In the meantime, a few values of $(1 + r)^n$ are presented in table 7-3 for readers who may wish to use their own assumptions about the appropriate value of r and use these in conjunction with data on actual earnings (Y_c) and years out of the labor force (n) to calculate Y_c^* using formula 7.8.

Summary

Our final suggested formula for child support and alimony combined, to be used when there are minor children in the home, is:

Table 7-3
Selected Values of $(1 + r)^n$

Out of the Labor Force (n)	Assumed Rate of Increase in Earnings per Year of Experience		
	$r = 1\%$	$r = 3\%$	$r = 5\%$
5 years	1.051	1.159	1.276
10 years	1.105	1.344	1.629
20 years	1.220	1.806	2.653

Source: Union Carbide Corporation, Compound Interest Tables, (New York: Union Carbide, 1964).

$$T = (1 - 1/k)\ \overline{Y}_{nc} - 1/k\ (Y_c - C). \qquad (7.7)$$

The first term represents the noncustodial parent's share of child support. This share depends on his or her income at the time of divorce and the number of own dependent children living in each household. The second term represents the custodial parent's share of child support, which depends on her or his current income net of child-care expenses, if any, and again on the number of own dependent children in each household. The number of own dependent children depends on the extent to which support of a new child is shared with a new spouse. For example, a child whose support is shared equally with a new spouse counts as half a dependent.

Once the children have all reached age eighteen (or perhaps age twenty-one, if still in school), then alimony alone is paid according to the following formula:

$$T_a = 1/2\ (Y_c^* - Y_c). \qquad (7.6)$$

This represents one-half the difference between the wife's current earning ability and what she could have earned had she never made any investments in homemaking. Alimony payments are not based primarily on the mother's current needs or the father's current ability to pay. Rather they are an obligation growing out of the homemaker's unpaid contributions to the family. As such, they represent deferred compensation, not a private welfare payment.

Two final comments are in order. First, there will always be exceptions to any set of rules. Thus, formulas of the type used here are most useful in producing an initial estimate of parental obligations for support. Where there are special circumstances that are difficult to capture in the formulas, some modification of these obligations might be appropriate. However, the burden should be on the aggrieved parent to show why an exception is necessary.

Second, any formula is ultimately based on a set of value judgments. The normative bases for equations 7.7 and 7.8 have been explicitly laid out here. Some alternatives based on other values have also been suggested. Still other alternatives are possible. In this sense, these formulas may be viewed as a springboard for further discussion and debate.

Comparing Actual to Expected Support

Data

The data used in comparing actual to expected support are from the Panel Study of Income Dynamics, a representative survey of five-thousand

American families who were first interviewed in 1968 and have been reinterviewed each year since. From this larger sample, we have selected all those families in which a couple with children was married at the start of the panel period but subsequently divorced or separated, creating a female-headed family, or remarried women with minor children (under eighteen) in 1973. There are 127 such families. Of these, 108 are headed by females and 19 are remarried. Remarried women are included in the sample since they remain legally eligible for child support. All of the tabulations are broken out by current marital status so that they can be excluded from the comparisons where it seems appropriate. Excluded from the sample are women over sixty-two and women whose ex-spouse has died.

Because many of the men involved attrited from the sample before 1973 (about 40 percent), we do not have sufficient data to look at their current (1973) characteristics. Moreover, those remaining in the survey in 1973 are undoubtedly a biased sample.

The original sample of five-thousand families was deliberately chosen to overrepresent lower-income families, but a set of sampling weights has been used that makes the results reported here generally representative of the U.S. population.

These data are inadequate to the task at hand. Not only is the sample small, but there is insufficient information about such matters as assets, property settlements at the time of divorce, and the current income and family status of the ex-husbands in the sample. Nevertheless, the results are suggestive and illustrate what could be accomplished with better data and analysis of this sort. Since the Panel Study was continued up to the present time, it would be possible to produce a somewhat larger sample by redoing this analysis including all those families that split subsequent to 1973. The advantage of these data, relative to others now available, is that information on the characteristics and economic status of the absent parent are available.

Formulas to Be Used to Calculate Expected Support

The Community Council Formula: The federal regulations (45 CFR 302.53) issued in conjunction with Title IV-D of the Social Security Act (Public Law 93-647) of 1974 require that states devise a formula for determining the child-support obligations of absent parents when no court order is in effect. The regulations include some general guidelines that suggest that the formula should be based on the resources of the absent parent and the needs of the child in a manner that treats all children of the absent parent equitably.

In an attempt to help the states come up with appropriate formulas, the Office of Child Support Enforcement and the Social and Rehabilitation

Service of the U.S. Department of Health, Education and Welfare funded the Community Council of Greater New York to translate the general principles contained in the regulations into a more specific set of guidelines. The council's report, "Guide for Determining the Ability of an Absent Parent to Pay Child Support," proposes that states use the following procedure:

1. Calculate the absent parent's economic resources after certain allowable deductions, such as for taxes and special needs.
2. Assume that unless the absent parent's resources are above a minimum level (the Bureau of Labor Statistics' lower-level living standard for a family of the size he currently supports), he should not be asked to provide any support.
3. Require that the absent parent devote a relatively high proportion (for example, 90 percent) of his income in excess of the minimum level to support his children living in another household as long as income in the custodial family is below the minimum level.
4. Once both families have incomes above the minimum level, any of the absent parent's remaining income should be divided equally between all legal dependents and the absent parent.[16]

Here we use the council's proposals, among others, to calculate expected child-support payments. Basically, the formula is:

$$T_{cs} = 0 \qquad \text{when } (Y_{nc} - D) < M_{nc}$$

$$T_{cs} = 0.9\,(Y_{nc} - D - M_{nc}) \qquad \text{when } (Y_c - D) < M_c$$

$$T_{cs} = \left(N_{c/N}\right) Y_{nc} - D - M_{nc}) \qquad \text{when } (Y_c - D) \overline{>} M_c$$

where: D = allowable deductions, M_{nc} = the BLS lower-level living standard for the noncustodial (absent-parent family), M_c = the BLS lower-level living standard for the custodial family, N_c = dependents living in the custodial family, N = the number of dependents of the absent parent (in both families) plus one (the absent parent himself), and M_{nc} and M_c vary with family size. New spouses are counted as dependents only if they have insufficient income to support themselves at the lower-level living standard for individuals. The values of M for different-sized families, as reported by the Community Council of Greater New York, are reproduced in table 7-4.

Several features of the council formula are worth noting. First, no account is taken of the resources of the custodial parent. Second, initial priority is given to the second family. Only when that family's income is above the established minimum (see table 7-4) is any support owed to the first family.

To apply the council formula to our data, a number of simplifying assumptions must be made since we do not have sufficient information to

Table 7-4
Family Maintenance Standard, by Family Size

Family Size	Equivalence Scale	Annual Standard in 1973 Dollars
1	1.00	$3,538
2	1.31	4,626
3	1.62	5,715
4	1.92	6,803
5	2.23	7,892
6	2.54	8,980

Source: From Mignon Sauber and Edith Taittonen, "Guide for Determining the Ability of an Absent Parent to Pay Child Support" (New York: 1977), Community Council of Greater New York, (1977), p. 31. Figures have been adjusted to a 1973 price level.
Note: Based on cost of lower budget for an urban four-person family.

make the more-refined calculations that might be desirable. Specifically, data are unavailable on the absent parent's current income and family status, although there are data on his earnings at the time of divorce. Therefore, we make the following compromises:

1. The absent parent's earnings at the time of divorce adjusted for inflation but not for other allowable deductions are used as a proxy for $Y_{nc} - D$. (Note that earnings are often less than total income and that earnings are likely to rise over time, lending a downward bias to our estimates of ability to pay. On the other hand, there is no deduction for taxes or special needs as required by the council.)
2. The non-AFDC, nonalimony, and child-support income of the custodial parent is used as a proxy for $Y_c - D$. We include some types of nonearned income in this case and measure income on a current basis, again without any adjustment for taxes or special needs.)
3. Since we have no data on the absent parent's current family status, we make two alternative assumptions. The first is that he has no new dependents. The second is that he has three new dependents. The expected level of support is calculated under both sets of assumptions.

The Absolute-Needs Formula: Some favor meeting children's minimum needs without attempting to relate those needs to the standard of living enjoyed by the family prior to a divorce. The absolute-needs formula was chosen to test the implications of this view against the data.

For this purpose, we have used a simple modification of the council formula. The modification consists of setting T_{cs} equal to zero whenever $Y_c + T_{cs}$ is greater than M_c. In other words, once the custodial family has been brought up to a minimum level of living, all support obligations cease. As in the original formula, initial priority is given to ensuring the minimum needs of the second family before any support is provided for the first family. Again, we use two sets of assumptions about the father's new dependents: (1) he has no new dependents and (2) he has three new dependents.

The Sawhill Formula: The final formula to be used is based on the standards developed earlier and incorporated into equation 7-7. This formula implicitly assumes:

1. A relative- rather than an absolute-needs standard.
2. Equal sharing of support responsibilities between both parents based on ability to pay.
3. Modest economies of scale associated with living in larger households (see table 7-1).
4. Some adjustments for the benefits that accrue to the custodial parent because she lives with the children and enjoys their standard of living. (This adjustment takes the form of using the father's earnings at the time of divorce, adjusted for inflation, rather than his current earnings as a measure of ability to pay.)

Because of data limitations, some compromises have been made: earnings have been used in place of income and no adjustment has been made for taxes, property settlements, asset positions, or new dependents. Child-care costs for the custodial parents have been crudely estimated. If the child is under six, child-care costs are estimated to be $0.32 times the hours worked by the mother; if the child is six or over, the child-care costs are estimated to be $0.05 times the hours worked by the mother.[17]

Many other variations on the above formulas could have been introduced. Given the existing data limitations, however, it was felt that these represented a reasonable set to use for exploratory purposes. To recapitulate, there are a total of five formulas:

1. Council formula A (no new dependents).
2. Council formula B (three new dependents).
3. Absolute-needs formula A (no new dependents).
4. Absolute-needs formula B (three new dependents).
5. Sawhill formula (no new dependents).

Results: We can begin by looking at the amount of support actually received by the women in the sample.[18] In 1973, this amount was $1,496 for the average divorced, separated, or remarried woman with custody of at least one child under eighteen. For those with a history of receiving some support (the group that is most likely to be operating under a court award or at least an informal agreement with the spouse), the average is $2,315. AFDC recipients were receiving $303 a year, and women whose husbands were employed and in the top quartile of the earnings distribution ($11,000 in 1973 dollars) at the time of divorce were receiving $2,859. Additional evidence on amounts actually received is included in tables 7.A1 through 7.A5 in the appendix. Support includes child support and alimony.

Table 7-5 explores the support gap (the difference between expected and actual support) implied by different formulas. Both the Sawhill formula and the council formula A yield large gaps ($2,875 and $3,767, respectively), while the absolute-needs formulas yield negative gaps (− $838 and − $1,101). The numbers suggest that the current system represents a compromise between an absolute- and a relative-needs standard tilted toward the absolute end of the scale.

Any positive gap is the product of two factors: (1) the inadequacy of support awards or agreements (by some standard) and (2) the probability of noncompliance (or partial compliance) with these obligations. With these data, we cannot neatly sort out these two factors, although the relatively large gaps shown for women with a history of receiving support suggests that the first factor is not unimportant.

The support gap for AFDC recipients is relatively large and remains positive even under the absolute-needs formulas. This brings us to table 7-6,

Table 7-5
Difference between Expected and Actual Support, for Various Groups

	Formula				
Sample	*Sawhill*	*Council A*	*Council B*	*Absolute Needs A*	*Absolute Needs B*
All eligible households (N = 127)	2,875	3,767	525	− 838	− 1,101
AFDC recipients (N = 33)	2,480	1,741	203	824	23
AFDC recipients who received some support, 1969-1973 (N = 9)	3,032	3,658	1,018	1,065	− 271
Women with relatively high earning employed spouses at time of divorce (N = 19)	4,338	6,307	1,332	− 2,092	− 2,111
Women who have a history of receiving some support (N = 65)	3,102	4,481	448	− 1,563	− 1,752

Note: Negative numbers mean that actual support is greater than expected support.

Table 7-6
Potential Savings in Welfare Costs from Eliminating the Support Gap

	Formula				
Sample	Sawhill	Council A	Council B	Absolute Needs A	Absolute Needs B
Support gap among AFDC recipients	$2,480	$1,741	$ 203	$ 824	$ 23
AFDC income	$2,354	$2,354	$2,354	$2,354	$2,354
Estimated potential welfare savings as percentage of existing outlays for this group	100 +	74	9	35	1

where the findings for the AFDC population are explored in greater detail. (We are now dealing with a sample of only thirty-three people, so the evidence should not be given undue weight.)

The first line of table 7-6 repeats the support gap for AFDC recipients from table 7-5. The second line indicates the average amount of AFDC income actually received by the group in 1973. (To the extent that these averages are representative, both sets of figures can be inflated to obtain estimates of aggregate additional support that might be obtained from absent parents and aggregate AFDC costs for this group of formerly married women.) The third line is the most revealing. It indicates the potential welfare savings associated with implementation of each of the five formulas. For example, under the Sawhill formula, welfare payments could be eliminated entirely without making the recipients any worse off. In the process, some of the absent parents and their new families would undoubtedly need assistance (remembering that there is no adjustments for any new dependents), so this tends to exaggerate the potential savings. Under the council formula B, on the other hand, every father is assumed to have three new dependents and to be providing for their minimum needs before transferring anything to his former family. So an estimate of 9 percent in cost savings would seem to set a lower bound on what could reasonably be effected (ignoring additional enforcement or collection costs). It is also apparent that the results are very sensitive to the assumptions built into the different formulas, especially assumptions about new dependents. For example, the 35 percent in cost savings associated with absolute-needs formula A suggests that there would be relatively large savings if the fathers of children on welfare were required to support these children at a minimum level before taking on any new support obligations.

An alternative way of looking at the numbers in table 7-6 would be to consider the support gap as a potential supplement to, rather than as a substitute for, welfare payments. That is, instead of returning the savings to the taxpayers, they could be used to increase the incomes of the poor, either through expanded coverage of the low-income population, or more generous payments to those already covered. Assistance would, in effect, be retargeted toward those most in need where need is defined in relationship to the income of both parents.

Taking this latter perspective, table 7-7 examines the potential increases in income among female-headed families with children from eliminating the support gap. (Remarried women are excluded from this set of tabulations.) It shows that these families would be substantially better off under the Sawhill formula (27 percent higher incomes) and the council formula A (38 percent higher incomes). They would be slightly better off under council formula B and somewhat worse off under the strict application of an absolute-needs standard. Under the first three formulas (which all give attention to relative needs), the biggest percentage gains in income would accrue to women with higher-income ex-husbands (see the appendix). Not surprisingly, these same women would also suffer the sharpest drop in income under an absolute-needs formula. This finding confirms our earlier statement characterizing the current system as a compromise between meeting absolute and relative needs with emphasis on the former.

Summary: The average amount of support received by divorced, separated, and remarried women with children in 1973 was $1,496. If the standards developed in the first section of this chapter had been in effect and if the fathers involved had not taken on any new support obligations, these women would have been eligible to receive $4,371, raising their income by 26 percent. Alternative formulas incorporating other basic principles would

Table 7-7
Potential Increases in Income among Female-Headed Families from Eliminating the Support Gap

			Formula		
Sample	Sawhill	Council A	Council B	Absolute Needs A	Absolute Needs B
Support gap among female-headed families	$2,692	$3,759	$ 477	$ – 909	$ – 1,204
Average family income	$9,903	$9,903	$9,903	$9,903	$9,903
Estimated increase (Decrease) in family income as percent of current family income from eliminating the support gap	+ 27	+ 38	+ 5	– 9	– 12

have quite different effects. The results are particularly sensitive to whether an absent parent has new dependents and the priority attached to their support.

The child-support standards currently in effect appear to be a compromise between basing support obligations on the absolute and the relative economic needs of children. One reason it is difficult to be more definitive is because it is not possible with these data to determine clearly whether any perceived shortfall in private transfers is the result of inadequate standards or the result of noncompliance with established standards. Data from the supplement to the 1979 CPS indicate that 59 percent of all eligible women had child-support awards. Of those who were supposed to receive payments in 1978, 72 percent actually did, although only one-half of them received the full amount.[19]

Conclusion

There is continuing discussion of the need for welfare reform. Reform is defined largely in terms of correcting various perceived inequities in the current system. Recently these reform efforts have been constrained by attempts to modify the system within a reasonably fixed budget. Most observers have concluded that the budget constraint dooms the effort to failure since there is a natural reluctance to improve the well-being of some groups by imposing losses on others.

Within this context, the significance of the present analysis is twofold. First, it identifies an inequity that has received little attention in the past. The inequity occurs because a child's eligibility for welfare and other types of assistance is usually conditioned on only one parent's income. (About nine out of every ten children on AFDC have an absent father.) Yet the income of this second parent is rarely counted as a resource in determining eligibility or benefit levels because it is viewed as not available to the child. The result is that children with relatively low-income (but present or financially responsible) fathers are denied assistance. The inequity has been only dimly perceived because the absent parent's income has been assumed to be nonexistent or impossible to collect. The accumulating evidence, some of it in this report, is that both assumptions are false.[20]

The second point to be made is that we have identified a possible new source of funding for welfare reform: the incomes of absent parents. As indicated in table 7-6, the cost savings associated with improving the flow of private transfers to children on welfare could be substantial. Tapping into this source of funds might have the added benefit of encouraging greater family responsibility. If the breaking up of a relationship did not deprive a child of continued access to both of his parents' incomes and if all of this income were counted in determining eligibility and benefits, then there would be less opportunity for financial incentives to influence family stability.

But it is not only the low-income population that is affected. The significance of the issues we have raised go far beyond their implications for welfare reform. With divorce becoming more common, there is a need to develop more-systematic ways of allocating financial responsibility for children. This chapter has tangled with some of the difficult normative questions that must be addressed. These questions are currently being resolved in an ad hoc fashion. The process is both inefficient and inequitable by almost any set of standards. The suggestions for change advanced here are tentative; the evidence presented is less than adequate; but both point in some new directions, which remain to be explored.

Notes

1. Heather Ross and Isabel Sawhill, *Time of Transition: The Growth of Families Headed by Women* (Washington, D.C. Urban Institute, 1975); Thomas J. Espenshade, "The Economic Consequences of Divorce," *Journal of Marriage and the Family* (August 1979).

2. Paul C. Glick, "Children of Divorced Parents in Demographic Perspective," *Journal of Social Issues* 35, no. 4 (1979):176.

3. For a good overview of this evidence, see chapter 4.

4. Carol Jones, Nancy Gordon, and Isabel Sawhill, "Child Support Payments in the United States," working paper 992-03 (Washington, D.C.: Urban Institute, October 1976). See also Judith Cassetty, *Child Support and Public Policy* (Lexington, Mass.: Lexington Books, D.C. Heath and Company, 1978).

5. Jones, Gordon, and Sawhill, "Child Support Payments," p. 77.

6. Ibid., p. 106.

7. U.S. Bureau of the Census, *Divorce, Child Custody and Child Support*, Current Population Reports, Series P-23, no. 84 (June 1979), p. 3.

8. U.S. Bureau of the Census, *Child Support and Alimony: 1978* (Advanced Report), Current Population Reports, Series P-23, no. 106 (September 1980), p. 1.

9. Kenneth R. White and R. Thomas Stone, Jr., "A Study of Alimony and Child Support Rulings with Some Recommendations," *Family Law Quarterly* 10, no. 1 (Spring 1976):75-91.

10. 45 CFR 302.53.

11. Jacques van der Gaag, "On Measuring the Cost of Children," *Children and Youth Services Review* (Spring 1982).

12. For a discussion of various types of adjustment and a plea for more automatic percentage escalation of awards, see Michael E. Gossler, *Washington Law Review* 55, no. 2 (April 1980).

13. 45 CFR 302.53.

14. Jacob Mincer and Solomon Polachek, "Family Investments in Human Capital: Earnings of Women," *Journal of Political Economy* 82 (March-April 1974); Steven H. Sandell and David Shapiro, "The Theory of Human Capital and the Earnings of Women: A Re-Examination of the Evidence" (Center for Human Resource Research, Ohio State University, September 1975).

15. Ibid. Also see Sawhill, "The Economics of Discrimination against Women: Some New Findings," *Journal of Human Resources* (Summer 1973).

16. Mignon Sauber and Edith Taittonen, "Guide for Determining the Ability of an Absent Parent to Pay Child Support" (New York: Community Council of Greater New York, May 1977).

17. Richard L. Shortlidge, Jr., and Patricia Brito, "How Women Arrange for the Care of Their Children While They Work: A Study of Child Care Arrangements Cost and Preferences in 1971" (Columbus Center for Human Resource Research, Ohio State University, January 1977).

18. Jones, Gordon, and Sawhill, "Child Support Payments," p. 67.

19. Also see ibid. for more data.

20. For additional evidence, see ibid.; S. Hoffman, "Marital Instability and the Economic Status of Women," *Demography* 14, no. 1 (February 1977); Comptroller General, General Accounting Office, "New Child Support Legislation—Its Potential Impact and How to Improve It" (April 1976).

Appendix 7A

Table 7A-1
Actual and Expected Support Payments Based on Sawhill Formula

	Sample Size	(1) Average Support Received, 1973	(2) Average Expected Support, 1973	(3) Difference (2-1)	(4) Average AFDC Income, 1973	(5) Average Family Income, 1973	(6) Expected Change in Family Income, 1973 (3 as a Percentage of 5)
Total eligible households	127	$1,496	$4,371	$2,875	$ 271	$10,962	26.2%
Received some support, 1969-1972	65	2,315	5,417	3,102	53	11,113	27.9
Received no support, 1969-1972	62	0	2,461	2,461	670	10,685	23.0
AFDC recipient	33	303	2,783	2,480	2,354	6,887	36.0
Non-AFDC recipient	94	1,652	4,578	2,926	0	11,493	25.5
Received some support, 1969-1972, and AFDC recipient	9	1,241	4,273	3,032	1,221	5,928	51.1
Husband employed[a]	80	1,502	4,315	2,813	310	11,250	25.0
Husband employed at time of divorce with earnings of:							
$0-1,925	12	28	409	381	718	8,769	4.3
$1,926-6,620	25	484	1,928	1,444	760	10,354	13.9
$6,621-11,134	24	885	3,486	2,601	260	11,400	22.8
More than $11,134	19	2,859	7,197	4,338	20	12,327	35.2
Husband unemployed at time of divorce	7	347	1,768	1,421	676	9,786	14.5
Husband retired, disabled, or student at time of divorce	9	0	1,123	1,123	2,112	4,996	22.5
Husband's employment status missing	31	1,688	4,938	3,250	29	10,896	29.8
Current marital status							
Married	19	552	4,489	3,937	123	17,087	23.0
Not married	108	1,659	4,351	2,692	297	9,903	27.2

Note: All amounts are in 1973 dollars and represent averages based on 1972 sampling weights.
[a]At time of divorce.

Table 7A-2
Actual and Expected Support Payments Based on Council Formula: Husband Has No New Dependents

	Sample Size	(1) Average Support Received, 1973	(2) Average Expected Support, 1973	(3) Difference (2-1)	(4) Average AFDC Income, 1973	(5) Average Family Income, 1973	(6) Expected Change in Family Income, 1973 (3 as a Percentage of 5)
Total eligible households	127	$1,496	$5,263	$3,767	$ 271	$10,962	34.4%
Received some support, 1969-1972	65	2,315	6,796	4,481	53	11,113	40.3
Received no support, 1969-1972	62	0	2,463	2,463	670	10,685	23.1
AFDC recipient	33	303	2,044	1,741	2,354	6,887	25.3
Non-AFDC recipient	94	1,652	5,683	4,031	0	11,493	35.1
Received some support, 1969-1972, and AFDC recipient	9	1,241	3,782	2,541	1,221	5,928	42.9
Husband employed[a]	80	1,502	5,297	3,795	260	11,250	33.7
Husband employed at time of divorce with earnings of:							
$0-1,925	12	28	0	-28	718	8,769	-.3
$1,926-6,620	25	484	1,687	1,203	760	10,354	11.6
$6,621-11,134	24	885	4,452	3,567	260	11,400	31.3
More than $11,134	19	2,859	9,166	6,307	20	12,327	51.2
Husband unemployed at time of divorce	7	347	1,230	883	676	9,786	9.0
Husband retired, disabled, or student at time of divorce	9	0	609	609	2,112	4,996	12.2
Husband's employment status missing	31	1,688	5,867	4,179	29	10,896	38.4
Current marital status							
Married	19	552	4,369	3,817	123	17,087	22.3
Not married	108	1,659	5,418	3,759	297	9,903	38.0

Note: All amounts are in 1973 dollars and represent averages based on 1972 sampling weights.
[a]At time of divorce.

Table 7A-3
Actual and Expected Support Payments Based on Council Formula: Husband Has Three New Dependents

	Sample Size	(1) Average Support Received, 1973	(2) Average Expected Support, 1973	(3) Difference (2-1)	(4) Average AFDC Income, 1973	(5) Average Family Income, 1973	(6) Expected Change in Family Income, 1973 (3 as a Percentage of 5)
Total eligible households	127	$1,496	$2,021	$ 525	$ 271	$10,962	4.8%
Received some support, 1969-1972	65	2,315	2,763	448	53	11,113	4.0
Received no support, 1969-1972	62	0	665	665	670	10,685	6.2
AFDC recipient	33	303	506	203	2,354	6,887	2.9
Non-AFDC recipient	94	1,652	2,218	566	0	11,493	4.9
Received some support, 1969-1972, and AFDC recipient	9	1,241	1,142	-99	1,221	5,928	-1.7
Husband employed[a]	80	1,502	2,073	571	310	11,250	5.1
Husband employed at time of divorce with earnings of:							
$0-1,925	12	28	0	-28	718	8,769	-.3
$1,926-6,620	25	484	0	-484	760	10,354	-4.7
$6,621-11,134	24	885	1,296	411	260	11,400	3.6
More than $11,134	19	2,859	4,191	1,332	20	12,327	10.8
Husband unemployed at time of divorce	7	347	288	-59	676	9,786	-.6
Husband retired, disabled, or student at time of divorce	9	0	0	0	2,112	4,996	0.0
Husband's employment status missing	31	1,688	2,205	517	29	10,896	4.7
Current marital status							
Married	19	552	1,351	799	123	17,087	4.7
Not married	108	1,659	2,136	477	297	9,903	4.8

Note: All amounts are in 1973 dollars and represent averages based on 1972 sampling weights.

[a]At time of divorce.

Table 7A-4
Actual and Expected Support Payments Based on Absolute-Needs Formula: No New Dependents

	Sample Size	(1) Average Support Received, 1973	(2) Average Expected Support, 1973	(3) Difference (2-1)	(4) Average AFDC Income, 1973	(5) Average Family Income, 1973	(6) Expected Change in Family Income, 1973 (3 as a Percentage of 5)
Total eligible households	127	$1,496	$ 658	$ −838	$ 271	$10,962	−7.6%
Received some support, 1969-1972	65	2,315	752	−1,563	53	11,113	−14.1
Received no support, 1969-1972	62	0	486	486	670	10,685	4.5
AFDC recipient	33	303	1,127	−824	2,354	6,887	12.0
Non-AFDC recipient	94	1,652	597	−1,055	0	11,493	−9.2
Received some support, 1969-1972, and AFDC recipient	9	1,241	2,306	1,065	1,221	5,928	18.0
Husband employed[a]	80	1,502	707	−795	310	11,250	−7.1
Husband employed at time of divorce with earnings of:							
$0-1,925	12	28	0	−28	718	8,769	−.3
$1,926-6,620	25	484		−363	760	10,354	−3.5
$6,621-11,134	24	885	859	−26	260	11,400	−.2
More than $11,134	19	2,859	767	−2,092	20	12,327	−17.0
Husband unemployed at time of divorce	7	347	13	−334	676	9,786	−3.4
Husband retired, disabled, or student at time of divorce	9	0	559	559	2,112	4,996	11.2
Husband's employment status missing	31	1,688	619	−1,069	29	10,896	−9.8
Current marital status							
Married	19	552	125	−427	123	17,087	−2.5
Not married	108	1,659	750	−909	297	9,903	−9.2

Note: All amounts are in 1973 dollars and represent averages based on 1972 sampling weights.

[a] At time of divorce.

Table 7A-5
Actual and Expected Support Payments Based on Absolute-Needs Formula: Three New Dependents

	Sample Size	(1) Average Support Received, 1973	(2) Average Expected Support, 1973	(3) Difference (2-1)	(4) Average AFDC Income, 1973	(5) Average Family Income, 1973	(6) Expected Change in Family Income, 1973 (3 as a Percentage of 5)
Total eligible households	127	$1,496	$ 395	$ -1,101	$ 271	$10,962	-10.0%
Received some support, 1969-1972	65	2,315	563	-1,752	53	11,113	-15.8
Received no support, 1969-1972	62	0	88	88	670	10,685	.8
AFDC recipient	33	303	326	23	2,354	6,887	.3
Non-AFDC recipient	94	1,652	403	-2,149	0	11,493	-10.9
Received some support, 1969-1972, and AFDC recipient	9	1,241	970	-271	1,221	5,928	-4.6
Husband employed[a]	80	1,502	443	-1,059	310	11,250	-9.4
Husband employed at time of divorce with earnings of:							
$0-1,925	12	28	0	-28	718	8,769	-.3
$1,926-6,620	25	484	0	-484	760	10,354	-4.7
$6,621-11,134	24	885	484	-401	260	11,400	-3.5
More than $11,134	19	2,859	748	-2,111	20	12,327	-17.1
Husband unemployed at time of divorce	7	347	0	-347	676	9,786	-3.5
Husband retired, disabled, or student at time of divorce	9	0	0	0	2,112	4,996	0.0
Husband's employment status missing	31	1,688	357	-1,331	29	10,896	-12.2
Current marital status							
Married	19	552	42	-510	123	17,087	-3.0
Not married	108	1,659	455	-1,204	297	9,903	-12.2

Note: All amounts are in 1973 dollars and represent averages based on 1972 sampling weights.
[a]At time of divorce.

8 Setting Appropriate Levels of Child-Support Payments

Barbara Bergmann

In thinking about how high child-support payments from an absent parent ought to be, the first thought that might come to mind would probably be, How much does it cost to raise a child? The second question might be, How much can the absent parent afford to send? A third question might be, How much does the custodial parent need help? None of these questions has a short answer. The task of putting together a mathematical formula on the basis of which child-support payments in particular cases can be computed is the task of deciding how important each of these questions is and what we mean by each of them.

Suppose we were to adopt the philosophy that the purpose of child support is to pay for some fraction of the cost of the child to the custodial parent. The formula would have to be based on some measurement of those costs. As we started to think about measuring those costs in practice, it would become obvious that the term *cost* needed further definition. For example, it would not be appropriate to define cost as the amount needed to keep a child barely fed, clothed, and housed in a poverty setting. The estimate of cost would need to be based on a more-generous standard. But which? The amounts that parents spend on children obviously depend on the type of clothing, toys, sporting equipment, lessons, and vacations provided to the child, which in turn depends on the income of the household in which the child lives. So cost becomes an elastic concept. Moreover, the amount spent on the food and clothing of a child whose parents are separated will depend on the level of the child-support payments. All in all, measuring cost on which to base child-support payments seems problematical and difficult, if not downright circular.

It may be this difficulty in finding a simple, single, usable definition of cost that would be acceptable to reasonable people that has probably pushed those who have thought about normative standards (notably Sawhill and Cassetty) to move from what we might call a cost-sharing approach to an income-sharing approach.

Sawhill's formula takes the aggregated income of the custodial and noncustodial parent and, after special allowances for certain costs, which are assumed to be paid off the top, imputes a share of the remainder to each of the adults and children involved.[1] A treatment of the determination of child-support payment levels along similar lines was developed by Judith

Cassetty, who suggests as an appropriate guiding principle that child-support payments should be such as to bring into equality the living standards in the separate households of the former spouses.[2] Thus Cassetty's major principle, like that of Sawhill, can be characterized as income sharing.

One simple form of an "income sharing" formula would be

$$\begin{array}{l} \text{child} \\ \text{support} \\ \text{payment} \end{array} = \begin{array}{l} \text{father's} \\ \text{income} \end{array} - \left(\frac{\text{father's income} + \text{mother's income}}{\text{number of persons}} \right).$$

The second term on the right is the father's allotted share of the combined income of the mother and father. The formula calls for the father to turn over as child-support payment any of his income over and above his allotted share. In some applications, a child is counted as a fractional person, and taxes and certain child-care expenses may be subtracted from the incomes before the father's share is computed. In some versions, the mother's income does not appear in the formula at all; only the father shares his income, and the amount he is required to give is not affected by the size of the mother's income.

Formulas based on an income-sharing approach implicitly call for an extension into the postdivorce or postseparation period of financial arrangements conventionally thought to be appropriate when both parents live in one household. These arrangements include income pooling by mother and father, the mother's option to refrain from paid work and be supported by the father, and the sharing by the mother, the father, and the children in the life-style made possible by the pooled monies.

Formulas developed under the income-sharing approach have little chance of acceptance and implementation, and rightly so. The major problem with the approach is that the income-sharing formulas embody no presumption that the custodial mother will take paid work. The assumption that a mother has a right to stay home with her young child full time if she chooses to do so is clear to some people. Some even refer not only to a right to stay home but to an obligation to do so. We must examine the economics of this right or obligation for a single mother to be a full-time homemaker before adopting a formula that allows for that right.

When the single mother of a child works for pay, she is in a position to take care of her own expenses and to contribute part of the expenses of the child. When the mother does not work for pay, payments from outside the household must expand to cover the entire expenses of both the child and the expenses of the child's full-time caretaker. This means that the payment from outside the home to a nonworking mother must be double or triple the level of payments to a working mother, if the former and the latter are to have the same living standard. For this reason, the Sawhill formula requires a separated father to give more than half of his income to the mother of his children in the case where she chooses not to work.

Why should this opportunity not be extended to her? First, a high and increasing proportion of mothers already do work. As of March 1980, 47 percent of mothers with children under six were in the labor force and 64 percent of mothers with children six to seventeen were in the labor force. Thus the woman who wants to stay home full time is asking for a status that many other women have chosen to give up. If such a woman were to get a judge to award her support payments according to Sawhill's formula and if she were actually to collect them, she would be staying home at the cost of precluding for her former husband anything but life as a low-income single. Many would not consider this just. Thus, Sawhill's formula is not a likely candidate for the formula on which to erect our child-support reform. In too many cases it gives an answer many would find wrongful.

In the end we are thrown back to a cost-sharing formulation despite all its difficulties. One possible such formula would be

$$\text{child support payment} = \left(\frac{\text{father's income}}{\text{father's income} + \text{mother's income}} \right) \times \text{cost of child} \; .$$

How might the cost of a child be estimated? One possibility would be to try to estimate expenditures for children by single mothers at various incomes. If we did that, the cost we came up with would vary with the wage-plus-alimony income of the custodial parent. The father would then pay as child support some share of that. He might pay a share equal to his share in the sum of the incomes of the ex-spouses, as suggested in the second formula.

Another variant might be to add to the out-of-pocket costs for the child some estimate of the monetary value of the personal services given to the child by the custodial parent and to credit the mother with having made that contribution. One such formulation might be

$$\text{child support payment} = \left(\frac{\text{father's income}}{\text{father's income} + \text{mother's income}} \right) \times \text{money cost} + \tfrac{1}{2} \times \text{imputed value of unpaid personal services} \; .$$

It might be argued that a child is entitled to live at a standard appropriate to the father's income, or to a standard appropriate to the sum of the father's and mother's incomes, or to a standard somewhere between the father's and mother's. Women typically earn lower salaries than men, principally because of employment discrimination. By choosing the standard appropriate to the mother's income, we have implicitly chosen a relatively low level of child-support payment. This, however, is the only choice that makes it unlikely that monies allocated to child support will allow the mother herself a higher standard than she might have had with no child and no child support. The third formula somewhat redresses the balance.

Any income-sharing or cost-sharing formula that takes the mother's income into account will call for different payments from two fathers having the same income but having former wives with different earnings. By some definitions, such formulas would be treating men who are similarly situated differently. Perhaps for this reason some of the formulas used in practice exclude the mother's income from the calculation. Such an exclusion may also stem from the belief in the father's obligation to support the child entirely, without financial help from the mother.

Notes

1. See chapter 7.
2. Judith Cassetty, *Child Support and Public Policy* (Lexington, Mass.: Lexington Books, D.C. Heath and Company, 1978), pp. 121-133.

Developing Normative Standards for Child-Support Payments: A Critique of Current Practice

Carol S. Bruch

Recent attention to the plight of single-parent families has prompted efforts to redefine the standards that control child-support awards. Economists and judges are at work constructing tables and formulas to specify award levels for various family sizes and income levels.[1] If these efforts are to prove equitable and successful, they must be based on a principled development and application of child-support theory. How much does it or should it cost to raise children in single-parent households? What are and should be the relative contributions of the children's parents to their support and rearing? Are adjustments to the legal method for setting support needed, or is reform possible within the context of traditional support theory? This chapter examines long-standing child-support theories, discusses the issues raised by recent economic insights, and proposes a new application of existing theory that could significantly improve current practice.

The Parental Obligation to Support

Child-support law currently posits two hallmarks for support awards: the child's needs and parental ability to pay.[2] Parents are expected to supply a child's minimal needs, even at considerable sacrifice to themselves. Beyond this basic obligation, should the parents' income permit a higher living standard, the child is entitled to share in their good fortune. The parents' marital status is theoretically irrelevant, although its practical ramifications are great. For intact families, the standard-of-living rule rarely presents problems because the children share housing and amenities with their parents.[3] Following divorce, however, disputes and legal efforts to enforce the rule are common.[4]

In practice, child-support awards have rarely implemented either the goal of meeting a child's minimal needs or that of ensuring the child of the promised standard of living. Support orders are typically for less than one-half the amount needed to provide the child with even a low-cost standard of living.[5] The major financial responsibility for child rearing, accordingly,

119

falls on the custodial parent. If that parent is unable to provide this disproportionate share of the child's expenses, public funds must often fill the gap.[6] Even in less-dramatic circumstances, almost no child of divorce maintains a standard of living comparable to that of the noncustodial parent. Instead children live with their mothers in the vast majority of cases and share sharply reduced circumstances with them in the postdivorce years.[7] Their fathers, freed of many former household costs, benefit from a concomitant increase in their own living standards.[8]

These disparities, which begin at the time of divorce, have multiple causes. First, judges rarely have an accurate understanding of child rearing costs. Their misconceptions, which are reflected in the inadequate awards they enter, are shared by many. For example, middle-income parents who spent approximately 40.7 percent of their annual income to raise two children estimated their child-rearing expenses at only 14.7 percent of their annual income.[9] Further, judges frequently assume that a support award that exceeds 30 percent of a father's net income will be dishonored and reason that such orders therefore should not be entered.[10] Finally, judges seek to protect a father's financial ability to build a new life for himself, even if that future is secured at serious cost to his children and former wife.[11]

Time exacerbates the inequity. Because children's needs grow as they do,[12] the support ordered at divorce provides proportionally less of the child's needs with each passing year. At the same time, the purchasing power of the orginal order is eroded by inflation, further reducing its effectiveness.[13] And custodial parents in states that mandate child support only for minor children frequently become the sole source of parental financial support for a child's college education. Finally, each time that a support payment is delayed or missed and enforcement is ineffective, financial imbalance is increased.[14]

Further disproportion can be discerned if the parents' nonmonetary contributions to the care of their children are examined. Indeed, nonmonetary and monetary support burdens are frequently linked. A child's caretaker devotes substantial time and physical effort to the satisfaction of the child's needs. Typically, following divorce, one parent will bear far greater or sole responsibility for child-care tasks. If funds are sufficient, some duties can be assigned to housekeepers and sitters or can be minimized through the purchase of more-costly prepared foods, laundry services, and the like. For most custodial parents, however, financial resources to provide such relief are simply not available, and caretaking duties absorb long evening and weekend hours when they are not working outside the home.[15]

These dual problems of disparate financial and caretaker support contributions deserve greater scholarly attention. Public concern has focused on welfare-avoidance programs. However needed, this perspective neglects the larger problems faced by the members of postdivorce households across the socioeconomic spectrum. Fortunately, social scientists and legal scholars (primarily, although not exclusively, female) are now addressing these issues.[16] Their research has identified the plight of children and custodial parents and has shed new light on the policy implications of current practices. The reasons for their insight and willingness to confront policy are unclear. It is possible that women researchers are more sensitive to these issues because they identify with former wives rather than former husbands, and it is former wives whose needs have long been ignored. Recent psychological inquiry, however, suggests a more-subtle explanation. This research reports that women tend to view morality in terms of responsibility in personal relationships, while men's moral concerns address the rights of individuals to noninterference.[17] If this is so, female concern for interpersonal responsibility may explain mothers' greater willingness to assume the burdens of child care following divorce. A 1977 study in Los Angeles, for instance, revealed that although 57 percent of sampled divorced fathers reported that they wanted physical custody of their children at divorce, only 38 percent asked their attorneys about their chances of receiving custody, and only 13 percent actually requested custody on the divorce petition.[18] The men who requested custody were much more likely to want custody of teenage children.[19] In contrast, 96 percent of the divorced women reported that they wanted custody.[20] Clearly most, if not all, of these women asked the court for custody: 88 to 90 percent of the final decrees entered that year in Los Angeles County awarded the sole physical custody of children to their mothers.[21] Women scholars' interest in sustaining the postdivorce parental obligations of both parents may be similarly rooted in this same moral concern for issues related to interpersonal responsibility.[22] On the other hand, male moral attention to noninterference may explain both the existing judicial pattern of deference to fathers' postdivorce lives[23] and the related interest of many male scholars in justifications for minimizing, avoiding, or terminating child-support obligations.[24] Whatever the reasons, one can only hope that the newly expanded dialogue will increase our understanding of the needs and appropriate obligations of all family members after divorce.

What Does It Cost to Rear Children?

Current estimates of the costs—both monetary and nonmonetary—of providing a home for a child are woefully inadequate. For example, much of the literature relies upon spending patterns of selected families in the early 1960s (for urban and rural nonfarm estimates) and early 1970s (for farm estimates) and employs data "which did not measure family consumption that might be attributed to stocks of durables, past expenditures, income-in-kind, gifts, or the value of community services. Similarly, no account was made for the value of personal services performed by family members or for earnings given up while raising children."[25] Although these measurement tools may therefore be relevant in defining the floor below which support levels are clearly inadequate,[26] their several omissions make them underinclusive as indicators of actual costs in divided households. Far more precise data are needed.

Account must be taken, for example, of the additional child-care costs that are incurred when children live with only one adult. California sources indicate that day-care expenses alone can exhaust child-support awards,[27] leaving the custodial parent with total responsibility for all other support needs. More generally, studies must recognize that custodial parents have two sources of increased service needs. First, chores formerly performed by the noncustodial parent must now be handled in some other fashion. Second, the caretaker herself will have less time and energy to devote to household tasks if she now works longer hours outside the home. However, she may well have no resources with which to purchase relief. Data on out-of-pocket expenses in single-parent families will therefore underestimate true living costs unless account is taken of the custodial parent's dramatically increased nonmonetary service contributions. Further, the increased cost of those items she does buy, given her decreased ability to spend time on comparative shopping, is relevant and should be recognized through application of the economic concept of search costs.[28]

California data reveal that a woman with a predivorce household income of $20,000 to $29,000 must run her household one year after divorce on $6,300 per year, while her former husband has $20,000 for his household needs.[29] To state that this woman does not employ a housekeeper or gardener or purchase convenience foods is to state the obvious. A relevant inquiry must ask not only what she actually spends but also what child-care services or substitute (surrogate) services she would purchase if her household income were to permit a standard of living comparable to that of her former husband, the children's father. Of course, any transfer of additional support to her household would reduce the father's disposable income; both adjustments must be accounted for in assessing appropriate spending patterns.

Finally, the parents' contributions to their children's needs are affected by custody orders in ways that should be considered. For example, financial support awarded to a custodial parent may be based upon an assumption that the children will have permanent housing with her but will spend weekends in their father's care. This plan may entail two new kinds of support costs: travel costs and redundant costs (the costs of duplicating housing, clothing, and equipment such as bicycles and toys in the father's household). Together with a share of the children's food and entertainment expenses, some or all of these additional costs may appear in the father's budget rather than the mother's. However, if deviations from the ordered pattern occur (for example, the father's failure to exercise visitation or custodial rights), significant direct costs and caretaker responsibilities may be shifted from one parent to the other,[30] and redundant costs may disappear. This problem, which frequently arises under traditional custody patterns, will be exacerbated by joint-custody decisions if they unrealistically anticipate divided-time arrangements. Should the children develop problems in shifting back and forth between homes, or one parent become disenchanted with the inconvenience of significant child-care responsibilities, the pattern established by a joint-custody order may be abandoned. If so, any related child-support order will be similarly outdated, and increased support transfers will be needed to compensate the parent who assumes greater financial and non-financial burdens than those originally contemplated.

Even if some principled means is developed to ensure an appropriate living standard to children at the time of divorce and shifts in the temporal allocations of custody orders are avoided, the support order will nevertheless be rendered inadequate by the increasing needs of growing children and inflation. Should there be independent changes in parental living standards due to promotions, ill health, or other circumstances, existing child-support orders may be rendered even more inappropriate.

Allocating Costs between Parents

Certainly the relative poverty of households headed by women is now well known. Less well recognized are the human costs associated with this sudden plunge into poverty for many women and their children.

Wallerstein and Kelly document serious repercussions from the economic effects of divorce. First is the disruption of children's school and social lives as they move to less-costly housing.[31] Second is the decreased time for children with their custodial parent if she must increase her employment outside the home (at a time when they are also adjusting to their father's absence).[32] Third is the depletion of the mother's human resources, and, sometimes, parenting capacity, as she struggles to make financial ends meet and fulfill the weighty home and child-care functions that are her lot.[33] Finally, both the children and their mother will suffer a pervasive, enduring bitterness if their living standard is sharply inferior to that of the children's father, a frequent problem for formerly middle-class families.[34] Not yet identified and measured are the undoubtedly great societal costs of a disproportionately high number of young people who are being raised in poverty or near poverty, including the ultimate consequences for their eventual education, employment, and offspring.

All of these impacts could be eased if child-support practice were brought more closely in line with legal theory, and support costs were more equitably apportioned between the children's parents. Thus, knowledgeable writers recognize that the equal parental-support obligations imposed on mothers and fathers by gender-neutral laws require equality in the standard to be met (support for the child's needs according to the parent's ability to pay) and not mathematical equality in the parents' dollar contributions.[35]

This concept of relative ability to pay is frequently ignored or misapplied, however, when concrete proposals are made. Some proponents of joint physical custody, for example assert that no support transfers are required if children will spend equal amounts of time in each parent's household. Their approach potentially relegates the child to two highly disparate living standards, contrary to the goals of custody and support law that seek continuity and stability in children's life circumstances. It may also prompt distorted contribution levels for major purchases or expenses, such as music lessons, tuition, or orthodontic care.

Sawhill points out that children can share in their father's living standard only if the household in which they live also partakes of that standard.[36] This analysis makes both economic and human sense. If, as now, children are expected to live at the standard that their mother's income will provide, with but a few additional amenities such as private schooling, summer camp, or music lessons, these luxuries in the midst of otherwise constrained finances can be expected to foster intrafamilial tensions. Yet if the children do not share in any of the educational or cultural experiences that are appropriate to the circles in which their father moves, their relationship with him may erode in subtle yet important ways. The policies that ensure children a standard of living comparable to that of their parents are founded in basic attitudes about parenting and nurturance; to sacrifice them for the selfish interests of one parent seems inconsistent with long-standing concern for the welfare of dependent family members. So long as the parental relationship continues, so does the propriety of comparable wealth for parents and their minor children.

Many who recognize that equal dollar amounts should not be demanded of parties in unequal financial positions conclude that support costs should be allocated according to the ratios of the parents' incomes.[37] Unless this reasoning is further refined, it, too, is seriously flawed. First, relative ability to pay may not be measured by taxable income streams alone. Courts often pay inadequate attention to wealth that is held in growth assets and produces little or no cash flow, such as land, but build parental wealth as surely and significantly as income-producing employment or investments. Similarly unscrutinized are many of the company cars, entertainment expenses, and related perquisites of the self-employed. Next, once a realistic net income figure is reached, some further amount must be deducted for a parent's self-support before disposable income is identified.[38] This is necessary because of the large gap between men's and women's incomes and the resulting proportional difference in the amounts necessary for self-support. It is the ratio established by these final income figures net of the amount necessary for equivalent levels of self-support that should dictate the parties' relative responsibilities for the costs of their children's care. Failure to make this last deduction will result in an overpayment by the parent with lesser income—usually the mother.[39] Finally, even with these adjustments, the validity of this approach turns on the accuracy of the child-rearing cost figure that is used. Dollar amounts currently cited as reflecting child-support needs seriously understate the true costs of raising children, including the costs of freeing the custodial parent for employment. Further, there are virtually no data relevant to families who are capable of providing a comfortable living standard. Reliance on current materials will therefore result in placing total responsibility for all unstated or understated expenses on the shoulders of the child's primary custodian. This burden will be borne in addition to that parent's fair share of the recognized expenses. Similar disproportion will occur whenever support awards are permitted to lag behind increasing costs. In each of these instances, the unacknowledged true costs will nevertheless remain to be absorbed by the child's primary caretaker, to her relative disadvantage.

An alternate approach has been attempted by some scholars, who seek to identify that portion of a family's net income typically devoted to child-rearing expenses.[40] Once this percentage is determined, the discussion then turns to its use as a support assessment tool after divorce. The basic appeal of this approach lies in its apparent simplicity: the court need only consider the income situation of the person from whom support is sought, applying a simple percentage rather than a complex formula. Additional contributions appropriate to his or her income situation are then expected from the custodial parent, though no support order is entered, since such support occurs automatically in a shared household.

This approach shares many of the serious limitations already identified because it also relies on cost figures from studies of intact families. First, these studies incompletely measure costs in intact families. Next, their results have not been adjusted to reflect the significantly changed needs of family members after divorce. Further, the percentage approach may pay inadequate attention to differences between families of varying economic strata. Finally, and most importantly, this work ignores the goal of comparable living standards, which can be achieved only if relative incomes are considered.

Should improved tools for measuring costs in intact families be developed, however, and should a principled (normative) means be found to accommodate those results to postdivorce households (taking into account such factors as surrogate and redundant costs), this approach does meet the test of practicality. Indeed, unless courts are given access to computer technology that can make sophisticated analyses of relative income data, judges are likely to be content with general approaches that offer rough equity. Given this constraint, a thoughtfully constructed percentage-of-income test may be useful for affluent families. For those of more-modest means, however, it will inevitably pose a substantial threat that the custodial parent will bear a disproportionate share of child-rearing expenses.

The Relevance of Subsequent Mates and Children

There are sound reasons why the parent-child relationship, rather than more-transitory liaisons, should remain central to child-support policy in the postdivorce years. Stepparents or other adult household members have usually not been held responsible for child support.[41] This is based in part on the role assigned to the nuclear family by our society, and in part on a frank recognition of the undesirable features of other solutions. If stepparents were required to support their stepchildren, for example, a negative dower would be created. Rather than bringing the once-traditional dowry to marriage, a woman with custody of her children would bring financial liabilities with her, decreasing the already-impaired likelihood of her remarriage. Because disincentives to cohabitation are rapidly disappearing, it is likely that a stepparent support obligation would merely channel what might otherwise have been legally acknowledged family units into informal ones. To the extent that this would negatively affect other forms of mutual obligation, ultimate societal costs might well be increased. At base, suggestions that children look to the adult males in their household for support rather than to their fathers is but a recasting of the old gender-based notion that women and children belong to, and are the responsibility of, whatever man shares their lives.[42] Such proposals deny the legitimacy of women's and children's own identities and of claims based on their own legal and biological relationships.

On the other hand, income made available to either parent from new mates may well be relevant to an assessment of that parent's support capability.[43] Similarly, costs associated with new families may be deemed relevant to support obligations to former family members. Related policy issues are more difficult in this context, however. Should children from prior relationships have superior claims to their parents' resources? Constitutional law limits the degree to which the state may discriminate between groups of children[44] or may impinge on reproductive freedom.[45] However, because the classification in this case is not entitled to heightened scrutiny of the kind applies to discrimination based on legitimacy or illegitimacy, some latitude is clearly available to make reasonable policy-based distinctions.[46] And recent Supreme Court opinions suggest that certain burdens may be placed on a person's reproductive choices.[47] It remains to be seen whether this language applies only to impede a woman's decision not to bear children or whether it would also sustain financial disincentives for fathers who are considering more children. Reason and economic theory both suggest that the problems of inadequate support for children of multiple relationships would be alleviated if parents were discouraged from having more children unless they were capable of contributing adequately to the needs of all of their offspring. Legal theory has embraced this view as courts have held that an assumption of additional parental obligations does not justify a downward modification of an existing child-support decree. Once again, however, theory and practice frequently diverge.[48]

Changes in Employment

Possible changes in employment are a final concern for those who contemplate the fairness of support awards over time. If orders are to accurately access and maintain support at a level consistent with living standards, both favorable and negative financial changes for either parent may be deemed relevant. Other authors in this book, for example, have sometimes assumed or asserted that it is unfair to maintain support orders at previous levels if an obligor ceases to work or earns less money than at the time of the initial order.[49] Although this is certainly true for many families, closer analysis is needed.

First, there is a well-established support doctrine that imputes earnings, whether or not received, to parents at the level available to them were they to make a good-faith effort to earn. This sensible doctrine has seen frequent, effective use when threats to cease or reduce profitable employment are made in an effort to avoid or minimize support responsibilities.[50] Next, focusing exclusively on earned income omits other relevant sources of wealth from consideration: savings and other assets may permit continued support contributions, and unemployment benefits, worker's compensation, disability insurance, and pensions frequently maintain income streams during periods of nonemployment.[51] If grounds for a reduction of support do exist, prompt review of the existing order should be required so that the custodial parent can, to the extent possible, make appropriate adjustments in spending and earning behavior. Allowance of nonpayment, followed by return to payment status once the custodial parent is seemingly owed enough to justify the costs of enforcement litigation, is unconscionable. Retroactive adjustment of court orders and wholesale debt forgiveness are permitted in no other sphere. Even bankruptcy law, which permits a limited form of relief from some debts, recognizes that support obligations deserve greater, not lesser, respect than other court-established debts.[52] Fairness to both parents and their children requires that parties be permitted to rely on court orders until they are changed and that speedy access to court at reasonable cost for modification requests be available for those who find themselves unable to maintain payment under existing orders.

The Legal Framework

If the basic legal rules that allocate responsibility for the rearing of children to their parents according to the children's needs and the parents' abilities to pay are sound, how can their application be made more equitable?

First, better measures of child-rearing costs, including the costs associated with the employment of both parents outside the home, must be developed. These should be accompanied by greater consensus regarding appropriate living standards for children whose parents are capable of more than minimal support. Next, a principled allocation of these costs between the child's parents must be implemented. And finally, means must be developed for incorporating anticipated changes in children's needs and parents' incomes in a less burdensome fashion. Because an individual's earnings generally rise at a rate that exceeds price increases (due to the combined impact of merit or seniority raises and inflation-related wage adjustments),[53] this final reform could be accomplished by imposing cost-of-living adjusters,[54] which should become a standard feature of every support order. The resulting figures would more closely track those provided by *de novo* review than do the static orders of today. Of course, as under current law, modification hearings must remain available, should one parent feel that the amount imposed by this approach improperly measures the child's needs or parental ability to pay.

The courts' authority to implement such reforms is clear. Less certain is judicial willingness to confront these issues. Although courts do not have the expertise or resources to develop more-adequate measures of child-rearing costs, they are capable of incorporating the best available information into published guidelines that will determine support levels absent unusual circumstances. Current support tables, most of which have an unfortunate history of ignoring rather than implementing economic insights, may have to be developed under legislative directives if courts persist in avoiding the impartial assessment of postdivorce finances that is their charge. Similarly courts can no longer in good faith refuse to tie child-support awards to reasonable cost-of-living figures that approximate actual increased needs. Judicial protestations that such orders require impermissible predictions of the future are totally inconsistent with the well-established, yet far less defensible, judicial practice of ordering that spousal support be reduced by stated amounts at stated intervals in the future. Such orders are often supported by no more than the judge's hope that self-support will increase. Courts are involved in assumptions about the future course of economic events every time they enter a lump-sum award for wrongful-death damages or discount anticipated retirement benefits to present value. Tying child-support obligations to a cost-of-living increase is a far more precise initial order and one that also remains subject to further refinement through modification proceedings. But however compelling the logic, judicial resistance may require that this reform, too, be legislatively mandated.

In the meantime, parents and scholars should present the best available data in settlement negotiations, court proceedings, and legislative hearings until the much-needed educational process bears fruit.

Notes

1. D. Chambers, Making Fathers Pay 39-43 (1979); Uniform Domestic Relations Local Rules for Bay Area Superior Courts 15 (1979) (Alameda, Contra Costa, Marin, San Francisco, San Mateo, Solano and Sonoma Counties, California); BNA, *Practice Aid No. 13,* Fam. L. Rep. Ref. File 513:0001, 0004 (February 27, 1979); Franks, *How to Calculate Child Support,* Case & Com., 3; Holloway, *Delaware,* in A Legislator's Guide to Child Support Enforcement 21 National Conference of State Legislatures (1980); M. Day, Draft Outline—Policy and Procedures for the Determination of Child Support (April 1981) (unpublished proposed Wisconsin child-support guidelines available from Wisc. Dept. of Health and Social Services, Div. of Econ. Assistance); Hall and Family Law Committee of Seattle-King County Bar Association, Proposed Support Schedules for Children of Divorced Parents (1st draft 1973); Hall and Family Law Committee of Seattle-King County Bar Association, Proposed Support Schedules for Children of Divorced Parents (1975).

2. Uniform Marriage and Divorce Act § 309; H. Clark, Law of Domestic Relations in the United States 496 (1968); H. Krause, Family Law in a Nutshell § 18.2 (1977).

3. *But see, e.g.,* Calif. Welf. & Inst. § 903 (West 1972) (child's support owed when placed in facility by order of juvenile court); *In re* H, 2 Cal. 3d 513, 523, 86 Cal. Rptr. 76, 81, 468 P.2d 204, 209 (1970) (applying Cal. Welf. & Inst. Code § 903.1: parents must reimburse county for legal services rendered to children in juvenile proceedings); Greenspan v. Slate, 12 N.J. 426, 97 A.2d 390 (1953) (child's medical expenses).

4. *See, e.g., In re* Marriage of Aylesworth, 106 Cal. App.3d 869, 165 Cal. Rptr. 389 (1980); Straub v. Straub, 213 Cal. App.2d 792, 29 Cal. Rptr. 183 (1963) (cases requiring wealthy parents to provide private-school education for their children).

5. Seal, *A Decade of No-Fault Divorce: What It Has Meant Financially for Women in California,* Fam. Advocate Spring 1979 at 10, 11-15; Weitzman and Dixon, *Child Custody Awards: Legal Standards and Empirical Standards for Child Custody, Support and Visitation After Divorce,* 12 U. Cal. D. L. Rev. 473, 494-501 (1979).

6. 4 Survey Research Center, University of Michigan Institute for Social Research, Five Thousand American Families—Patterns of Economic Progress 7, 34, 41 (G. Duncan and J. Morgan eds. 1976).

7. Chambers, *supra* note 1, at 43-58; Survey Research Center, *supra* note 6, at 8, 17; Weitzman and Dixon, *The Alimony Myth: Does No Fault Divorce Make a Difference?* 14 Fam. L. Q. 141, 173-179 (1980).

8. Sources cited at note 7 *supra.*

9. *See* note 5 and accompanying text *supra*; Espenshade, *The Value and Cost of Children,* 32 Population Bull. 43 (1977).

10. *See* Baldus, Book Review, 78 *Mich. L. Rev.* 750, 751 (1980).

11. *See* Zablocki v. Redhail, 434 U.S. 374 (1978); Bernstein, *Shouldn't Low Income Fathers Support Their Children?,* 66 Pub. Interest 55 (1982). *Cf.* Chaps. 16, 19.

12. C. Edwards, USDA Estimates of the Cost of Raising a Child 2, 4 (1981); Espenshade, *supra* note 9, at 28-29.

13. Eden, *How Inflation Flaunts the Court's Order,* Fam. Advocate, Spring 1979 at 2; L. Weitzman, C. Bruch, & N. Wikler, *Support Awards and Enforcement,* in National Judicial Education Program, Judicial Discretion: Does Sex Make a Difference? 53-56, 90-95 (1981).

14. *See* J. Cassetty, Child Support and Public Policy: Securing Support from Absent Parents (1978); D. Chambers, *supra* note 1, at 43-58; note 6 *supra.*

15. *See* J. Wallerstein and J. Kelly, Surviving the Breakup 110 (1980).

16. *See, e.g.,* J. Cassetty, *supra* note 14; Family Policy: Government and Families in Fourteen Countries (S. Kamerman and A. Kahn eds. 1978); H. Ross and I. Sawhill, Time of Transition: The Growth of Families Headed by Women (1975); J. Wallerstein and J. Kelly, *supra* note 15; Bodenheimer, *Equal Rights, Visitation, and the Right to Move,* Fam. Advocate, Summer 1978 at 19; (1978); Bruch, *Making Visitation Work: Dual Parenting Orders, id.* at 22; Hetherington, Cox & Cox, *Divorced Fathers,* 25 Fam. Coordinator 417 (1976); Seal, *supra* note 5; Weitzman and Dixon, *supra* note 5; L. Weitzman, C. Bruch & N. Wikler, *supra* note 13.

17. Saxton, *Are Women More Moral than Men?,* 1 *Ms.* 63-64 (1981) (interview with Professor Carol Gilligan concerning Gilligan's forthcoming book, In a Different Voice).

18. Weitzman and Dixon, *supra* note 5, at 517-518.

19. *Id.* at 517 n.127.

20. *Id.* at 517.

21. *Id.* at 503.

22. *See, e.g.,* chapters 1, 7, 8, 15.

23. *See* note 11 *supra* and accompanying text.

24. See chapters 16, 19.

25. *Supra,* note 12, at 9.

26. *See* D. Chambers, *supra* note 1, at 43-45; Seal, *supra* note 5, at 13-14; Weitzman and Dixon, *supra* note 5, at 494-500.

27. J. Emerson and Bay Area Child Care Project, Children's Council of San Francisco Report (Dec. 1980); L. Weitzman, C. Bruch, and N. Wikler, *supra* note 13, at 78.

28. *See* Stigler, *The Economics of Information,* 69 J. Pol. Econ. 213, 216, 223 (1961).

29. Weitzman and Dixon, *supra* note 7, at 174.

30. *See* Bruch, *supra* note 13, at 41-42.

31. J. Wallerstein and J. Kelly, *supra* note 15, at 183.

32. *Id.* at 42-43.

33. *Id.* at 42, 108-110, 155-157, 185-186.

34. *Id.* at 22-23, 150-152, 172, 185-186, 230-231.

35. H. Clark, Cases and Problems on Domestic Relations 601-602 (3d ed. 1980); H. Krause, *supra* note 2, at 201; Brown, Emerson, Falk, and Freedman, *The Equal Rights Amendment: A Constitutional Basis for Equal Rights for Women,* 80 Yale L.J. 871, 944-946 (1971). *Cf.* Orr v. Orr, 440 U.S. 268 (1979) (spousal support).

36. *Cf.* chapter 7.

37. *See, e.g.,* chapter 8; Franks, *supra* note 1, at 4-9. *Cf.* Smith v. Smith, 290 Or. 675, 626 P.2d 342, 346-48 (1981).

38. H. Holloway, *supra* note 1; M. Day, *supra* note 1.

39. L. Weitzman, C. Bruch and N. Wikler, *supra* note 13, at 13-16, 69, 70, 72, 73.

40. Hall and Family Law Committee of Seattle-King County Bar Association, two studies cited at *supra* note 1. These unpublished works rely on T. Espenshade, The Cost of Children in Urban United States 26 (1973) (Population Monograph Series No. 14, University of California, Berkeley, Institute of International Studies).

41. H. Clark, *supra* note 2, at 188-189; H. Krause, *supra* note 2, at 217-219.

42. Chapter 19.

43. *In re* Marriage of Fuller, 89 Cal. App. 3d 405, 152 Cal. Rptr. 467 (1979) (income of obligor parent's nonmarital partner relevant); *cf.* Gammell v. Gammell, 90 Cal. App. 3d 90, 93, 153 Cal. Rptr. 169, 171 (1979) (income of obligor's new spouse relevant in spousal support case).

44. *See* Trimble v. Gordon, 430 U.S. 762 (1977); Gomez v. Perez, 409 U.S. 535 (1973); Weber v. Aetna Casualty, 406 U.S. 164 (1972); Levy v. Louisiana, 391 U.S. 68 (1968) (classification based on legitimacy).

45. Skinner v. Oklahoma, 316 U.S. 535 (1942); *cf.* Buck v. Bell, 274 U.S. 200 (1927) (sterilization nevertheless ordered).

46. *Contra,* chapter 16.

47. *See* Harris v. McRae, 448 U.S. 297 (1980) (Medicare may fund childbirth without funding abortions). *See also* Poelker v. Doe, 432 U.S. 519 (1977) (county hospital need not provide abortions).

48. *See, e.g.,* Wilson v. Howard, 266 Ala. 636, 98 So. 2d 425 (1957); Warren v. Warren, 218 Md. 212, 146 A.2d 34 (1958); Crosby v. Crosby, 272 N.C. 235, 158 S.E.2d 77 (1967). *But see* Berg v. Berg, 116 R.I. 607, 359 A.2d 354 (1976); Steinkamp v. Luthjens, 370 So. 2d 655 (La. App. 1979).

49. *See* the views expressed in chapter 16.

50. *See, e.g.,* Pencovic v. Pencovic, 45 Cal. 2d 97, 287 P.2d 501 (1955); Meagher v. Meagher, 190 Cal. App. 2d 62, 11 Cal. Rptr. 650 (1961).

51. *See, e.g., In re* Marriage of Loehr, 13 Cal. 3d 465, 531 P.2d 425, 119 Cal. Rptr. 113 (1975).

52. "A discharge in bankruptcy shall release a bankrupt from all of his provable debts . . . except such as . . . (7) are for alimony due or become due, or for maintenance or support of wife or child. . . ." 11 U.S.C. § 35 (1970).

53. Eden, *supra* note 13, at 5.

54. *See In re* Marriage of Stamp, 300 N.W.2d 275 (Iowa 1980).

**Part IV
Social and Emotional
Implications of the
Economics of Divorce**

10 Bread and Roses: Nonfinancial Issues Related to Fathers' Economic Support of Their Children Following Divorce

Judith S. Wallerstein and
Dorothy S. Huntington

The noncustodial father maintains a significant and long-lasting psychological presence in the lives of his children in the postdivorce family. Whether this presence is reinforced by continued visiting over the years or reinforced, sometimes more powerfully, by absence or abandonment, he remains influential, often beyond his own awareness or expectation.

Although child support is unquestionably one of the major strands in the relationship between fathers and children during the years following divorce, its relevance to the other aspects of this important relationship has been relatively unexamined. Traditionally, economic analysis and psychological analysis have remained separate from each other despite the complex interweaving of economic and psychological factors within the fabric of family life. As a result, the multifaceted interaction of economic and psychological factors in family life and family relationships within the intact as well as the divorced family urgently awaits analysis and understanding. As a specific result, efforts to examine the workings and consequences of current child-support policy with reference to the economic and psychological benefit or detriment of children in the postdivorce family have been severely hobbled.

We propose in this chapter to cross the lines between these two fields of inquiry in order to examine the convergence of economic and psychological factors in the financial support that the father provides for his children during the postdivorce years and to illuminate some of the psychological consequences of the different patterns of child support for the children within these families. The following questions have guided us. (1) To what extent do parent-child or former spousal relationships influence levels of child support? Are fathers who visit their children more likely to support them, and if so, at what levels and for how long? Is child support primarily related to the predivorce or postdivorce father-child relationship? Does the prior or

Funding for this study was provided by the San Francisco Foundation and the Zellerbach Family Fund.

ongoing relationship between the divorced adults influence patterns of support? To what extent does remarriage or need or other circumstance of the mother affect patterns of support? (2) What characteristics of the father are related to child support? Does the psychological status of the father, his educational attainment, or his social role as remarried husband or new stepparent influence support of the children of his prior marriage? (3) To what extent and in which ways does the father's fulfillment or nonfulfillment of his economic obligations affect the child's overall psychological, social, or academic adjustment? Are children aware of support issues and how do they regard these within the context of the family relationships? How, if at all, does the father's economic support affect the child's attitudes and feelings toward himself or herself, toward the father, and perhaps toward adult society? (4) Finally, what recommendations for public policy ensue from these conclusions?

Findings from a psychological study of 60 divorcing families with 131 children drawn from a northern California population—largely, but not entirely, white and middle class—provided the context for this preliminary analysis. The advantage that the study provides is in the detailed illumination of the adjustment of children and adults and the patterning of the postdivorce family relationships that have been observed closely at several checkpoints over the five-year period following the marital breakup, as well as the detailed observation of attitudes, feelings, and overall psychological and social adjustment of the adults and the children over the same time span. The major disadvantage is the fact that the sample is small and is not intended to be representative. The findings, of course, may be representative of middle-class populations elsewhere throughout the country. Psychological findings from the project have been remarkably congruent with a comparable study of a middle-class population in Virginia, and it may be that child-support patterns will have a similar generalizability to comparable socioeconomic populations in other places.[1]

The economic findings are set within a specific context. In California and in many other states, the court sets levels of child support at the time of the final decree, but the order is not enforced vigorously unless the divorced wife applies for welfare or following successful litigation initiated by the divorced wife. In the main this policy relies on voluntary compliance with the court order over the postdivorce years until the child becomes legally adult at age eighteen.

Father-Child Relationships in the Postdivorce Family

Fathers and children encounter formidable difficulties in establishing and maintaining the part-time parent-child relationships outside the home, separate from the shared experiences of daily family life. We have reported earlier as a major finding that the predivorce relationship did not predict the relationship between father and child that later evolved.[2] Notwithstanding the change of the postdivorce relationship, the importance to the child's development of continued contact with the father remained undiminished over the years and was significantly correlated at the five-year mark with good psychological adjustment of both boys and girls of varying ages. The psychological significance of this continuing tie between father and child did not diminish following the marital rupture and, despite the passage of time, remained a powerful factor in the child's self-esteem. Conversely, psychological dysfunction and clinical depression in both boys and girls were associated with disrupted or erratic, unreliable contact with the non-custodial father during the postdivorce years.[3] Thus, the psychological dependence of the child on the continuing relationship with the father is co-equal with economic dependence.

The California Children of Divorce Study

The data presented derive from a longitudinal, clinical investigation that began in 1971 and ended in 1977. The objectives of that project were three-fold: (1) to examine the divorce-related experience of children and adolescents, tracing their developmental course from the marital rupture through the five-year aftermath; (2) to study patterns of continuity and change in the parent-child relationship over the same time span; and (3) to delineate the adult's experience and adjustment, including the early years of the re-marriage, when this occurred. Each of the 131 children and adolescents from 60 families, together with their parents, were studied intensively during a six-week period close to the time of the decisive separation. Each family member was reexamined again at eighteen months and once again at five years after separation.

The Population of the Study

By the end of the five-year period, two of the families were lost to followup, and two others remarried each other and were dropped from the sample. Additionally for the analysis of the material presented here relating specifically to noncustodial fathers' economic support of their children, one father-custody family with two sons was dropped. The final sample, then, consists of sixty-four girls and fifty-three boys from fifty-five families. The children who were lost from the sample did not differ significantly from those remaining in sex, age, or original assessment of psychological function.

Their families did, however, fall into a somewhat lower socioeconomic group than the families remaining in the sample. All of the children were in the legal and physical custody of their mother. Those youngsters who had already reached their eighteenth birthday by the time of the five-year followup have been included in the analysis, but child support has been defined here as extending through high school graduation or the child's eighteenth year.

Socioeconomic Data

In their socioeconomic distribution, the families reflected the population of the county in which they resided. Of the sixty original families, 88 percent were white, 3 percent were black, and 9 percent were interracial with one Asian spouse. They were largely, but not entirely, within the middle-class range. In accord with the Hollingshead two-factor index, 23 percent were in class I, 20 percent in class II, 28 percent in class III, 18 percent in class IV, and 10 percent in class V at the time of the marital breakup. The average age of the men at separation was 36.9; the average age for women was 34.1. They had been married an average of 11.1 years prior to the final separation. The couples averaged 2.2 children per family.

Characteristics of the Children

Prior to the family disruption, all of the children in this study had reached appropriate developmental milestones. They were performing at age-appropriate levels in school, and none had been referred for psychological or psychiatric intervention. They represented, therefore, a group somewhat skewed in the direction of psychological health, or at least psychological normalcy, a population at considerable variance from the usual clinic population on which most other divorce studies have been based.

Many of the children had been well cared for during the troubled marriage. At least 25 percent had enjoyed the care of two devoted parents, and at least 30 percent had parents who were fully in accord regarding child-rearing practices and values. At the far end of the spectrum, 40 percent of the father-child relationships were impoverished or overtly psychopathological. And at least 25 percent of the children were poorly cared for by abusive or disinterested mothers.

Economic Changes Following Divorce

Five years after the marital breakup, half of the men continued to be solidly upper or middle class. Their social and economic status and standard of living were either unchanged from the position achieved during the marriage or showed the increase expectable with greater seniority in their field. At the other end of the spectrum, 25 percent of the men were economically unstable, including those who had not worked regularly during the marriage, as well as those who had deteriorated psychologically following the divorce. Several of the men who earned less than they had during the marriage had voluntarily sought a less-competitive life-style and less-demanding employment following the divorce.

By contrast, most of the women who had started from a position of economic privilege during the marriage were poorer at the five-year mark than they had been earlier. Only 20 percent of the women enjoyed economic security five years later. Thirty-three percent of the women were engaged in a daily struggle for survival, including chronic worry over meeting monthly bills. Additionally, 7 percent were newly on welfare. The reduction in the standard of living was especially difficult for those women who had enjoyed the economic and social privileges of being wives of professional men. A significant number of these women failed to adjust to the change and remained socially withdrawn and depressed for many years.

At the five-year mark, 75 percent of the women were gainfully employed in full-time jobs outside the home as compared with the 34 percent who had worked full time outside the home during the marriage. Many of the working women were frustrated with their poor earnings and sought in vain to improve their financial position. About half of the 25 percent of the women who did not work full time suffered chronic or recurrent physical or psychiatric dysfunction.

Patterns of Child Support

Four different patterns of child support could be distinguished at the five-year mark, as follows. Group I had twenty fathers of forty-four children who during the entire five-year postseparation period had provided reliable and adequate support in accord with court order or arrangement at the time of the decree. In the main, they had done so unfailingly, but even when there had been occasional lapses, sometimes of several months' duration, families were included in this group if the overall intention of the father was to abide by his obligations in full and had done so with expectable regularity. Group II had fourteen men with twenty-seven children who throughout the same five-year period had provided child support that was customarily not reliable or full in relation to court-ordered support or agreement but that had remained during the entire five-year period at a sufficient level to be an economically important contribution to the rearing of their children. Group III had twelve fathers with twenty-seven children whose support during that time was erratic, poor, and essentially made no important economic contribution to the planning for or rearing of the children. Group IV had nine fathers with nineteen children who had provided nothing or almost nothing in support of their children during the five years.

These patterns of support are considerably higher than other reports.[4] The higher level of support may reflect the greater affluence of the fathers in our population. It may also reflect bias in the original sample in the direction of greater commitment by the fathers to their children. Although we were not impressed with any special commitment of fathers to their children at the time of the marital rupture and, in fact, were concerned with the high incidence of alcoholism and psychiatric illness among fathers, our judgment may have been unduly harsh.

Perhaps the high degree of continuing support reflects our brief counseling (two to four interviews) at the time of the marital breakup that was geared in part to reversing the attitude of many of the men that they were no longer needed by their children and had been rendered both expendable and replaceable by the divorce. A significant number of men remembered our counsel vividly and at the five-year interviews told us of their efforts to remain in close touch with their children.

Socioeconomic Characteristics of Fathers and Child Support

There were significant socioeconomic and employment differences among the men in each support category. Men in groups I and II were employed full time. Several men in group III were employed only part time, and one was unemployed. In group IV, half of the men were employed full time and the remainder were unemployed. Similarly, most of the men in group I enjoyed a higher socioeconomic status. Those in group IV were at the lower end of the socioeconomic scale. Nevertheless, there was a wide economic scatter in all of the groups, which reflected the presence of many confounding factors.

Educational attainment prior to the divorce did not correlate significantly with membership in each of the four support groups. This may have reflected the downward economic course and changed life-styles of professional men in groups II and III who were earning well below their capacities. Additionally, several men in groups III and IV had graduate degrees, but alcoholism and other psychiatric difficulties prevented their full economic use of these academic achievements. A comparison of the four economic support groups yielded no significant differences in the number of children in the family or in the age of the children at the time of the breakup or their gender.

Child Support and the Relationship between
the Divorced Adults

Child support was not significantly associated with the relationship between the divorcing adults at the time of the marital rupture or at the five-year mark. There were friendly relations between the divorced adults, as well as those that were hostile in each of the four support groups. Some men who paid full support flew into a rage at the mention of their former wife's name. Others who spoke kindly, even lovingly, of their wives provided no support. Nor was there any relation between support patterns and communication frequency between the adults. The amount of communication varied widely but did not link to different support patterns.

There was no significant relation between the extent of the postdivorce litigation betwen the divorced adults and child-support patterns. Litigation occurred among approximately one-third of the families in each of the four groups. There was, however, a difference in the content of the legal dispute. Visitation was more likely to be litigated among families where child support was higher, while litigation over money occurred more often among the poorly supported families.

Child Support and the Circumstances of
the Former Wife

Child support at the five-year mark was not significantly related to the attributes of the mother: her emotional stability or instability, her happiness or her unhappiness, her health or ill health, her social isolation or social involvement, her employment or remaining at home. The mother's circumstances were essentially of no influence on the support patterns, even among divorced adults who called each other at emergencies or helped each other in crises. Only the economic success of the mother was relevant and led to diminished child support. Thus, women who successfully entered the job market on their own following the divorce and outdistanced their husbands economically were likely to receive less support for their children. Women's economic failure or economic need did not appear to influence fathers to increase their support, however.

Child Support and Remarriage

Economic support of the children was unrelated to single or remarried status of either men or women, nor was it related to the presence or absence of a lover or series of lovers for either spouse, or to the social isolation of either spouse.

The presence of stepchildren or natural children in the father's remarriage or live-in relationship did, however, significantly diminish support for children of the prior marriage. In part, this decline reflects the economic burden of supporting two family units. Nevertheless, the decline in support following the presence of children in the father's new marriage also occurred when the men could well afford to support both families. Altogether there was little spontaneous adherence among fathers to the idea of equalizing opportunities for all of the children despite the children's open, frank preoccupation with this concern. Sometimes we were able to observe this course of change in the father's attitude. For example, one father who was devoted to his young children in the prior marriage initially told his new wife when she wished to become pregnant, "But, my dear, I already have children." Subsequently when she became pregnant, his several-times-a-week visits to his children and his generous support of them began to fade. Soon after he provided only the obligatory support, and his visits diminished greatly.

Psychological Functioning of the Father and Child Support

The psychological intactness or psychopathology of the father was powerfully and significantly related to patterns of child support. We found a higher correlation between the psychological stability of the father and the payment of child support than between economic stability and such payment. The high incidence of psychological illness among divorcing populations has been reported and well documented.[5] Our observations regarding our own population affirm these grave findings.

The men in group I who fulfilled their economic obligation in full over the years were clearly more intact psychologically than their peers within the other groups. Although 25 percent of the men in group I suffered with psychological symptoms, these fell well within the neurotic range of sexual dysfunction, emotional constriction, and social withdrawal. Their symptoms did not affect their earning capacity or full-time employment.

One-third of the fourteen fathers in group II were severely alcoholic. Although these men were able to sober up enough to work successfully and to earn well, their after-work activity was often largely under the influence of alcohol. Wife abuse had been high in this group. One father was a compulsive gambler, and another man was frequently on drugs. It was characteristic of these men, however, that they were able to hold good jobs despite their dysfunction.

At least half of the fathers in group III had psychological problems of varying severity, including a high incidence of character problems. These men were impulsive and irresponsible, making their living by a combination of luck and shrewdness. The payment of child support often paralleled the fathers' cycles of success and failure in these enterprises or reflected sudden impulses of generosity toward their children followed by prolonged disinterest. Additionally, several men in group III had come under the influence of the counterculture ideology and opted out of their earlier career commitments.

Finally, the high incidence of disabling psychological dysfunction among fathers who failed to support was striking. Half of the men in group IV were severely troubled, suffering from paranoid schizophrenia, manic-depressive psychosis, or severe alcoholism. Several of these men appeared dilapidated, were habitually unemployed despite educational attainments, and had been supported during the marriage by their own parents or the divorced wife.

The number of years that the men required to stabilize following the divorce crisis was significantly related to child-support issues. Men in group I required an average of two years to reestablish continuity and stability in their lives. Groups II and III required an average of two to three years, and several of the men in group IV were still unstable at the five-year mark.

Men who supported their children in full were more likely to be contented with the results of the divorce and its aftermath. A striking 70 percent of the men in group I were pleased with the divorce as compared with only 20 percent of the men in group IV. In addition, men who were happier with their remarriage than they had been during the earlier marriage were more likely to support their children well.

The psychopathology of the fathers and the failure to provide child support did not necessarily translate into poor quality of father-child relationships. We have noted earlier that parent-child relationships can remain relatively conflict-free spheres of functioning.[6] Some of the more-troubled men also evoked both compassion and love from their children. One seven-year-old poignantly described her father who had visited her infrequently, supported her poorly, and dealt with her over the years with little understanding or sympathy: "Daddy does what he can."

Patterns of Postdivorce Visiting and Child Support

It is widely held that child support is linked to visiting access and to a good father-child relationship. In this view women are well advised to encourage the frequency of visitation in order to increase the likelihood of support. Our findings do and do not support these conclusions. There are, as so often happens, many confounding factors, which also change over the years and affect visiting patterns.

There was no connection between visiting during the first six-months postseparation and the level of subsequent child support by the father. As we have reported elsewhere, there was, indeed, no link between visiting at the six-month mark and the predivorce father-child relationship.[7] Further, there was no significant connection between the overall quality of the predivorce father-child relationship and subsequent child support. The sole dimension of the visiting relationship that at the time of the marital rupture predicted future support was whether the visiting plans were predicated entirely on the father's wishes or whether they were arranged with relative flexibility in ways that reflected the child's interest as well. In effect, the capacity and willingness of the father to perceive the child's needs as separate from his own and his willingness to bend responsively seemed related to subsequent child support.

Other dimensions of the visiting relationship at the time of the breakup failed to show a similar linkage. Anger between the parents during visits at the breakup time was not related to subsequent support. Visiting at that time was likely to be as much encouraged by the mother's friendliness as by her anger.

The second checkpoint of our study at eighteen-months postseparation showed a growing link between frequency of visiting and child support. Children who were fully supported (group I) were visited more frequently than children in the remaining three groups. Moreover, disruption of contact between parent and child emerged very strongly in group IV at this time.

Frequency of contact was a less-significant measure of the father's interest than the pattern of the visit and the duration of each visit. Weekend visits and overnight visits were highly correlated with child support. Children who regularly visited their fathers over the weekend were found primarily in group I. Children in groups II and III were much less likely to spend the weekend at the father's home, and no one in group IV spent the weekend with the father at the eighteen-month mark. Weekend visits had very special meaning to children and were much preferred by them to visits restricted to daytime hours. During weekends children felt integrated into the father's household and were able to banish the nagging sense of time that burdened daytime visits. The children did not require a separate room but were content to bring sleeping bags or to curl up on makeshift arrangements in order to remain over the weekend or at least overnight.

At the eighteen-month mark the father's capacity to respond flexibly to his children regarding planning the visits was highly correlated with continued support. Friendliness between the parents and encouragement from the mother facilitated visits and enabled children to visit more often, but anger between the parents over visitation did not necessarily discourage visiting at this time.

By the five-year mark, the frequency, duration, and patterning of the visit and the flexibility of the parent were all significantly linked to child support. At this time 72 percent of fathers in group I were highly invested in frequent visiting, compared with 46 percent in group II, 24 percent in group III, and 22 percent in group IV. The close correlation between frequency of visiting with child support at the five-year mark is evident along many mea-sures of the visiting. Those children visited once a week or more at that time constituted 35 percent of group I, 29 percent of group II, 8 percent of group III, and 6 percent of group IV. Similarly, children who were not visited at all by their father constituted 14 percent of group I, 21 percent of group II, 31 percent of group III, and 56 percent of group IV. Children who were not visited at all occurred largely in group IV.

The visiting pattern and duration of the visit continued also to show strong and telling linkages with patterns of child support, so much so that the pattern of the visiting itself seemed to parallel the pattern of child support Thus, fleeting patterns of contact were exemplified by the father in group III who characteristically parked his car in the driveway of the children's residence, spoke with them for a few minutes, and then drove away, leaving his children frustrated and miserable. This father provided support erratically and always well below that which he had been ordered to pay. Such patterns of fleeting contact were absent in group I and rare in group II but were not uncommon in groups III and IV. Similarly, weekend visits were part of the regular pattern of visiting for 61 percent of the children in group I who saw their father not only during the weekends but also had midweek contact with him as well. This pattern may be considered quite remarkable in terms of the previously considered expectable visiting patterns of the noncustodial parent after a period of years. Children in groups II, III, and IV fell far below the frequency and duration of the contacts that were common for the children in group I. Thus, visiting patterns that were disappointing to the children oc-curred in all groups but were more likely to occur in the poorly supported groups. Ten percent of the children in group I and 37 percent in group IV ex-perienced patterns of visiting that the children felt were disappointing.

Despite the powerful link between visiting and child support, within each support group were subgroups of fathers who had a very limited in-terest in visiting their children. Ten percent of the fathers in group I had no interest in visiting, and an additional 18 percent had only a limited interest in visiting. At the other end of the spectrum, 55 percent of the children in group IV had fathers who failed to visit and an additional 22 percent whose interest was limited.

Work for Child-Support Payments

Frequent visits do not necessarily reflect a loving or concerned father. We have seen several examples of frequent visiting combined with full child support over the five-year period that were not only unrelated to a loving father-child relationship but that economically and psychologically exploited the child.

Doris was eleven years old when her parents divorced. In response to the bitter feuding of her parents (which continued over the years), the girl was ordered by the court at the time of the divorce to spend every other weekend from 9 A.M. on Saturday to 6 P.M. on Sunday in the company of her father. During the years that followed until she graduated from high school, Doris abided in full by the court order. Although at times she pleaded with her father to permit her to attend a school dance or an outing with her friends, he rarely agreed, threatening to cut off her child support if she disobeyed him and failed to appear at his home at the appointed time. His threat succeeded, and the youngster acquiesced. Throughout her high school years, the lonely girl spent every other weekend doing household chores for her father, essentially working for her child-support payments. Feeling alternately intense anger or pity for her father, recognizing his social isolation, loneliness, and dependence on her, as well as his economic control, Doris waited desperately for the day when she would graduate from high school and leave for college.

Thus, while frequency of visitation and the duration and patterning of the visit linked highly to full and good child support, they do not necessarily reflect either a caring father-child relationship or the calming of angers and bitterness between the parents. Although it is not possible to build a close, loving relationship without a reliable visiting structure, it is quite possible to build a visiting structure that lacks a loving relationship. Child support closely correlated with visiting may reflect emotional dependence on the child, anger at the former partner, and economic exploitation.

Good Father-Child Relationship and Child Support

We turn now to the father-child relationships that were associated with different patterns at the five-year mark. We refer here to the quality of the father-child relationships that is distinguishable from the visiting patterns of the postdivorce period.[8] There are overall significant linkages between the quality of the father-child relationships and the patterns of support evident at the five-year mark. There are also important subgroups that emerged that are not represented within the dominant patterns.

Although most children were visited at the five-year mark, a significantly smaller number had fathers who continued to exercise a parental influence.[9] Father-child relationships within this group had kept pace psychologically with the developmental changes in the youngsters and had successfully avoided the hazards of remaining psychologically fixated to the developmental stage of the child when the divorce occurred. The significant link between an age-appropriate, loving father-child relationship and good child support over the years is striking. This link emerged eighteen months after the marital breakup and continued during the years that followed.

Those good parent-child relationships that survived the many vicissitudes of the postdivorce years or that grew under the difficult conditions of the postdivorce family occurred largely within group I where the children were fully supported, with some sprinkling into groups II and III. Within these relationships fathers continued to combine many functions of parenting, including child support. Youngsters in this group were also likely to be supported in part or in full during their college years.

Full Child Support within the Context of a
Poor Father-Child Relationship

Several subgroups within group I reflected patterns that were at marked variance with these beneficial relationships. A striking example is the experience of two youngsters who were supported fully over the entire five-year period by their father who mailed his support check in an envelope without a return address. From the postmark the children could read that the father was residing close by, although they remained ignorant of his whereabouts. Their rage and sense of rejection were in no way assuaged by the child support that their mother received. Their distress may well have been magnified by the recurrent monthly reminder that their father lived close by and chose not to visit them. The son at sixteen years of age angrily told us, "I have no feeling for my dad. It's like he's not my dad. He doesn't know me and I don't know him." We were not surprised to learn that this very angry boy had been involved in several delinquent episodes and had experienced a stormy adolescence, from which he was gradually emerging. His sister was also profoundly troubled, preoccupied over the years with low self-esteem, suffering an acute sense of having been rejected, and a continuing intense anger that did not diminish over time.

These youngsters and others who were fully supported without a good relationship with their father at no point regarded the child support as representing interest or affection. They may indeed have found it more difficult to forgive their father because his ability to support them fully was evidence to them of the competence of his functioning and his conscious choice not to see his children.

Several other youngsters in group I who were regularly and fully supported but visited erratically or infrequently struggled for many years with anguish over their hurt and humiliation. Additionally, a small group of youngsters who were well supported continued to reject their father in his efforts to reestablish a friendly relationship with them. As one such youngster said, "Why doesn't my father understand that when he shoots arrows at my mother they go through my body?"

Perhaps it should be said with some allowance for misperception and skewed perspective, that the children in the main gauged their father's interest with reasonable accuracy. Generally the children were generous in understanding the father's failure to maintain regular contact; they were eager to recognize realistic bars to visiting such as geographical distance and expense and their mother's opposition, and they were quick to forgive failure. What they found intolerable at the five-year mark, as they had earlier, was the conclusion that they were loved insufficiently for the maintenance of regular contact. Their inability to deal directly with these feelings of being rejected did not diminish notably over the years except where the youngster was able to recognize the serious psychological disturbance of the father as the root cause of the discontinued relationship. Child support without the relationship that the children sought provided no comfort to them and no defense against their hurt feelings.

Poor Child Support within the Context of a Poor Father-Child Relationship

Although there were good and poor father relationships in all of the economic support groups, the more limited and impoverished relationships were significantly linked to poor support and absence of support. In groups III and IV the poor or limited relationships between father and child predominated. By and large, these relationships emerged at eighteen months and continued within the same mold.

The poor relationships in groups II and III fell into a range of patterns. Some fathers in these two groups preferred one sibling over another and did not hesitate to express their preference openly, disregarding the hurt feelings of the remaining child or children. Fathers in group III were more likely to appear irregularly at indeterminate intervals after an absence of several months or more and to sweep the child up into a very exciting but all too brief reunion. These father-child relationships often paralleled a pattern of economic support that was also erratic in amount and irregular over time. The constancy and loyalty of the children in these relationships appeared in marked contrast to the inconsistency of the father both in his relationships and in the support he provided.

Poor Child Support within the Context of a
Loving Father-Child Relationship

Sometimes the absence of child support from the father nevertheless went hand in hand with a loving father-child relationship. Some of the fathers in group IV lived for many years on the periphery of their former families. In one instance the disturbed father continued to live in the same apartment house as his divorced wife and children. In several of these relationships the children took the initiative in reaching out to their troubled fathers and maintained their relationship with him over the years.

Mary, at age sixteen, talked movingly and compassionately about her father, a disturbed man who had lived nearby and had provided no support during the years following the divorce. She said that she resented her father's not being able to help the family, "but resentment comes from mom. . . . He is my father and he says he respects me and I believe him, and I believe also that he is very interested in me. . . . He should never have had a family. . . . Someday I will get a car and I will drive dad out to the ocean. He would like that. . . . Dad doesn't lie deliberately. . . . He just has such different impressions about so many things." Several youngsters like Mary were able to forgive their fathers and to maintain a loving relationship over the years despite their mother's anger and the absence of economic or emotional support from their father.

Attitudes of the Children and Child Support

The children's love for their father was entirely unrelated to issues of child support. Their yearning to be reunited with him was also unrelated to child support. Children who were well supported were significantly less likely to feel rejected by their father, however. Few youngsters in group I felt rejected; a bimodal distribution emerged in group II, whereas most of the children in group III and some in group IV suffered intensely with the recurrent concern that their father did not love them.

Children who were well supported were less angry about the divorce or at their parents than their less-well-supported peers. The children's anger at the father where this persisted is not significantly linked to child support. Sadly and ironically, the anger of the poorly supported children at their mother appears significantly related to the father's support pattern. Children in groups II and III where the support was erratic and inadequate and where the father did not appear dysfunctional were likely to blame their mother for the father's capriciousness or inconsistency. Where the former husband continued to live fairly well economically and the mother and children daily faced poverty or a significantly lower standard of living, the mother and children were likely to be angry and depressed for many years and to remain preoccupied with this discrepancy in living standard. Sometimes children in such situations were angry at both parents.

Respect for and trust of the father correlated highly with child support. There was considerable respect for the father among the children in group I, a predominance of moderate respect for him in group II, and little or no respect for their father as a parent in groups III and IV.

There were other distinguishing differences in children in each of the support groups. Children in the well-supported group were likely to have more-positive attitudes toward adults and other people in authority positions. These attitudes and accompanying social skills could be of considerable help to them in both school and subsequent employment. Although only 10 percent of the children were involved in serious trouble with school authorities, all of these youngsters were from less-well-supported groups. Youngsters in group I were altogether less likely to feel psychologically needy or emotionally deprived and more likely to have good impulse control.

Finally, youngsters who regarded the divorced family as an improvement over the predivorce family were more heavily represented in groups I and II than in the remaining groups. Oppositely, children who found no relief in the divorced family and looked backward longingly and nostalgically to an unrealistically idealized intact family were significantly more numerous in the poorly supported groups.

Psychological and Social Adjustment of Children and Child Support

The child's adjustment at the five-year mark was a product of multiple determinants, which include family relations, the social environment, and individual psychological characteristics of the child at a particular period during the growing-up years. The mother-child relationship was central in these various outcome configurations. By and large, child support, while pivotal to the mother's concern and life-style, did not affect significantly the emotional quality of the relationship between mother and child. The stress that the mother experienced during the postdivorce years was, however, significantly related to issues of child support. Although the emotional stresses of custodial parenthood were high throughout, they were significantly higher in groups III and IV. Additionally, life routines differed. Groups II and III contained the highest percentage of fully employed women, whereas a greater number of women were in part-time employment or remained at home in groups I and IV. (Women on welfare were entirely in group IV except for one family in group I where full child support did not cover the expenses of the chronically unemployed new husband and the new household.) Thus, the child-care arrangements, the mother's schedule, and particularly the availability of the mother differed considerably among the four groups.

Therefore it is not surprising to find that children who had many interests and participated in activities outside the home clustered in group I and occurred significantly less in the remaining three groups. Mothers in group I were much more able to arrange transportation, as well as to seek out the appropriate activities for their children. Fathers in group I were more likely to take their children to sports or cultural events or on hikes and camping expeditions during the visits and their vacations together.

In keeping with these differences in the social milieu is the additional finding that there was a significant relationship between good child support and stability in residence over the five-year postdivorce period. Children in group I were much more likely to have remained over the years within the same residence and the same school district than were their less-well-supported peers. Poorly supported children were more likely to have sustained three or more moves, usually to less-expensive neighborhoods and more-crowded homes, including moves to trailer communities. Thus, for many children who were well supported by fathers, the good features of their predivorce family were likely to have remained in place, and the adjustment required of them was often of a lesser magnitude than that faced by their less-well-supported peers. In effect, the pleasures and opportunities provided, as well as the required adjustments to change, differed among these groups.

There were no significant differences among the children in the different groups in their relationships with peers, in their capacity for empathy, or in their clarity regarding adults and adult relationships. Not unexpectedly, the children who were poorly supported were significantly more independent than their better supported peers.

In sum, good psychological adjustment among the children was significantly associated with adequate, stable child support over the years. Analysis of rating scales devised within the project to assess each individual youngster in his or her psychological, social, and academic performance revealed that children who rated at the top of the scale were more likely to be well supported by their fathers. Thus, of twenty-six children who placed consistently at the top of the scales, fourteen were in group I; the remaining twelve were distributed throughout the other three groups. In the same view children who did well academically in relation to their estimated potential, clustered at the five-year mark disproportionately in group I.

Poor psychological adjustment appeared unrelated to issues of child support. Depression of childhood, which was the most frequent clinical diagnosis in this population, was evenly distributed among all four groups.

Similarly, children who were experiencing learning difficulties and were performing at school well below their intellectual capacities were distributed across the board, with no significant linkages to issues of child support.

Thus, within the constraints of this small sample, poor child support by the father was apparently not a critical factor in poor learning or poor adjustment. Good economic support, however, was significantly linked to successful academic achievement, to good school adjustment, and to psychological health. Good economic support was significantly associated with a good father-child relationship, with a psychologically intact father, and with appropriate visitation patterns over the years following the divorce.

Discussion

The various patterns of fathers' support for their children during the five years following the divorce reflect a mix of economic and psychological factors. As expected, adequate and regular child support is associated with the full employment and higher socioeconomic status of the father. Poor or erratic child support was associated with the father's erratic employment or unemployment and lower socioeconomic status. Psychological and social factors emerged significantly as well.

Some of the findings are surprising and challenge generally held assumptions. Contrary to expectations, a father's economic support was not associated with the relationship between the divorcing adults at the time of the separation or at the five-year mark. People who were friendly or feuding were as likely or unlikely to provide economic support for their children. Support was not significantly related to the physical or mental health or the economic straits of the mother, even in families in which the father had maintained an active parenting role during the marriage and had been concerned about leaving his children in the care of a psychologically or physically ill mother.

Nor was the father's economic support of his children related to remarriage of either spouse. The presence of stepchildren in the father's remarriage, however, or children born in the new union significantly diminished economic support of the children of the former marriage even when the father seemed economically able to maintain the two households. The preference of many fathers to provide economic support first to the children or stepchildren of the new marriage is fully congruent with our psychological findings regarding the difficulties that remarried fathers experience in maintaining a psychologically important relationship with the children from the earlier marriage when children are present within the remarriage.

We were interested to discover that there was, in the sample, no significant link between the father-child relationship in the predivorce family and subsequent patterns of child support by the father. Here, too, economic patterns reinforce one of the major findings of our project: that the marital breakup represents a nodal point of change in father-child relationships and that relationships that evolve following divorce are not likely to be continuous with relationships that obtained during the marriage. This conclusion, combined with the tendency of the father to a primary concern with children in the new marriage, would reinforce the inadvisability of basing future expectations for support on the father's past performance or ties to his children or on a voluntary system of compliance with court-ordered support.

The relationship between child support and visiting, while of little moment at the time of the separation, grew increasingly important over the years that followed. Both the pattern of relationship and the participation of the child in the visiting plan, the willingness of the father to recognize the children's wishes, and the father's capacity to be flexible and sensitive to the child all correlated very highly with child support at the five-year mark. In many postdivorce families, then, child support was an important component of the father-child relationship.

From the child's perspective, the father's attitude and performance were watched carefully over the years for indications of love and continuing interest. Child support was carefully scrutinized by children for its meaning within this frame of reference. It appears from our data that child support alone without a visiting relationship that was gratifying for the child or a sense of caring by the father was associated in the child's mind with a rejection and generated responses of hurt and anger. Such children did not benefit psychologically from the economic support however much they may have benefited by an improved standard of living.

The high correlation that emerged between the psychological intactness of the father and good economic support of the children is striking and reflects the complex interweaving of psychological and economic data. Clearly in this study, those fathers who provided continuous and adequate support during the five years following the divorce were more intact psychologically, were more likely to be contented with the divorce, and exhibited a capacity, a sensitivity, and a willingness to perceive and act on their children's needs separate from their own. Their children were, in turn, less likely to feel rejected, more likely to respect and trust their fathers, and more likely to regard the postdivorce family as an improvement over the earlier marriage. These children were also significantly better adjusted and more likely to engage in activities and interests outside the home and to perform well at school and on the playground. They were more likely than their less-well-supported peers to have a positive view of adults and of adult society.

By contrast, the fathers who provided essentially little or no support during the same time period were more likely to suffer psychological dysfunction, and to continue to disapprove of the divorce, and in many in-stances they found it impossible to recapture the level of their earlier func-tioning or to go beyond it. There were limited and impoverished father-child relationships in this group accompanied by failure to visit or infrequent visits that disappointed the children. Although these fathers were by and large loved by their children and not infrequently pitied and treated with much compassion, they evoked little respect from their children, who, in turn, found hardly any relief in the postdivorce family and looked back longingly and unrealistically to an idealized predivorce family five years after the marital rupture. Thus, the failure in the father-child relationship, including its child-support functions, prolonged the emotional stresses of the marital breakup and rendered it more difficult for the children to reach closure on the divorce experience.

Conclusions and Recommendations

A variety of far-ranging implications for public policy derive from the find-ings of this study of the interlocking of psychological with economic sup-port factors in the postdivorce lives of affected children. Although the study itself was a small one, there is no reason to assume that the close connection we have found that endures and, in fact, increases over the postdivorce years between economic and psychological support factors would differ in broader studies of middle-class populations.

It is clear that the present system of child support that is ordered by a court and that depends for its good functioning on the voluntary compli-ance of the father operates well for a particularly advantaged segment of children affected by divorce. These are the children mostly of group I, in which there is an adequate postdivorce relationship with a psychologically healthy father who is concerned with the children and their well-being and is willing and able to maintain financial support and a life for the children, one that is economically buttressed as close to the predivorce level as pos-sible. It is in such instances that the divorce has truly given the parents (or at least the instigating parent) the desired and/or needed second chance with the fullest mitigation possible of adverse impact on the children.

At the other end of the spectrum are those group III and IV situations where psychological impairment and/or irresponsibility, especially on the part of the father, are reflected—postdivorce—in a deteriorated father-child relationship and erratic and inadequate economic support, if any. The present child-support system, so heavily dependent on voluntary compliance (unless the mother can, through expensive litigation, successfully force payments from an ex-husband with attachable resources), plays into the perpetuation or the accentuation of disadvantage for the children in these groups. Whatever the degree of relief obtained by one or the other parent through the divorce, the affected children in these instances are often not only no better off but considerably worse off. Previously present and perhaps concerned and attentive fathers are no longer there, and previous material supports within an intact family (at whatever level) are no longer available. For so many custodial mothers and their children, divorce brings about a major downward shift in economic well-being and security.

The major public-policy implication from this is that of the strong benefits that would emerge for all parties from a nonvoluntary economic-support system. In this system, it is envisioned that monies would be automatically deducted from the father's wages or income, supplemented by governmental allowance where the father's earning capacity proved inadequate to the support needs of his children. In this way, economic support would be automatic, adequate (or at least as adequate as can be), and divorced from the unhappy interlocking of economic and psychological factors that exists at the present time.

Notes

1. E.M. Hetherington, M. Cox, and R. Cox, "Divorced Fathers," *Family Coordinator* 25 (1976):417-428; E.M. Hetherington, M. Cox, and R. Cox, "The Aftermath of Divorce," in J.H. Stevens and M. Mathews, eds., *Mother-Child Relations* (Washington, D.C.: NAEYC, 1978); E.M. Hetherington, M. Cox, and R. Cox, "Play and Social Interaction in Children following Divorce," *Journal of Social Issues* 35 (1979):26-49.

2. J. Wallerstein and J. Kelly, "Effects of Divorce on the Visiting Father-Child Relationship," *American Journal of Psychiatry* 137 (1980): 1534-1539.

3. J. Wallerstein and J. Kelly, *Surviving the Breakup: How Children and Parents Cope with Divorce* (New York: Basic Books, 1980).

4. H. Ross and S. Sawhill, *Time of Transition: The Growth of Families Headed by Women* (Washington, D.C.: Urban Institute, 1975); D.L. Chambers, *Making Fathers Pay: The Enforcement of Child Support* (Chicago: University of Chicago Press, 1979).

5. B.L. Bloom, S.W. White, and S.J. Asher, "Marital Disruption as a Stressful Life Event," in G. Levinger and O.C. Moles, eds., *Divorce and Separation* (New York: Basic Books, 1979), pp. 184-200.

6. Wallerstein and Kelly, *Surviving the Breakup.*

7. Wallerstein and Kelly, "Effects of Divorce."

8. Wallerstein and Kelly, *Surviving the Breakup.*

9. Ibid.

11 Economic Support of Children by Fathers Following Divorce: Some Theoretical and Empirical Considerations

Martha J. Cox

In an early review of the literature on divorce, Herzog and Sudia suggested that many differences in adjustment of children in one-parent and two-parent families could be explained by economic differences in these families.[1] Since that review some research has been directed toward the role of economic factors in postdivorce adjustment of families, although the impact of economic factors is still far from clear. In general, it appears that income as a single variable does not play as powerful a role in determining the adjustment of one-parent families as Herzog and Sudia have suggested. Adjustment of children and parents is determined by many factors, with quality of parent-child relationships apparently being primary.[2] What is suggested is that economic factors indirectly affect children and that their impact is mediated by such variables as the stress imposed upon the mother or custodial parent by economic factors, the implication of economic factors for changes in parent-child relationships, and the implications of economic factors for significant changes in the child's environment.

The Economic Situation of Divorced Families

The number of children and parents experiencing divorce has increased dramatically since 1960. The country's divorce rate has more than doubled since 1965, and it is estimated that more than 40 percent of current marriages will eventually end in divorce. Children under eighteen years are involved in 60 percent of these divorces; thus, the number of children who live or will live in one-parent homes also has increased dramatically.[3] Whereas in 1960 only about 14 percent of children would have been expected to experience a parental divorce before the age of eighteen, on the basis of current divorce rates, Glick projects that by 1990, 33 percent of children will experience a divorce of parents before the age of eighteen.[4]

157

Only 10 percent of all children live with their fathers following divorce, and this proportion has not changed significantly since 1960.[5] Therefore, most children in a postdivorce home are residing with the mother.

What is the economic situation of these families? First, it appears that most postdivorce homes with children experience significant drops in income. Second, this drop in income is much more severe for mother-custody than for father-custody homes or for fathers in general.

Divorce occurs more often in poorer families.[6] And it also leads to a significant drop in income for women across the income spectrum. Hoffman suggests that the drop may be as much as 30 percent.[7] Espanshade reports that whereas in 1977 the median income for male-headed families was $17,517, the median for female-headed families was only $7,765.[8] In addition, in 1977 female-headed families accounted for about 14 percent of all families, but they accounted for nearly 50 percent of all families in poverty, with approximately 32 percent of all mother-headed families earning below the poverty level.

Part of the explanation of the relative poverty of female-headed families seems to be due to the fact that income decreases after divorce for women but not for men.[9] In a study of sixty predominantly middle-class families, Wallerstein and Huntington found that only 20 percent of women enjoyed economic security five years after divorce (although economic security was not clearly defined).[10] In contrast, 50 percent of the men experienced either an unchanged or increased standard of living. Spanier and Castro found that 23 percent of the men in their sample reported that they were worse off financially after divorce but not significantly so.[11] The rest, 77 percent, reported being as well off as before. In contrast, only 39 percent of the women, primarily younger women, reported being as well off. Duncan and Morgan provide specific details concerning this trend for greater relative poverty in women after divorce.[12] They found that for males, becoming divorced between 1967 and 1973 did not change the probability of becoming poor. However, women who were poor in 1967 had a 45 percent chance of being nonpoor in 1973 if they stayed married but only a 26 percent chance of being nonpoor if they divorced. More dramatic is the converse; women who were nonpoor in 1967 had only a 6 percent chance of being poor in 1973 if they stayed married but a 33 percent chance of being poor if they divorced. Duncan and Morgan also found that in 1973, children of divorced parents had greater economic well-being if fathers rather than mothers gained custody, although they point out that economically advantaged fathers may be awarded custody for the very reason that they are economically advantaged. Other researchers, however, also have found that mother-custody homes experience significant drops in income whereas father-custody homes do not.[13]

The drop in income for women can be attributed to several factors. Only about one-third of husbands provide support either because they have not been ordered by courts to do so or because they have been ordered but have failed to do so.[14] Winston and Forsher found that the ex-husbands of divorced women on AFDC were not from low-income categories particularly but represented the occupational and income distribution of men in general.[15] Kriesberg found that poverty of divorced mothers was unrelated to their previous socioeconomic status.[16]

The drop in income for women after divorce is also attributable to the fact that, although a large proportion go to work, their lack of education and seniority confines them to low-paying jobs.[17] The average educational level of mothers in one-parent families is still relatively low but has been rising. The rise is due to the fact that between 1970 and 1977, while the increase in mother-headed families where the mothers had not graduated from high school was 95 percent, among those who had attended college, the increase was 167 percent. Even so, in 1977 as many mothers in single-parent homes had not graduated from high school as had attended college.[18]

Many of these divorced women are employed outside of the home; 77 percent of divorced women as compared to 48 percent of married women worked in 1977. In 1977, among divorced mothers of school-aged children, the percentage was even greater; 82 percent worked, while 66 percent of divorced mothers with preschool children were employed. With such high labor-force participation rates, it is somewhat surprising that 28 percent of the families are still in poverty. Clearly, this reflects the fact that many divorced women work for extremely low pay.[19]

One can conclude from these data that divorced women and their families lack economic resources when compared to their married counterparts. But determining the implications of this lack of resources for the adjustment of children and parents after divorce is more difficult.

The Impact of Economic Factors on Postdivorce Adjustment

Complexity of the Problem

Relatively few studies have been reported that address the question of the role that economic factors play in family adjustment after divorce. Moreover, when the question is studied, researchers often use different indexes of economic situation, so results are not comparable. For example, it appears that studies should distinguish between income and economic resources. Most studies have investigated the relationship between adjustment and either income or level of child support; however, the actual economic resources of a family may not be reflected accurately by income or level of child support. Espenshade suggests that because of the importance of such assets as homes and savings to financial well-being, when economic well-being is based completely on current income, the relative economic deprivation of divorced women and their families may be overstated.[20]

Another problem with research relating economic factors to adjustment in divorced families is that most studies have been correlational with relevant variables measured at one point in time. Longitudinal studies would describe more accurately changes in family process and family adjustment that were caused by increases or decreases in economic resources.

Of those studies reported, only two were longitudinal, and each used different indexes of economic situation.[21] Wallerstein and Huntington report data on level of economic support by the father, while Hetherington and coworkers measured the income of the mother. Earlier Wallerstein and Kelly reported on the relationship between family adjustment and economic decline in families.[22] All these, of course, are different variables. Economic support and income may even be inversely related for some families, as Wallerstein and Hungtington found evidence that as working mothers became more successful financially, level of support by the father decreased. Because few divorced women achieve significant financial success, however, for most families levels of support and income are positively, though not perfectly, correlated.

Hetherington discusses the problem of specifying which index of economic condition is critical for the family's response to divorce.[23] She notes that current level of income, change in level of income, expected level of income, as well as the custodial parent's concerns about income are all potentially important in determining a family's subjective feeling of economic stress. The relative importance of these variables in determining a family's response to divorce cannot be assessed from current research; however, it appears that the associations one finds vary, depending on the variable studied.

In the Wallerstein study, economic support was found to be associated with some, but not all, of the important aspects of the child's behavior measured in this study.[24] Wallerstein and Huntington found that children in full support groups were significantly better adjusted, were more likely to have positive attitudes toward adults, were less likely to feel needy and deprived, were less likely to be depressed, and had better impulse control. Economic support, however, was not significantly associated with relationships with peers, capacity for empathy, understanding adult relationships, happiness, and academic ability. Clearly many other factors are at work. Moreover, the fact that economic support is associated with some characteristics of the child does not necessarily mean that it plays a causative role in determining those characteristics. Other alternative explanations are as feasible. For example, Wallerstein and Huntington found that economic support was strongly related to the father's adjustment. The adjustment of parents is certainly an important factor in determining the adjustment of children. The association between economic support and the adjustment of children, then, may be due to their relationships to a third variable, the father's adjustment. Suggestive of this is the fact that economic support was related to the adjustment of the child but not changes in adjustment over time after divorce.

In contrast, Wallerstein and Kelly reported that economic decline in the same sample (as opposed to economic support) was not strongly related to psychological ajdustment of children after divorce.[25] Likewise, Hetherington et al. report little relationship between income and adjustment of children.[26] It may be that economic support from the father communicates to children that the father is interested in them and thus has a meaning for children that income and income decline do not have. The samples of both Wallerstein and Huntington and Hetherington et al. were primarily middle class, however. It may be that the economic decline experienced by these families was not severe enough to result in meaningful differences for families. Wallerstein and Huntington also suggest that their sample may have been too small and too homogeneous to show sufficient variation in economic situations.[27] In a more heterogeneous sample, income and income decline may show greater relationship to adjustment. In a correlational study, one group of researchers reports a direct association between drop in income and children's adjustment (as measured by parental ratings only).[28] However, the number of subjects was small ($N = 25$), and maladjustment was found in only five subjects, each of whom came from a family that experienced a decline in income of 50 percent or greater. Because neither social class nor income was reported for the subjects, this study adds little to understanding whether an investigation of a more heterogeneous sample or a more economically deprived sample would yield a relationship between economic decline and adjustment.

Both studies, as well as others, suggest that economic factors may have an impact on family relationship, environment, and parental adjustment variables that have been found to be related to the adjustment of children in divorced homes. In other words, these variables may mediate the impact of economic factors on children's adjustment after divorce.

Mediating Factors

The impact of economic factors on the adjustment of children may be mediated by parental adjustment, parent-child relationships, and environmental variables.

Parental Adjustment: Several studies suggest that financial strain is a source of depression, anxiety, and distress to the custodial parent, who is usually the mother.

Brown, Felton, Whiteman, and Manela interviewed 192 men and women who were in the process of marital dissolution.[29] Economic resources were measured by actual income and anticipated financial strain. The investigators assessed the relationship of these two variables to distress (subjects were asked how often in the last two weeks they had felt blue, tense, worried, or hopeless). Anticipated financial strain, but not income, contributed significantly to distress in both men and women. In another study, Pearlin and Johnson measured economic hardship by asking subjects, "How often does it happen that you do not have enough money to afford 1) the kind of food your family should have, 2) the kind of medical care you (your family) should have, and 3) the kind of clothing you (your family) should have?"[30] In each category of marital status, Pearlin and Johnson report, economic hardship was related to depression. The relationship was particularly strong for unmarried individuals. In addition to being more vulnerable to depression caused by economic strain, unmarried individuals experience economic strain more often.

Wallerstein and Huntington also report an effect of financial hardship on the emotional reactions of mothers.[31] Over 33 percent of the women in their sample had a daily struggle to meet expenses, leading them to experience significant anxiety about payment of bills. Moreover, Wallerstein and Huntington suggest that a significant number of women who experience the most severe decline in economic standards (those who have been wives of professional men) respond with social withdrawal and clinical depression.

The emotional adjustment of the mother after divorce has been associated significantly with the child's adjustment.[32] Thus, to the extent that economic stresses increase the depression and anxiety of custodial mothers, they may also jeopardize her ability to deal with her children.

There is also evidence that financial matters affect the amount of conflict between divorced couples. Hetherington et al. found that financial matters were the main source of conflict between ex-spouses.[33] Ahrons also found that current finances were a major source of conflict between ex-spouses.[34] It is unclear, however, whether conflict over finances occurs equally in couples at all income levels or whether it occurs more frequently at low income or low support levels. Wallerstein and Huntington found no significant correlation between economic support of the child and the relationships between divorcing spouses (which presumably included conflict), suggesting that it occurs equally at all levels. The question is far from resolved, however. Because conflict between ex-spouses has been found to be such an important predictor of postdivorce adjustment in children, this is certainly an important area for further investigation.[35]

Parent-Child Relationships: Economic factors appear to affect child-rearing practices, amount of parent-child interaction, and role relationships in the home.

Colletta found that low-income divorced mothers were more restrictive in their child-rearing practices.[36] They expected more-immediate obedience. With boys, mothers were less likely to respond to children's attention demands. This more-restrictive approach to child rearing, where control is unilateral and conformity to rules is stressed, has often been associated with low social interaction with peers and obedience but lack of spontaneity, affection, curiosity, and originality.[37]

In addition, the economic situation of the mother after divorce seems to be significantly related to the frequency with which mothers seek employment, and employment of the mother may alter the parent-child relationship. The majority of divorced women (77 percent) are employed, many beginning employment at the time of divorce.[38] Although Wallerstein and Huntington suggest that they find no relationship between economic factors and employment of mothers, it appears from their data that such a relationship exists but that it is curvilinear rather than linear.[39] That is, the best- and least-supported mothers in their sample were less likely to work than the mothers falling in the middle. The best-supported mothers apparently did not need to work as often for financial security, and the least well supported more often relied on public assistance. Although the relationship between economic factors and employment needs further support, it is reasonable that more mothers will work in families where economic resources are in short supply.

The employment of mothers in one-parent families appears to have implications for the adjustment of children, although few studies are designed to assess this relationship directly. Hetherington et al. found a higher rate of behavior disorders in children when mothers began work at the time of divorce, perhaps reflecting the impact of decreased maternal time with the child as a result of greater task overload for the mothers. In their study, there was a pattern of less adult attention, more disorganization in homes, and less regular scheduling when mothers experienced task overload. Cox and Cox studied the impact of maternal employment on five-year-old first-born children in one- and two-parent lower-middle-class homes.[40] They found less adult supervision, less adult-child interaction, and greater social isolation in one-parent working-mother homes than in two-parent working-mother homes, but only when the single-parent working mother was not living in an extended family situation. Many of these divorced working mothers had moved into the home of their parents. Children in these homes received as much or more supervision and adult interaction as children in two-parent working-mother homes. In this study, lack of adult supervision and low adult-child interaction were both associated with behavioral problems in children.

The relationship between maternal employment and adjustment of children in mother-headed homes is not simple. However, it appears that when maternal employment results in task overload, adult-child interaction and supervision of children may be significantly decreased, which in turn may place the child at greater risk for behavioral disruption.

Weiss has suggested that task overload may be associated with both positive and negative outcomes for children.[41] He suggests that in divorced families where the mother is overloaded with tasks, premature adult role taking and too early assumption of responsibility by school-aged children may occur. These children, however, may also show positive characteristics, such as greater self-sufficiency. Similarly, Wallerstein and Huntington seem to suggest that these greater maturity demands may lead to positive outcomes for children.[42] They found that the least well economically supported children showed greater independence than those with more support. However, both researchers have cautioned that the push toward early independence and self-sufficiency can lead to feelings of incompetence, lack of support, feelings of resentment, and anger at the unavailability of the mothers.[43]

Wallerstein and Huntington also have suggested that level of support can affect the child's preoccupation with anger and feelings of rejection.[44] Children who were well supported economically were less likely to feel rejected by the father. Intrestingly, although children who were poorly supported were not more likely to be angry with the father, they were more likely to be preoccupied with anger at the mother. Particularly where the former husband lived relatively well and the mother and child faced daily poverty, the child was preoccupied with intense anger and depression, most of which seemed to be directed at the mother. Hess and Camara have suggested that a child's preoccupation with the divorce would absorb mental and emotional energy of the child, divert energy from social and school-related activities, and disrupt the normal progress of development.[45] There are insufficient data to confirm this path of effects, although the hypothesis that preoccupation of the child with anger and resentment may disrupt development is a plausible one.

Certainly anger at the mother would be expected to have a negative impact on the mother-child relationship. Several studies have suggested that that relationship is critical to the child's adjustment after divorce.[46]

Environmental Variables: Economic factors appear to be associated with a number of environmental variables that have been implicated in the adjustment of children after divorce. Children whose families lack economic resources are more likely to experience moves to poorer housing in poorer neighborhoods. Wallerstein and Huntington found that there was a significant relationship between good father support and stability of residence during the five years after divorce.[47] Poorly supported children were more likely to have experienced three or more moves, usually to poorer neighborhoods where homes were more crowded. Thus, with less economic support, children were more often required to give up a familiar environment, familiar school, friends, and, in many cases, a safer, more crime-free environment. There is also some suggestion that a family's social isolation is increased by moving.[48] Moreover, most people experience moves as a stress.[49] The greater social isolation of these families may be associated with fewer support systems and greater depression in mothers.[50]

Satisfaction with housing seems to be lowest among low-income, unmarried parents. In Colletta's study, 71 percent of low-income divorced mothers compared to 38 percent of moderate-income divorced mothers and 33 percent of married mothers expressed dissatisfaction with housing.[51] Displeasure with housing was particularly characteristic of divorced mothers who had moved in with their families after divorce, with 86 percent of this group expressing dissatisfaction and concern about the tension produced by such an arrangement.

Economic resources also seem to affect divorced mothers' satisfactions with support and help from friends and family. Colletta found that low-income mothers were least satisfied with support. She speculates that because help from others was so crucial to the functioning of the low-income mother, support systems were unable to meet the day-to-day needs of the low-income families. On the other hand, moderate-income mothers did not have to rely as much on support systems, so that the support systems were more likely to satisfy their needs. For low-income mothers, satisfaction with support was related to parenting practices; the less the satisfaction, the poorer the parenting.

Economic resources also have an impact on how children spend their time. Wallerstein and Huntington found that in homes with good economic support, children were much more likely to be involved in many interests and activities outside of the home such as sports, horseback riding, science groups, music, dance, art, and drama lessons.[53] Moreover, mothers were more able to provide safe transportation and arrange appropriate activities for their children.

Methodological Shortcomings of Current Research and Future Directions

The research that has been reported leaves many unanswered questions about the impact of economic factors on the adjustment of families after divorce. First, it is unclear which aspect of the family's financial situation is most salient. Are total income, income-needs, income decline, perceived

financial situation, income support, or some other variable the most important index of a family's economic situation? Most studies have not considered the possibility that these variables might have differential impact
and have measured either income or support.

Moreover, most studies have not utilized a broad enough range of
economic resources in families, so that lack of association of economic factors with family adjustment variables may be due to lack of variability in
the economic index variable. Longitudinal studies of a broad socioeconomic range of families are needed, not only to assess the impact of level
of resources on adjustment but also the impact of changes in resources.

Longitudinal studies are also needed to trace paths of influence of
economic factors. It appears that the impact of economic variables may be
mediated by their effects on other critical variables, such as adjustment of
parents, parent-child relationships, family processes and environmental
stability and quality. Only by following families over time can these relationships be revealed.

Further, in current studies researchers have failed to investigate age differences and sex differences in the impact of economic factors. There is considerable research suggesting that the impact of divorce varies with age and
sex of the child.[54] It seems very likely that these variables would also be important in a consideration of the impact of economic factors. For example,
young children may be more adversely affected when economic conditions
result in unstable and changing environments or significant decreases in
parental attention. Older children, on the other hand, may be more affected
when economic factors result in premature adoption of adult roles.

Male children may be more susceptible to the stress resulting from
economic hardship in general. Rutter suggests that males are more vulnerable than females to a number of stressors.[55] These include marital
discord and divorce.[56] The reason for greater behavioral disruption in males
exposed to marital conflict or divorce is unclear. Hetherington hypothesizes
that the answer may lie in differences in characteristics and response styles
in boys and girls and in differences in responses of others to boys and girls.[57]
She notes that the behavior of boys after divorce is more difficult and nox-
ious than that of girls (boys are less compliant, more coercive, and more
demanding), and boys receive less positive support, nurturance, and
solicitude after divorce than do girls.

Conclusions and Policy Implications

The conclusions that can be made concerning the impact of economic factors
on children's adjustment are tenuous; however, there is some evidence for
certain critical paths of influence between economic factors and children's

behavior. The most likely of these paths involves the impact of economic hardship on depression, anxiety, and stress in the mother, and environmental stability. There is also a possibility that economically stressed conditions lead to different, less-effective child-rearing practices, but this result was found in only one study.

What does this mean for our policies of economic support? First, the distress and depression of the mother seems as much associated with economic decline as actual level of income. That is, when support does not allow a mother-headed family to maintain a standard of living anywhere near the previous standard, that situation is detrimental to the mother's emotional adjustment and thus may adversely affect her children. This association, if valid, suggests that policies should be altered such that changes in standard of living after divorce are more nearly equal for men and women (currently men tend not to experience this decline, while women do).

Economic support from the father will not always be sufficient for the mother-headed family, however. Not all fathers are capable of providing support, and economic support alone may not solve the problems of the mother-headed family. One-parent families, particularly those with few financial resources, are very likely to suffer from role strain, lack of support and back-up in emergencies, and an inability to solve their own problems through purchase of services. Public welfare services are currently designed primarily to intercede only after families are failing to function appropriately in the wake of a crisis. Very few supportive services are available to prevent family breakdown in a crisis. Dependable supportive services provided at the onset of crisis, such as illness, loss of work, accident, or many other uncontrollable events, as well as ongoing services such as day care, could theoretically decrease the depression, stress, and anxiety in mother-headed families who lack support from friends, relatives, or ex-spouses.

Environmental stability also seems to be particularly important in a family's adjustment after divorce. Families who experience economic hardship and severe economic decline are the ones who are most likely to have to change residence, usually to a poorer, less safe, more crowded environment. For families who are particularly lacking in economic resources, these moves may be frequent, resulting in many disruptions of friendship, support groups, school progress, and adaptations to familiar surroundings. Thus, policies that make stability of residence more likely for children after divorce are desirable. Policies that seek to ensure that mother-headed families do not experience significant economic decline after divorce should have the effect of ensuring greater environmental stability in that mothers would be less likely to move for financial reasons. Public welfare policies that sought to help families remain, if not in the same housing, at least in the same neighborhood and school systems may also be important to the postdivorce adjustment of children and families.

For all families, public policies that decrease stress, increase support, and lead to greater environmental stability are desirable. The family experiencing the stress of divorce, however, may particularly require more stability of environment, continuity of support, and continuity of standard of living. Rutter suggests that children can deal with one stressor, but cumulative or chronic stress can have a negative impact on adjustment.[58] Thus, children who are coping with changed circumstances due to divorce may need the stability of a continued standard of living and the same neighborhood, school, and residence.

Notes

1. E.G. Herzog and C.E. Sudia, "Children in Fatherless Families," in B.M. Caldwell and H. Riccuiti, eds., *Review of Child Development Research* (Chicago: University of Chicago Press, 1973).

2. R.D. Hess and K.A. Camara, "Post-Divorce Family Relationships as Mediating Factors in the Consequences of Divorce for Children," *Journal of Social Issues* 35 (1979):79-96; E.M. Hetherington, M.J. Cox, and R.D. Cox, "Effects of Divorce on Parents and Children," in M. Lamb, ed., *Nontraditional Families* (Hillside, N.J.: Laurence Erlbaum Associates, 1981).

3. P.G. Glick and A.J. Norton, "Marrying, Divorcing, and Living Together in U.S. Today," *Population Bulletin* 32 (1978):3-38.

4. P.G. Glick, "Children of Divorced Parents in Demographic Perspective," *Journal of Social Issues* 35 (1979):170-182.

5. Ibid.

6. R.A. Brandwein, C.A. Brown, and E.M. Fox, "Women and Children Last: The Social Situation of Divorced Mothers and Their Families," *Journal of Marriage and the Family* 36 (1974):490-514; P. Brown, B.J. Felton, V. Whiteman, and R. Manela, "Attachment and Distress Following Marital Separation," *Journal of Divorce* 3 (1980):303-317; L.L. Bumpass and J.A. Sweet, "Differentials in Marital Instability: 1970," *American Sociological Review* 37 (1972):754-766; P. Cutright, "Income and Family Events: Marital Stability," *Journal of Marriage and the Family* 33 (1971):291-306; P.C. Glick and A.J. Norton, "Frequency, Duration, and Probability of Marriage and Divorce," *Journal of Marriage and the Family* 33 (1971):307-317; E.M. Havens, "Women, Work, and Wedlock: A Note on Female Marital Patterns in the United States," *American Journal of Sociology* 78 (1973):975-981; H. Pope and C.W. Mueller, "The Intergenerational Transmission of Marital Instability," *Journal of Social Issues* 32 (1976):49-66; H.L. Ross and I.V. Sawhill, *Time of Transition* (Washington, D.C.: Urban Institute, 1975).

7. S. Hoffman, "Marital Instability and the Economic Status of Women," *Demography* 14 (1977):67-76.

8. T.J. Espenshade, "The Economic Consequences of Divorce," *Journal of Marriage and the Family* 41 (1979):615-625.

9. M.J. Bane, "Marital Disruption and the Lives of Children," *Journal of Social Issues* 32 (1976):103-117; Espenshade, "Economic Consequences"; Hoffman, "Marital Instability"; S. Hoffman and J. Holmes, "Husbands, Wives, and Divorce," in G.J. Duncan and J.N. Morgan, eds., *Five Thousand American Families—Patterns of Economic Progress* (Ann Arbor, Mich.: Institute for Social Research, University of Michigan, 1976), vol. 4; G.B. Spanier and R.F. Casto, "Adjustment to Separation and Divorce: A Qualitative Analysis," in G. Levinger and O.C. Moles, eds., *Divorce and Separation: Contexts, Causes and Consequences* (New York: Basic Books, 1979).

10. Chapter 10.

11. Spanier and Casto, "Adjustment to Separation."

12. G.J. Duncan and J.N. Morgan, "Introduction and Overview," in Duncan and Morgan, *Five Thousand American Families.*

13. Espenshade, "Economic Consequences"; J.W. Santrock and R.A. Warshak, "Father Custody and Social Development in Boys and Girls," *Journal of Social Issues* 35 (1979):112-125.

14. L. Kriesberg, *Mothers in Poverty* (Chicago: Aldine, 1970).

15. N.P. Winston and T. Forsher, *Non-Support of Legitimate Children by Affluent Fathers as a Cause of Poverty and Welfare Dependence* (Santa Monica, Calif.: Rand Corporation, 1971).

16. Kriesberg, *Mothers in Poverty.*

17. Brandwein, Brown, and Fox, "Women and Children Last."

18. Glick, "Children of Divorced Parents."

19. Brandwein, Brown, and Fox, "Women and Children Last."

20. Espenshade, "Economic Consequences."

21. Hetherington, Cox, and Cox, "Effects of Divorce"; chapter 10.

22. J.S. Wallerstein and J.B. Kelly, *Surviving the Breakup: How Parents and Children Cope with Divorce* (New York: Basic Books, 1980).

23. E.M. Hetherington, "Effects of Father Absence on Personality Development in Adolescent Daughters," *Developmental Psychology* 7 (1972):313-326.

24. Chapter 10.

25. Wallerstein and Kelly *Surviving the Breakup.*

26. Hetherington, Cox, and Cox, "Effects of Divorce."

27. Chapter 10.

28. J. Desimone-Luis, K. O'Mahoney, and D. Hunt, "Children of Separation and Divorce: Factors Influencing Adjustment," *Journal of Divorce* 3 (1979):37-42.

29. Brown, Felton, Whiteman, and Manela, "Attachment and Distress."

30. L.I. Pearlin and J.S. Johnson, "Marital Status, Life Strains, and Depression," *American Sociological Review* 42 (1977):704-715.

31. Chapter 10.

32. E.M. Hetherington, M. Cox, and R. Cox, "The Aftermath of Divorce," In J.H. Stevens, Jr., and M. Matthews, eds., *Mother-Child, Father-Child Relations* (Washington, D.C.: National Association for the Education of Young Children, 1978).

33. Ibid.

34. C.R. Ahrons, "Joint Custody Arrangements in the Post-Divorce Family," *Journal of Divorce* 3 (1980):189-205.

35. Hetherington, "Effects of Father Absence"; Hetherington, Cox, and Cox, "Effects of Divorce on Parents and Children"; L.H. Tessman, *Children of Parting Parents* (New York: Aronson, 1978); Wallerstein and Kelly, *Surviving the Breakup.*

36. N.D. Coletta, "Support Systems after Divorce: Incidence and Impact," *Journal of Marriage and the Family* 41 (1979):837-846.

37. E.E. Maccoby, *Social Development: Psychological Growth and the Parent-Child Relationship* (New York: Harcourt Brace Jovanovich, 1980).

38. Glick, "Children of Divorced Parents."

39. Wallerstein and Kelly, *Surviving the Breakup.*

40. M.J. Cox and R.D. Cox "Maternal Employment in Intact and Father-Absent Families: Mediating Factors" Unpublished manuscript, 1982). (Available from M.J. Cox, Timberlawn Foundation, 2750 Grove Hill Road, Dallas, Texas 75227).

41. R. Weiss, "Single Parent Households as Settings for Growing Up" (Paper presented at the National Institute of Mental Health Conference on Divorce, Washington, D.C., February 1978).

42. Chapter 10.

43. J. Wallerstein, "Children and Parent Eighteen Months after Parental Separation: Factors Related to Differential Outcome" (Paper presented at the National Institute of Mental Health Conference on Divorce, Washington, D.C., February 1978); Weiss, "Single Parent Households."

44. Wallerstein and Kelly, *Surviving the Breakup.*

45. Hess and Camara, "Post-Divorce Family Relationships."

46. Ibid; Hetherington, Cox, and Cox, "The Effects of Divorce on Parents and Children"; Wallerstein and Kelly, *Surviving the Breakup.*

47. Chapter 10.

48. D. Marsden, *Mothers Alone: Poverty and the Fatherless Family* (London: Allen Lane, Penguin Press, 1969); Pearlin and Johnson, "Marital Status."

49. J. Weissman and E. Paykel, "Moving and Depression in Women," *Society* 9 (1972):24-28.

50. Pearlin and Johnson, "Marital Status."

51. N.D. Coletta, "The Impact of Divorce: Father Absence or Poverty," *Journal of Divorce* 3 (1979):27-35. (a)

52. Coletta, "Support Systems after Divorce."

53. Chapter 10.

54. E.M. Hetherington, "Children and Divorce," in R.W. Henderson, ed., *Parent-Child Interaction* (New York: Academic Press, 1981).

55. M. Rutter, "Sex Differences in Children's Response to Family Stress," in E.J. Anthony, ed., *The Child in His Family* (New York: John Wiley, 1970); M. Rutter, "Maternal-Deprivation, 1972-1978: New Findings, New Concepts, New Approaches," *Child Development* 50 (1979): 283-305.

56. Hetherington, Cox, and Cox, "Effects of Divorce on Parents and Children"; G. Porter and D.K. O'Leary, "Marital Discord and Child Behavior Problems," *Journal of Abnormal Child Psychology* 8 (1980): 287-295; J. Tuckman and P.A. Regan, "Intactness of the Home and Behavior Problems in Children," *Journal of Child Psychology and Psychiatry* 7 (1966):225-233; Wallerstein, "Children and Parent."

57. Hetherington, "Children and Divorce."

58. M. Rutter "Protective Factors in Children's Response to Stress and Disadvantage," in M.W. Kent and J.E. Rolf, eds., *Primary Prevention of Psychopathology,* vol. 3: *Promoting Social Competence and Coping in Children* (Hanover, N.H.: University Press of New England, 1978).

12 The Father-Child Postdivorce Relationship and Child Support

Neil J. Salkind

The role of the father has changed dramatically over the past one hundred years. From the English law notion of ownership of all property, his role has moved toward an equal and justified involvement in all the activities that surround the economic and parenting concerns of the family.

Margaret Mead's comment that fathers are a biological necessity but a social accident points out that in some cases, fathers have been almost conspicuous by their absence. Even in the animal kingdom, there is evidence that the full-time father was developed in order to double the number of parents young offspring had to protect them from the harshness of a hostile environment of predators, accidents, and disease, that was exacerbated by a missing mother who had to seek food constantly for her growing young.[1]

In the case of divorce, child custody, and child support, the father's role has changed as well. While twenty years ago few if any fathers had custody of their children following divorce, in 1975, 8.4 percent of children were with their fathers. Of those children, the majority are school age rather than preschool.[2] In addition, by 1990 several million more new households consisting of single or previously married men living alone or with children is expected.[3]

Changes in who receives custody of the children are paralleled by other economic and social changes that are taking place in the nature of the family itself and the effect these changes have on the relationship between parents and their children. With some 40 to 50 percent of the children born in 1970 living in single-parent families, our concerns about the impact of divorce on child support are well founded. It is essential that a relatively ignored dimension of this issue, the father's role, be investigated more fully.

What We Know about Children and Divorce

It would be impossible to discuss the role that the father occupies in the divorced family without first reviewing some of the general information about divorce that has accumulated over the past decade. There are three reasons within the context of this chapter (and this book) that such an overview is important. First, the community of psychologists, sociologists, and other professionals interested in divorce has not been sufficiently effective in bringing their empirical and conceptual knowledge to forums where policy decisions are made. Consequently, information contained in this chapter (as well as chapters 10 and 11) might serve to enlighten those people most directly involved in formulating policy concerning child support and child custody: economists, judges, and attorneys. Unfortunately, the professional literature in these fields has not yet developed along some of the lines of information these people should have available. Second, no family, whether intact or in a state of transitional stress as many divorced families are, operates as a set of individual members. As Skolnick suggests, there are as many marriages in a family as there are members.[4] Before we can understand the impact of divorce on the father and in turn how that impact affects his willingness to provide child support, we should first examine the effects of divorce on the family as an integrated unit. Finally, there is a meager amount of information available about the father's role in the postdivorce setting.

To get some idea as to the state of our knowledge concerning the effects that divorce has on children, some of the critical points might be summarized as follows.

During the first year following divorce, there seems to be a set of steps that characterize the development of new family patterns and functioning.[5] The initial increase in the amount and type of stress leads to a sense of disequilibrium and disorganization, followed by the use of certain coping mechanisms, the development of a new pattern of functioning in the single-parent household, and final adjustment on the part of the children to a new stepparent relationship. This stress that is associated with divorce is aggravated by concomitant economic and interpersonal problems that frequently arise.

These stress points can be introduced in three general areas; practical problems that deal with economic and occupational issues, emotional stress, and the maintenance of significant interpersonal relationships.[6] For example, Hetherington, Cox and Cox report how men in their sample had difficulty managing the house cleaning, shopping, and laundry.[7] Economically some fathers were forced to take additional jobs to provide adequate support and be able to keep up with the costs of maintaining two separate households. It is important to remember that child support often includes providing an additional set of resources at the father's (or noncustodial parent's) place of residence.

The second transition point is identified by the emotional stress that accompanies changes in family status and associated change in self-perceptions, self-concept, and general level of well-being. Many fathers who are separated from their children experience an intense sense of loss and rootlessness in that their lives lack any significant structure. Following the divorce, both mothers and fathers felt "anxious, depressed, angry, rejected and incompetent," making it increasingly difficult to provide necessary support.[8]

Finally, the maintenance of relationships with significant others becomes a point of potential stress. After initially being very active in interpersonal interactions immediately following divorce, support from friends tends to decrease, and a rather inconsistent pattern of ups and downs begins. These relationships, however, eventually stabilize by the second year following the divorce.

Recently divorced parents cope less well than those in intact families. In summarizing the literature, Levitan reported that divorced parents made fewer maturity demands on their children, used discipline in a less-consistent manner, showed less affection, and communicated less effectively.[9]

A cycle of negative parent-child interaction between mothers and sons, especially during the first year following divorce, has been described by Hetherington, Cox, and Cox.[10] This cycle is characterized by noncompliant and aggressive behavior by the son, leading to feelings of inadequacy and incompetence on the part of the mother, which in turn can lead to difficulties in parenting. This destructive cycle can continue to repeat itself until some type of intervention is introduced. The type of intervention and when it is introduced plays a key role in the successful post-divorce adjustment of the entire family and the maintenance of child-support payments.

Children at different developmental levels deal with the issues and consequences of divorce in different ways.[11] Just as the affective component of a child's functioning mediates the impact that divorce might have, so does one's cognitive level act as a filter for these significant events. How a child understands divorce can have a significant impact on the later interaction between the child and/or both parents.

Predivorce characteristics of the family and personal interactions between members are highly unreliable as predictors of postdivorce behavior, including child support.[12] Eighteen-month follow-ups "point to serious limitations in relying on the predivorce relationship between father and mother (or mother and child) as a reliable predictor of the postdivorce relationship."[13]

This finding raises some interesting questions about how much we actually understand the divorce process. Perhaps one measure of that understanding is the use of a criterion measure such as payment of child support that successfully predicts any one of many possible outcomes. For now, however, we have yet to ascertain that such a criterion, or set of criteria, exists.

Although it has not been a popular notion in our society, divorce can act as a functional adaptation by some families to deal with the stress associated with discordant relationships. This is especially true when an agreement can be reached that is acceptable to all parties (including the children) as far as child custody and support issues are concerned. Weiss reports that adolescents whose parents separated were happier and felt more secure than those children whose parents remained married but were unhappy.[14] Further supporting this notion of acceptable divorce, Edwards and Hoover cite how divorce is preferable to rearing a child in a tension-filled two-parent home.[15]

Fathers who are custodial parents have many of the same concerns that custodial mothers have, such as managing a home, providing emotional support for their children, and dealing with issues such as sex education.[16] Interestingly, after a period of readjustment to managing a family singlehandedly, many fathers view their parenting skills and child relationships as very satisfactory, in spite of some rather humorous anecdotes in the literature about fathers' initially not knowing how to cook the most basic foods or what foods their children like or dislike. In the single-parent, father-headed family, the pattern of discordant mother-son interaction has been found to be reversed. Warshak and Santrock found that girls in father-custody families are less well adjusted than girls in mother-custody families.[17]

Finally, fathers who are attached to their children prior to the divorce indulge them and find it especially difficult to withdraw from this relationship. They consider the separation from their children to represent a significant loss.[18] The amount of interaction between separated fathers and children tends to increase immediately following the divorce, and it declines rapidly, as does the high degree of indulgence. The impact of the loss on the father tends to remain.

These noneconomic factors that are related to the payment of child support have been the least well studied of all the factors discussed in this book. Historically, child support continues to be the province of economists and lawyers who are not concerned with the complex set of human factors that contribute to postdivorce adjustment and child support.

The Father's Role

The role of the mother in child rearing has been extensively studied, and the dynamics of this dyadic relationship are well on their way to being understood. The tender-years presumption and the tacit implication that mothers belong at home with their children has always strongly influenced the awarding of custody to the mother. Yet for the father, there is reason to be optimistic. The second half of the 1970s has been characterized as the era of paternal rediscovery; fathers are no longer being considered as by-products of the family's process of development and change but, instead, as an integral part of this process.[19]

The reasons for this historical emphasis on the mother's influence upon child rearing can be found in at least two sources. One is the biological preparedness that accompanies pregnancy and the inferred biological connectedness that has been discussed by Lewis and Weinraub.[20] Further, in experimental settings, mothers have been found to interact in a more caregiving way than fathers, whose role has been one involving play rather than nurturance. The second reason is that with the introduction of an industrial society, the division of labor between men and women became more pronounced, and the tasks associated with child rearing fell to the female.

In spite of the fact that in the past, fathers have been seen as somewhat unobtrusive influences on their child's development, the social and economic mores of our times coupled with the impact of the women's movement has encouraged, liberated, and sometimes required men to assume parenting and child-rearing roles. The two-parent working family is now more often the rule rather than the exception; in the past fifteen years, two-parent working families have increased some 30 percent. Given changes in personal and economic conditions, mothers can no longer remain as the primary caretaker or parent. Similarly, fathers are called upon to contribute in the less directly financially rewarding areas of being a supportive houseworker, including the duties that such a responsibility entails.

This reintroduction of the father into the mainstream of the family has raised an especially difficult and enigmatic issue. In light of the small number of fathers who are given legal custody of their children, it is unrealistic to expect fathers to have the opportunity to continue a close and consistent relationship with their children following divorce. This creates for the father a conflict between the encouragement and social pressure to participate fully in the upbringing of the child yet the denial of the benefits of equal parenting should the marriage be dissolved. This is only one of the many factors that might contribute to a stressful postdivorce relationship and the subsequent lack of any encouragement or incentives to provide child support.

There is almost a father backlash, which results from the new expectations of equal responsibility for child rearing on the father's part balanced against clearly unequal recognition. This can create, at the least, the potential for a good deal of dissonance in the family, affecting the well-being of the father-child relationship in the postdivorce situation and child-support payments.

What We Know about Fathers

Measured against what we know about mothers and their children, our knowledge about fathers is meager. Although this is not the place for an extensive review of what literature is available on this topic, it might be useful to review briefly some of the information we have that defines the father's role in the family.[21] It is essential to remember, however, that the father's influence on the dynamics of the family certainly cannot stand alone. In fact, the dyadic interactions (mother-child or father-child and mother-father) that have caught the fancy of so many investigators during the past as the logical units of analysis in the family are being replaced by an interest in the mutual relationships represented by the mother-father-child interaction. In light of Skolnick's comments about the multiplicity of relationships within any marriage, this knowledge that we have about fathers has to be considered relative to other available information.

Perhaps the most significant finding about the relationships between fathers and children is that fathers are as nurturant and supportive as mothers.[22] This is especially important since it helps to demystify the prominent influence that mothers continue to have, as well as elevating the father to a position commensurate with his capabilities.

The majority of studies relating the influence of fathers to child development, however, have focused on the effects of father absence and separation from the child. Beginning with Carlsmith's study on the effect of father absence on scholastic aptitude, additional work has been completed that seems to substantiate her conclusion that the absence of a father in the family is somewhat related to a depressed level of cognitive performance.[23]

The latter-day version of this same type of study has replaced the absent father with stepparents, examining the effects of stepparent presence on cognitive and personality variables. Chapman studied the effects of father absence and stepfather presence on the cognitive performance of ninety-six college-age students.[24] He compared father-absent families, families where a stepfather was present, and intact families and found that father absence is somewhat related to lower scores on standardized achievement tests and an increase in field dependence (an indicator of analytic versus global cognitive problem solving strategies). The most interesting finding was that the presence of a stepfather tended to mediate this trend of decreased or depressed performance.

Such findings raise two important issues. The first is the lack of information we have in general about the impact of stepparents on the child's postdivorce adjustment and subsequent relationship with the noncustodial parent. Most divorced parents remarry—30 percent more in 1978 than in 1960—and the child needs to establish a relationship with two sets of parents, as well as reestablish a relationship with the noncustodial parent given his or her new spouse and associated changes.[25] The second issue is that we have little idea if the effect of an absent father is due to the lack of stimulation and contributions that fathers may provide for the family or the introduction of stress related to and resulting from the father's absence, or the divorce itself. Lamb differentiates these two sources of influence from one another in what he calls direct sources (those influences due to the absence of a parent) and indirect sources (those due, for example, to the stress introduced in the mother's daily life).[26]

Another area that has recently received attention is the sex role that the parent assumes and its relationship to the psychological sex role adopted by the child. Students of psychoanalytic theory recognize that the major influences on a child's development take place during the early formative years. One of these major factors is the presence of an appropriate sex-role model after which the child models his or her behavior that subsequently can be reinforced.

Chapman argues that an important influence on the relationship between children and their fathers, and the extent to which the father actively participates in the rearing of his children, is the father's concept of sex-appropriate behavior.[27] Sex-appropriate behavior may be better labeled *gender-appropriate behavior* since it is not concerned with biological sex as much as it is with the degree to which an individual incorporates masculine and feminine characteristics into his or her own personality. In her extensive work in this area, Bem has found that androgynous people indeed incorporate both kinds of behaviors into their repetoires.[28] In her standard measure of androgyny, people are defined as masculine (high on masculinity and low on femininity), feminine (high on femininity and low on masculinity), undifferentiated (low on both masculinity and femininity), and androgynous (high on both masculinity and femininity).

Chapman examined divisions of labor in child care as it relates to sex-role perceptions by fathers. He found that fathers classified as androgynous were more involved with everyday child-care activities than those fathers who were classified as masculine. Interestingly, no relationship was found between mother-perceived sex role and child care. This may be due to the fact that even mothers exhibiting predominantly masculine behavior are still bound by economic constraints and are forced to be the primary caretaker. In other words, the variablility among females in the sample may be artificially constrained.

Encouraging Child Support through Intervention

Beginning with the social and political reforms of the Great Society during the early 1960s, intervention programs as a general strategy for assisting selected groups of people have become very popular. Although expensive, many of the programs that aimed at assisting children from low-income families have proved to be valuable from a psychological perspective (for example, they have increased feelings of self-worth and led to other positive personality changes), as well as in terms of economic value. For example, an economic analysis of the Perry Preschool Project has revealed a significant decrease in the amount of special education required for children who participated in the preschool program versus those who did not.[29] Weber et al. estimated that the total savings, including all economic factors, is about $3,000 per child per year over a five-year period.

Although they have not been termed as such, intervention strategies are being used effectively in a variety of settings, including medical rehabilitation, preschool education, and programs for the developmentally disabled. For most of these, the same general questions are germane to the strategy regardless of the content. When should the intervention be initiated? At what level of intensity should the treatment take place? How should the outcomes of the intervention program be evaluated? Is the associated cost of the intervention justifiable given the outcomes?

As far as the provision of and assurance of child-support payments, there are two general intervention strategies that we might examine. The first focuses on the way in which the divorce process itself is completed and whether the settlement is litigated or mediated. The second is illustrated by the work of Wallerstein and her colleagues, which represents a specific intervention program aimed at the father's relationships with his children in the situation where the mother is the custodial parent.

Predivorce Intervention

The first of these intervention strategies deals with the process through which the divorce takes place: specifically, the relative effects of litigation versus mediation in intrafamily personal relationships.

The resolution of divorce disputes can be divided into three major classes according to how the major critical issues between the involved parties are to be settled: desertion (leading to no child-support payments), litigation, and third-party intervention or mediation.

In an analysis of mediation as an alternative to litigation, Bahr has demonstrated the enormous savings to taxpayers of some $10 million in court costs and over $90 million in savings concerning legal fees.[30] More important, however, are the noneconomic indicators of past divorce status. Bahr found that general satisfaction with custody arrangements using mediation was 94 percent, while the level of satisfaction without the use of mediation was 86 percent. Also impressive was the finding that satisfaction with the decision concerning money and property distribution was 100 percent for those who chose mediation versus only 49 percent for those who did not. Most important, however, was the finding that 53 percent of the people who chose mediation were very satisfied with the divorce decision, while only 15 percent of those who did not use mediation were as satisfied.

Bahr did not collect direct evidence concerning child support, but it is not too great a leap of logic to hypothesize that if mediation leads to increased satisfaction with property and monetary decisions and levels of general adjustment, then child support might also assume a less-hostile psychological valence than within a litigation setting.

What might these results indicate about the payment of child support? People who believe that the divorce settlement is more equitable may be more likely to direct less anger and aggression toward their former spouses who may be responsible for the care of the children. It is doubtful that when individuals have the choice, they would choose an uncomfortable relationship with their former spouse versus one that affords some comfort and even security. Although data concerning the impact of litigation versus mediation on the children of divorced families are not currently available, this question cannot go begging for long.

Postdivorce Intervention

The strategy that Wallerstein and her colleagues have used is based on the assumption that divorce carries the potential for disrupting the flow of the developmental process, and that this disruption could be reversed or modified by appropriate interventions with children and with their parents.[31] To this end, the Divorce Counseling Service in the San Francisco Bay area was established in 1970 to provide the types of interventions that would assist children in incorporating the divorce experience into their everyday functioning.

In light of the notorious lack of empirical evidence regarding recommendations and policies concerning child custody and support, Wallerstein's work is important. In spite of some of the methodological shortcomings, it is the first systematic attempt to understand (and show) how outside intervention can affect father-child postdivorce relationships. Although the policy implications of this work have not been considered up to now, potential links between the research and its policy outcomes might be better understood given the wider dissemination of these tentative findings.

The Wallerstein strategy is strongly stage-related. Intervention programs based on behavioral or cognitive developmental paradigms that have proved so useful in other settings have yet to be applied in this context.

Wallerstein and Kelly conducted a five-year longitudinal study of 131 predominantly white middle-class children from 60 divorcing families.[32] All of the children who participated in the study were between the ages of three and eighteeen years and did not have any history of clinical problems or any other complications that might distinguish them from the remainder of the experimental group. Over a six-week period, and within six months of the initial separation by the parents, a team of interviewers conducted clinical interviews with parents and their children. Additional interview data were collected again within one year of the initial interviews and then five years later. The follow-up rate of over 96 percent is unusually high and raises some interesting questions about the geographic and economic stability of the families who participated in the study, as well as their willingness to cooperate.

The intervention strategies suggested by Kelly and Wallerstein are grounded in the psychological stage of the child and the degree of crisis the divorce represents for the child given that stage of development. For example, work with preschool children focused on such intervention activities as teaching the parents specific techniques for communicating with their young child about the divorce process and related events taking place in the family's life, the treatment that parents could apply to symptomatic reactions to the stress introduced by the divorce, and a strong emphasis on the continuity of caretaking where visiting of the noncustodial parent is an integral part of the child's life.

On the other end of the spectrum, strategies with preadolescents might take the form of brief interventions where the therapist would fill the space (left by the ambivalent feelings on the part of the child) as to which parent he or she might choose to live with. Extended interventions could consist of something as simple as longer-term opportunities for the preadolescent or adolescent to discuss the dynamics of the divorce and the changing nature of the family with an objective or certainly noncondemning individual.

Because "Bread and Roses" represents the forefront of intervention and empirical work in this area, I feel obligated to offer some critical evaluation. My primary concern about the design of the study is the absence of a control group in the experimental comparison, in the form of intact families. The lack of such a group especially threatens the validity of this study since we cannot be sure at any point whether some of the changes (or differences) observed are due to the economic status of the family (including the father) or confounding variables such as cohort effects. This may be especially important since a developmental component is introduced into the design.

My other concern focuses on the assumption that the independent variable of greatest utility is the economic status of the family. Although of interest, I think that this one factor receives more attention than it may deserve. For example, children who come from intact homes might be characterized by some of the same destructive patterns of behavior as are children of those parents who are divorced or separated for any number of reasons. A single global variable, as is described in "Bread and Roses," leaves too much variability unaccounted for in the realtionships between family members and calls for some sort of multivariate analysis and design.

Another problem is the lack of attention to the psychometric characteristics of the assessment instruments and procedures. At best in any measurement setting, we should strive for minimal trait and method variance to ensure that the findings are replicable and generalizable over time. Given the subjective nature of the assessment procedures alluded to in Wallerstein and Huntington's work, I am not comfortable that this critical element was preserved throughout the research.

Finally, as rich and generative as the clinical tradition is, it does little as far as enhancing replicability. Perhaps future work that assesses similar traits using more-objective methods will yield confirmation or disconfirmation of these results.

Although these methodological and substantive criticisms of the Wallerstein and Huntington work cast some shadows on the credibility of the intervention strategy as defined, it is essential to remember that these criticisms are focused more on method than substance. For the most part, all of these criticisms address the improvement of a design that has already resulted in significant and interesting outcomes. In other words, although the research could have been conducted in a more-rigorous way, the outcomes reported have high credibility given the potential for competing explanations that did not reveal themselves in the final analysis.

Organizing the Factors Related to Postdivorce Adjustment

Because of the uniqueness of the family unit and its members, it represents something qualitatively different than the contributions of each of the members alone. For this reason we might seek some system or set of dimensions that will help us organize the ways in which these members interact with one another. Table 12-1 lists a set of factors related to postdivorce adjustment gleaned from the literature. To help us organize the potential interactions of these factors, we can classify each according to Kurdek's identification of four interdependent levels that describe the world of the child's postdivorce relationship; the macrosystem, the exosystem, the microsystem, and the ontogenetic system.

The macrosystem defines factors concerning cultural beliefs, attitudes and values generic to family life. The exosystem deals with the stability of the postdivorce environment and the nature of the social support system that is available to the newly formed single-parent household. The microsystem focuses on predivorce and postdivorce relationships, and the ontogenetic system focuses on the individual child and his or her competence in dealing with the stress associated with divorce.[33]

This classification system provides a context for examining how the different factors listed in table 12-1 might affect the father's adjustment following

Table 12-1
Factors Related to Postdivorce Adjustment

Factor	Reference	System	Question Posed
Vulnerability to sources of stress	Garmezy (1975)	Ontogenetic	How well can the child deal with the stress associated with divorce?
	Colleta (1978)		What impact do multiple sources of stress or conditions of chronic stress and extrafamilial factors have on the child?
Age of child at divorce	Tessman (1978) Hetherington (1979) Kalter and Rembar (1981)	Ontogenetic	What qualitative differences exist in children at different developmental levels as far as perceptions and interpretations of the divorce process?
Availability of noncustodial parent	Hess and Camara (1979)	Exosystem	Does physical distance from the noncustodial parent affect postdivorce adjustment?
Sex differences and postdivorce adjustment	Hetherington et al. (1978)	Ontogenetic, microsystem	Does the impact of divorce differ for boys and girls?
Changes in family patterns	Ross and Sawhill (1975)	Macrosystem, microsystem	How do postdivorce changes such as economic instability affect children?
	Brandwein et al. (1974)		What impact do changing parental breadwinner roles have on the child?
Parent-child relationship	Wallerstein and Kelly (1980)	Microsystem	How does the conflict between parents during the divorce process affect the subsequent parent-child relationship?
Absence of one parent	Hetherington et al. (1978)	Macrosystem	What is the effect of the absence of role models who can demonstrate a wide range of skills?
Predivorce and postdivorce relationship	Kelly (1978) Wallerstein and Kelly (1978)	Microsystem	Does the predivorce parent-child relationship have any predictive validity for postdivorce relationships?
			Does the equality of parent-child interaction change following divorce?
Nonnuclear support systems	Spicer and Hamper (1975)	Macrosystem, exosystem	Can kinship availability assist the child in postdivorce adjustment?
Marriage settlement	Wallerstein and Kelly (1980)	Macrosystem	Were decisions on child support, alimony, and other issues settled fairly via mediation?

Factor	Reference	System	Question Posed
Quality of post-divorce social relationships	Hetherington et al. (1978)	Exosystem	To what degree are the divorced parents satisfied with their social and interpersonal relationships?
Economic conditions following divorce	Hetherington (1979) Hoffman (1977) Desimone-Luis et al. (1979)	Macrosystem	How does a sharing of income or decrease in available resources affect the postdivorce adjustment
Sex-role differences	Russell (1978)	Macrosystem	How does a parent's concept of sex-appropriate behavior affect childrearing patterns?

Garmezy, N. The experimental study of children vulnerable to psychopathology. In A. Davids, ed., *Child Personality and Psychopathology*, Vol. 2, New York: Wiley, 1975.

Colleta, N.D. Divorced mothers at two income levels: Stress, support, and child rearing practices. Unpublished thesis, Cornell University, Ithaca, 1978.

Tessman, L.H. *Children of Parting Parents*. New York: Aronson, 1978.

Hetherington, E.M. Divorce: A child's perspective. *American Psychologist*, 1979, pp. 851-858.

Kalter, N., and Rembar, J. The significance of a child's age at the time of parental divorce. *American Journal of Orthopsychiatry*, 1981.

Hess, R.D., and Camara, K.A. Post-divorce family relationships as mediating factors in the consequences of divorce for children. *The Journal of Social Issues* 35 (1979):79-96.

Hetherington, E.M.; Cox, M.; and Cox, R. The aftermath of divorce. In J.H. Stevens, Jr., and M. Matthews, eds., *Mother-Child, Father-Child Relations*, Washington, D.C.: National Association for the Education of Young Children, 1978.

Ross, H.L., and Sawhill, I.V. *Time of Transition: The Growth of Families Headed by Women*. Washington, D.C.: Urban Institute, 1975.

Brandwein, R.A.; Brown, C.A.; and Fox, E.M. Women and children last: The social situation of divorced mothers and their families. *Journal of Marriage and the Family* 36 (1974):498-514.

Wallerstein, J.S., and Kelly, J.B. *Surviving the Breakup: How Parents and Children Cope with Divorce*. New York: Basic Books, 1980.

Kelly, J.B. *Children and Parents in the Midst of Divorce: Major Factors Contributing to Differential Response*. Paper presented at the National Institute of Mental Health Conference on Divorce, Washington, D.C., February 1978.

Spicer, J., and Hamper, G. Kinship interaction after divorce. *Journal of Marriage and the Family* 28 (1975):113-119.

Hoffman, S. Marital instability and the economic status of women. *Demography* 14 (1977):67-77.

Desimone-Luis, J.; O'Mahoney, K.; and Hunt, D. Children of separation and divorce: Factors influencing adjustment. *Journal of Divorce* 3 (1979):37-42.

Russell, G. The father role and its relation to masculinity, femininity, and androgeny. *Child Development* 49 (1978):1174-1181.

divorce. For example, the age of the child when parents divorce is a factor within the ontogenetic system, while the availability of a custodial parent most directly affects the family's exosystem. None of these factors can stand alone, nor can the father's role be separated from any other. This interdependence between the factors surrounding any divorce proceeding demands a consideration of the father in the context of the family and his interaction with his children before we can understand factors associated with child support.

A Workable Solution: Joint Custody

From an examination of the factors critical for both the father and children during the postdivorce adjustment period, it is clear that we are faced with a multidimensional set of forces that are just beginning to be investigated. The most common denominator across these different factors, however, is that they all influence the degree to which a father can, or is willing to, provide child support when he is the noncustodial parent. They also influence his position along a continuum that has total absence of the father on one end and, on the other, what we will call joint custody. The distribution of who actually gets custody seems skewed, with there being relatively few cases of joint custody or coparenting.

Single-parent custody awards have been popular. The argument for single-parent custody is most broadly based on the seminal work of Goldstein, Freud, and Solnit entitled *Beyond the Best Interests of the Child.*[34] Based on psychoanalytic theory, they cite a number of arguments why single custody as opposed to any other custody arrangement is optimal for the child's development. Four important examples of these arguments, cited by Stack, are as follows.[35] Their first, and most general, argument for single custody is that the nuclear family presents an environment for the child that is a "protective enclave." Their adherence to the notion that a family must be intact to provide protection and support is paramount to their stance on single custody and has some precedence in its importance to our society.

Second, they believe that any arrangement other than single custody produces a "pathological" outcome, where children grow up to be "malfunctional" and maladaptive as a result of a chaotic and inconsistent home environment.

Third, they argue that the continuity that is so important to successful child development is missing, resulting in a child who has difficulty establishing the appropriate identity given the confusion in role models. They argue that unless children have clearly defined limits as to who is responsible for them and their behavior, destructive loyalty conflicts can and will develop. What is especially puzzling about this position is their assumption that two adults being apart cannot perform necessary parenting duties.

Fourth, and perhaps most important for our discussion here, is that Goldstein, Freud, and Solnit suggest custody be given to only one parent, who then has complete control over the visitation rights of the noncustodial parent. For many reasons, not excluding the common sense of what is best for the child in the long run, this seems to be misguided advice.

If continued support from noncustodial fathers is in part contingent on the quality of the postdivorce relationship they have with their children (presumably controlled by the mother), to advise anything other than a policy that facilitates his contact with his children is at best self-defeating and at worst destructive for the postdivorce adjustment for all members of the family.

An arrangement where the mother (or in rare cases the father) has total control over visitation rights immediately places the custodial parent in a position of control and power. In an already strained relationship, this pits parents against each other, with children as the objects of victory or defeat. We know that the postdivorce adjustment period is very difficult for children of all ages, and it is highly questionable whether this added stress is beneficial for anyone involved. It is important to keep in mind that what is father absence for the child is also child absence for the father. Simply stated (and as endorsed by a good deal of available literature, including the longitudinal work of Wallerstein and Huntington), if the father is emotionally supported following divorce, it is more likely that he will continue to provide financial support. If the task at hand is to ensure child support, we should be examining policies that encourage coparenting participation rather than discouraging parents from wanting to have a continuing relationship with their children.

It is within this context that such an argument for joint custody can be effectively made. Perhaps the best operational definition of joint custody is offered by Steinman in her study of thirty-two children living in joint-custody arrangements.[36] She used a set of three criteria to define joint custody: (1) both parents have authority and responsibility for the decisions that are made concerning the child's welfare, (2) parents view themselves as being equally important to the children and "jointly responsible for their physical, emotional, intellectual and moral development," and (3) the children have two separate residences. Generally joint custody is an arrangement between two parents allowing the children to be the charges of two adults, who provide for all of their needs on an equal basis. Galper has used the term *coparenting* to describe the same situation.[37]

For many, however, and especially in light of our society's rejection of divorce as a sometimes healthy and necessary step, joint custody contains overtones of parental irresponsibility and ambiguity toward the child. These feelings are in part generated by a series of theories about joint-custody arrangements.

Among some of these theories is that one parent is not as good as two regardless of the disharmony between them, that two residences cannot provide the quality of home life that one can, that joint-custody parents care less about their children than parents in intact families (otherwise they would have never separated), that unsuccessful marriages breed unsuccessful children, and that joint custody encourages inconsistent parenting practices.

Although most of the literature on joint custody "has been based on personal and professional opinions rather than systematic study," recent studies have helped to clarify some of the confusion over joint custody and some of its advantages and disadvantages.[38] For example, Abarbanel, in an intensive case study of four families, found that parents were generally satisfied with joint parenting and that the children in the family accepted the arrangement as well.[39]

Two important and well-executed studies in this area support joint custody as a viable policy alternative. The first, a survey of forty middle-class divorced fathers, focused primarily on their relationship with their children and examined their perceptions of the postdivorce relationship.[40] Although the sample chosen for the study was somewhat select (white middle-class professionals) and probably not representative of the more-general population of divorced fathers, the importance of the outcomes should not be underestimated. For example, the greater the father's involvement in the rearing of his child, the greater is his sense of having an ongoing parental role in the child's postdivorce life. Besides directly involving him in the health and welfare of his child(ren), it is, as Greif calls it, "self-reinforcing: the more opportunity fathers have to act as fathers, the more they see themselves as fathers and seek to continue that involvement."[41] As a noneconomic factor that contributes to child support, father involvement is clearly important and something that seems to be increased through a joint-custody arrangement.

The second study, completed by Ahrons, is even more persuasive in its argument for coparenting.[42] She interviewed 54 divorced parents and found that the more contact the parents had with one another, the more supportive and mutually cooperative they were concerning parenting responsibilities. In her study, a total of 108 divorced parents were interviewed. The interviews were analyzed using the most sophisticated analytical techniques of any other studies in this area. Among the many variables examined were frequency and content of coparental interaction and quality of communication. The results support the development of a new descriptive concept presented by the author as the "binuclear family," where both a maternal and a paternal household is established. Ahrons points out that even though the process of divorce necessitates a dissolution of many of the traditional aspects of the nuclear family, the demands that are placed on postdivorce relationships can force the establishment of a new equilibrium represented by this new family structure.

Ahrons generally found that "parents who have a mutually supportive and cooperative co-parenting relationship also interact quite frequently and share much more besides child rearing.[43] In fact, those who did interact most frequently were also those who were the most supportive and cooperative parents.

As a policy alternative to single-parent custody, joint custody seems to have some attractive features. The increasing spiral of divorce, the increase in dual-career families that will experience divorce, plus the fact that in 1978, 54 percent of mothers with children less than six years of age were in the labor force speaks to the need for an arrangement that will facilitate the healthy development of children already under stress as a function of separation or divorce, yet will not compromise the psychological integrity of the noncustodial parent. Simultaneously, this arrangement should also allow the adult with the children to seek a fuller life while still remaining a competent parent.

If the primary argument that Goldstein, Freud, and Solnit make is that the child thrives best in the setting of a nuclear family, we must consider as well the evidence that the trauma of divorce is mediated by the child's accessiblity to both parents regardless of the family's structure.[44] As Greif effectively communicates, one way to maximize the amount of contact that children have with both parents is through a joint-custody arrangement. She points out how "structural arrangements such as custody and visitation are crucial to the postdivorce adjustment of fathers and, ultimately, of their children."[45] A different quality of psychological involvement grows out of the opportunity to take care of, to be a parent to, one's children rather than visit with one's child.

Conclusion

When one parent in a divorcing couple clearly poses a danger to a child, the decision on the part of the judge as to who should receive custody and furnish support may be relatively easy and straightforward. This is rarely the case, however. In spite of many parents' inability to meet some of the criteria that are related to adequate parenting, each parent often feels responsible and competent to undertake a difficult and often stressful job of raising a child in a single-parent family made even more difficult by postdivorce tensions and arguments over visitation rights.[46] The fact that over one-third of divorced families are involved in disputes over visitation and custody speaks to the fact that the status-quo awarding of children to one parent (usually the mother) leaves something to be desired in terms of establishing and maintaining a pattern of consistent noncustodial child relationships and subsequent child support.

Joint custody is an effective policy alternative for ensuring that child-support payments are met. The primary reasoning behind this conclusion is that the available evidence shows that under joint or coparenting conditions, postdivorce relationships of fathers, children, and mothers produce better-adjusted people who feel as if they are being treated more equitably.

For many years, decisions on custody and child support (which are very difficult, if not impossible, to separate one from another) have been based on personal opinion and subjective judgments. By far, all of the information we need about those factors mentioned in table 12-1 is not available and that which is is certainly not conclusive. But what is available is enough to seriously question present practices of awarding single-parent custody, including single-parent support as well.

Additional research is needed along some of the lines suggested in this chapter, and above all, social scientists and professionals outside of the disciplines of law and economics need to become more familiar with and involved in the policymaking process and thus communicate available information to those interested parties.

Notes

1. J. Pfeiffer, "Full Time Fathers," *Science* 80 (1980):32-34.

2. P.G. Glick, and A.J. Norton, *Marrying, Divorcing and Living Together in the U.S. Today.* Population Bulletin, 1978, *32,* 3-38.

3. G. Masnick and M.J. Bane, *The Nation's Families: 1960-1990* (Cambridge: Joint Center for Urban Studies of MIT and Harvard, 1980).

4. A. Skolnick, "The Family and Its Discontents," *Society* (January-February 1981): 42-47.

5. E.M. Hetherington, M. Cox, and R. Cox, "The Aftermath of Divorce," in J.H. Stevens, Jr., and M. Mathews, eds., *Mother-Child, Father-Child Relations* (Washington, D.C.: National Association for the Education of Young Children, 1978).

6. Ibid.

7. Ibid.

8. Ibid.

9. T.E. Levitan, "Children of Divorce: An Introduction," *Journal of Social Issues* 35 (1979):1-25.

10. Hetherington, Cox, and Cox, "Aftermath of Divorce."

11. N. Kalter and J. Rembar, "The Significance of a Child's Age at the Time of Parental Divorce," *American Journal of Orthopsychiatry* 51 (1981):85-100.

12. J.B. Kelly, "Children and Parents in the Midst of Divorce. Major Factors Contributing to Differential Response" (Paper presented at the National Institute of Mental Health Conference on Divorce, Washington, D.C., February 1978); J.S. Wallerstein and J.B. Kelly, "Effects of Divorce on the Visiting Father-Child Relationship," *American Journal of Psychiatry* 12 (1980):1534-1539.

13. Ibid.

14. R.S. Weiss, *Marital Separation* (New York: Basic Books, 1975).

15. E. Edwards and E. Hoover, *The Challenge of Being Single* (Los Angeles: J.P. Teacher, 1974).

16. H.A. Mendes, "Single Fathers," *Family Coordinator* 25 (1976):439-440; D.K. Orthener, T. Brown, and D. Ferguson, "Single-Parent Fatherhood: An Emerging Family Lifestyle," *Family Coordinator* 25 (1976):429-437.

17. R. Warshak and J.W. Santrock, "The Effects of Father and Mother Custody on Children's Social Development" (Paper presented at the Society for Research in Child Development, San Francisco, March 1979).

18. J. Wallerstein and J.B. Kelly, *Surviving the Breakup: How Children and Parents Cope with Divorce* (New York: Basic Books, 1980).

19. M.E. Lamb, "Fathers: Forgotten Contributors to Child Development," *Human Development* 18 (1975):245-266.

20. M. Lewis and M. Weinraub, "Sex of Parent X Sex of Child: Socioeconomical Development," in R. Rubart, R. Friedman, and J.R., Vande Wiele, eds., *Sex Differences in Behavior* (New York: Wiley, 1974).

21. L. Bonson, *Fatherhood: A Sociological Perspective* (New York: Random House, 1968; H.B. Biller, *Paternal Deprivation* (Lexington, Mass.: Lexington Books, D.C. Heath and Company, 1974); R.D. Parke, "Perspectives on Father-Infant Interaction," in J.D. Osofsky, ed., *Handbook on Infant Development* (New York: Wiley, 1979).

22. R.D. Parke and S. O'Leary, "Father-Mother-Infant Interaction in the Newborn Period: Some Findings, Some Observations, and Some Unresolved Issues," in K. Riegel and J. Meacham, eds., *The Developing Individual in a Changing World,* vol. 2: *Social and Environmental Issues* (The Hague: Mouton, 1975).

23. L. Carlsmith, "Effect of Early Father Absence on Scholastic Aptitude," *Harvard Educational Review* 34 (1964):3-21; R.W. Blanchard and H.B. Biller, "Father Availability and Academic Performance among Third Grade Boys," *Developmental Psychology* 4 (1971):301-305. E.A. Nelson, and E.E. Maccoby, "The Relationship between Social Development and Differential Abilities on the Scholastic Aptitude Test," *Merrill-Palmer Quarterly* 12 (1966):269-284.

24. M. Chapman, "Father Absence, Step Fathers, and the Cognitive Performance of College Students," *Child Development* 48 (1977):1155-1158.

25. J.C. Westman, *Child Advocacy* (New York: Free Press, 1979).

26. M.E. Lamb, "Paternal Influences and the Father's Role," *American Psychologist* 34 (1979):938-943.

27. Chapman, "Father Absence."

29. S.L. Bem, "The Measurement of Psychological Androgeny," *Journal of Consulting and Clinical Psychology* 42 (1974):155-162.

29. C.U. Weber, P.W. Foster, and D.P. Weikart, *An Economic Analysis of the Ypsilanti Perry Preschool Project* (Ypsilanti, Mich.: High/Schope Educational Research Foundation, 1978).

30. S.J. Bahr, "Divorce Mediation: An Evaluation of an Alternative Divorce Policy" (Unpublished manuscript, University of Utah, 1980).

31. Kelly, "Children and Parents."

32. Wallerstein and Kelly, *Surviving the Breakup.*

33. L.A. Kurdek, "An Integral Perspective on Children's Divorce Adjustment," *American Psychologist* 36 (1981):856-866.

34. J. Goldstein, A. Freud, and A. Solnit, *Beyond the Best Interests of the Child* (New York: Free Press, 1973).

35. C.B. Stack, *Who Owns the Child? Divorce and Child Custody Decisions in Middle-Class Families* (Durham, N.C.: Duke University, 1978).

36. S. Steinman, "The Experience of Children in a Joint Custody Arrangement: A Report of a Study," *American Journal of Orthopsychiatry* 51 (1981):403-414.

37. M. Galper, *Co-parenting: Sharing Your Child Equally* (Philadelphia: Running Press, 1978).

38. Steinman, "Experience of Children."

39. A. Abarbanel, *Joint Custody Families: A Case Study Approach* California School of Professional Psychology, Berkeley, Calif.: 1977).

40. J.B. Greif, "Fathers, Children, and Joint Custody," *American Journal of Orthopsychiatry* 42 (1979):311-319.

41. Ibid.

42. C.R. Ahrons, "The Continuing Coparental Relationship between Divorced Spouses," *American Journal of Orthopsychiatry* 51 (1981):415-428.

43. Ibid.

44. Hetherington, Cox, and Cox, "Aftermath of Divorce"; Wallerstein and Kelly *Surviving the Breakup;* Wallerstein and Kelly, "Effects of Divorce."

45. Greif, "Fathers, Children, and Joint Custody."

46. Westman, *Child Advocacy.*

**Part V
Parental Child-Support
Laws and Systems
in Developed Countries
Other than the
United States**

13 Child Support: A Global View

H. Robert Hahlo

"Parents are obliged to care for their childen and maintain their interests."[1]
If there is a natural law, written in the stars and observed even in the animal
world, one of its basic tenets is that parents have to support their children
until the children are able to support themselves. It is thus that the survival
of the species is secured.

There were times when in the common law the duty of parents to maintain their legitimate children was only indirectly enforceable and when an illegitimate child, being in law "no one's child" (*a filius nullius*), had no
claim to support against either parent.[2] Modern legal systems impose upon
both parents a duty to support their children, in proportion to their means,
and do not discriminate against the illegitimate child.[3]

The duty of parents to support their children is conditional on two requirements being satisfied: that the children cannot support themselves out
of their own income and that their parents are able to provide support. The
children may have inherited estates with income sufficient to maintain
them. Conversely, one of the parents may be destitute.

German law is exceptional: the duty of parents to maintain their
children goes further than any other support obligation. Whereas as a
general rule, a person is not deemed to be in need of support if he can maintain himself out of income or out of capital, a minor unmarried child is not
obliged to draw upon his capital before claiming support from parents.[4]
Again, whereas as general rule, no obligation to render support is imposed
upon a person who cannot render it without unduly depressing his own
standard of living, parents are obliged to share all of their disposable means
equally with their children, even if it means that they have to sacrifice their
own standard of living. This is subject to the proviso that in this case, and
only in this case, a minor who has capital of his own must exhaust it before
claiming support from parents.[5]

As long as parents and their children live together under one roof, questions of child support rarely arise. The needs of the child are taken care of in
the ordinary course of living. In the relatively rare cases where a young child
is abused or abandoned by parents or the parents fail to provide adequate
food, clothing, and medical aid, the parents are liable to criminal penalties.

It is in the case of the one-parent family that the question of child support becomes acute: the marriage of the parents has ended in divorce or
separation; the "common-law" union of which the child was born has

broken up; or the child was conceived in promiscuous intercourse. In the majority of cases, the child remains in the mother's custody, and the father's duty of support becomes transformed into an obligation to provide the mother with an appropriate contribution to the child's upkeep. The following analysis is based on the assumption that custody vests in the mother. The same principles apply, in reverse, where custody is awarded to the father or a third person. Here, the mother, if she has means, may be obliged to contribute to the child's maintenance. In many instances, no doubt, the father will fulfill this obligation willingly, without having to be taken to court. In most, the matter will come before the court.

Where, as part of a divorce or separation agreement, the parties have agreed upon the amount to be paid by the father, the mother will apply to court to make the agreement an order of court. If both parties were assisted by counsel and the agreement is not, on the face of it, unreasonable or unfair to one or other of the parties or the child, most courts will embody it in its decree without a detailed investigation of its terms. The court, however, if it so deems fit, can override the agreement of the parties. Nor can the parents of the child by their agreement deprive the court of the power to vary the agreement, should a change in the circumstances of the parties or the child call for it.[6] Failing an agreement between the parties, an application for child support by the father will be made to court by the mother or some public agency acting on her behalf.

Like problems tend to evoke like responses. There is a remarkable degree of uniformity among modern legal systems in their approach to child-support orders. The enabling statutes of virtually all Western jurisdictions refer to the needs of the claimant and the respondent's ability to pay as the main factors to be taken into account, leaving the rest to the courts. Thus, the French Code Civil, dealing with legitimate children, provides that "By the mere fact of their marriage, spouses contract the obligation to nourish, maintain, and educate their children."[7]

Regarding support obligations generally, the code lays down that "Maintenance is awarded in accordance with the need of the person claiming it and the means of the person owing it."[8]

As to the "subsidy" to be paid by the father of an illegitimate child, the French Code Civil lays down that "The maintenance is fixed in the form of periodical payments according to the needs of child, the resources of the debtor, and the situation of the family."[9]

The Quebec Code Civil states briefly that "spouses and relatives in the direct line, owe each other support."[10] It equates illegitimate children to legitimate children,[11] and as to the measure of support generally, the code states, "In awarding support, account is taken of the needs and means of the parties, their circumstances and, as the case may be, the time needed by. the creditor of support to acquire sufficient autonomy."[12]

The German B.G.B. ("Burgerliches Gesetzbuch"—Civil Code) prescribes that persons related to each other in the direct line are obliged to support each other.[13] It goes on to say that only a person who is unable to support himself is entitled to support[14] and that no support can be claimed from a person who is not able to render it without jeopardizing his ability to support himself.[15] In determining the measure of the support to be rendered for a child, the social position of the child's parents is decisive. Provision must be made for the necessities of life, including the costs of education and of an appropriate training for a trade or profession. Several provisions in the German code recognize that among support obligations, the duty of parents to support their minor children holds a special, privileged position.

German law requires the parents to support illegitimate children just as they would legitimate children.[16] Here, too, the position of both parents (and not, as in older German law, of the mother only) is taken into account in assessing the measure of support to be rendered.[17]

Unlike other legal systems, German law specifies a tariff fixing minimum accounts payable by a father as support for a child, legitimate or illegitimate, who is below the age of eighteen years and does not live in the father's household.[18] The amounts rise, as they ought to, with the age of the child—a certain amount for a child below the age of six years, more for a child from six to twelve, still more for a child from twelve to eighteen years. Where a child requires support after the age of eighteen, the court is at large in fixing the amount payable.

Perhaps the most detailed statement of the factors taken into account by the court when determining what financial provision should be made on divorce or the annulment of a marriage for a child of the marriage is found in the English Matrimonial Causes Act 1973. It enjoins the court to "have regard to all the circumstances of the case including the following matters":

a) the financial need of the child;
b) the income, earning capacity (if any) property and other financial resources of the child;
c) any physical or mental disability of the child;
d) the standard of living enjoyed by the family before the breakdown of the marriage;
e) the manner in which he was being and in which the parties to the marriage expected him to be educated or trained.[19]

These are obviously the main factors that any court anywhere will consider when dealing with child support.

Apart from ordering the father (or mother) to make provision for the maintenance of a child of the marriage by periodical payments or a lump-sum payment, the court may order either parent to settle property on the child.[20] The courts' powers are to be exercised so as to place the child, so far as it is practicable, "in the financial position in which the child would have been if the marriage had not broken down and each of [the parties to the marriage] had properly discharged his or her financial obligations and responsibilities towards him."[21]

In Canada, under the federal Divorce Act 1967/68, the courts are empowered, upon granting a *decree nisi* of divorce, to make an order requiring either the husband or the wife to secure or to pay such lump-sum or periodic sums as the court thinks reasonable for the maintenance of the other and/or the children of the marriage.[22] The section does not detail what the court should take into consideration, but merely states that the court is to have regard to "the conduct of the parties [husband and wife] and the condition, means and other circumstances of each of them." A child of the marriage is defined as a "child of a husband and wife who at the material time is (a) under the age of sixteen years, or (b) sixteen years of age or over and under their charge but unable, by reason of illness, disability or other cause, to withdraw himself from their charge or to provide himself with necessaries of life."[23]

British Columbia, one of the common-law provinces, provides in the Family Relations Act, R.S.B.C. 1979, c. 121 as follows:

1. Each parent of a child is responsible and liable for the reasonable and necessary support and maintenance of the child, taking into account the:
   a. cost of reasonable residential accommodation, housekeeping, food, clothing, education, recreation, and supervision for the child;
   b. child's need for a stable and supportive environment; and
   c. financial circumstances and obligations of each person liable for the support and maintenance of the child.
2. The making of an order against one parent for the maintenance and support of a child does not affect the liability of another parent for the maintenance and support of the child or bar the making of an order against the other parent.[24]

In Ontario, which considers all children as legitimate, the Family Law Reform Act 1978 holds that "every parent has an obligation, to the extent the parent is capable of doing so, to provide support in accordance with need, for his or her child who is unmarried and is under the age of eighteen years."[25] Among the factors to be taken into account by the courts in determining the measure of support, mention is made of the capacity of the child to provide for his own support, the capacity of the parent to provide support, and "the child's aptitude for and reasonable prospects of obtaining an education." The other provinces have similar provisions.

Since modern legal systems impose child-support obligations upon both parents, the court, in assessing the amount to be paid by the father to the mother, will have due regard to the income and earning capacity of the mother, for she too has to contribute her share. Where the mother has no means and her circumstances are such that she cannot be expected to work outside the home while the husband is well off, the whole financial burden of maintaining the child will fall on him. Where the mother has an adequate income, the courts, in determining how the financial burden is to be divided between father and mother, will bear in mind that the mother has to see to the daily care and upbringing of the child, a task that however rewarding, requires much time and effort on her part.

In the past, the father's duty of support ended automatically when the child reached a fixed age—sixteen years, eighteen years, the age of majority. Most modern systems have no automatic cutoff date, and even where the governing statute mentions a terminal age, the courts are inclined to regard it as no more than a guideline, which in an appropriate case, may be ignored. When the child comes from a family where going to college or university is traditional and the child possesses the necessary aptitude, the parents may have to support the child until he or she has completed the university course, long after attaining majority. Said Mr. Justice Ritchie in the Canadian Supreme Court case of *Jackson* v. *Jackson,* "The line is to be drawn at such point as the Court granting a *decree nisi* of divorce thinks it just and fit to draw it in all the circumstances of the particular case at issue having 'due regard to the conduct of the parties and the condition, means and circumstances of each of them,' "[26]

In England, it is now settled law that a court will not allow a man to absolve himself from his obligation to his family at public expense. Said I.J. Ormrod in *Clarke* v. *Clarke*:

> Reduced to a simplistic outline it [the defendant's argument] was this: people whose marriages broke down should have their wives and children maintained by social security unless they were rich enough to be able to provide for them without any appreciable inconvenience to themselves. This was really getting too much.[27]

The courts, however, will never push a man (and, if he has one, his second family) below subsistence level. When the means of the parties are of such modest proportions that an order against the husband, based on what otherwise would be a fair figure, would result in his being left with a sum quite "inadequate to meet his own financial commitments," the court may have regard to the fact that social security benefits will be available to his wife and children.[28]

In some countries, child-support awards invariably take the form of orders for periodic payments. In others, including England, orders may be made for periodic payments or for lump-sum payments.[29] In connection with a divorce, English courts may also order secured periodical payments and/or property adjustments, such as the transfer of the matrimonial home from husband to the wife for the benefit of the children.[30]

There is much to be said for flexible awards—awards that take into account future changes that are virtually certain to occur, such as the increasing needs of the child as she or he grows older or the effects of inflation. They obviate the need for repeated applications for variation on the grounds of a change in circumstances.

In Quebec, indexing of alimentary pensions is mandatory. The Civil Code provides that

> the court orders, on the motion of the creditor or, in the absence of such motion, *ex officio,* that support payable as a pension be adjusted in accordance with the annual Pension Index established pursuant to . . . the Quebec Pension Plan, unless the circumstances of the parties justify the fixing of another index.[31]

And in the province of Ontario, where no such express provision exists, the family court of Toronto has recently inserted an indexing clause in a maintenance award made in favor of a divorced wife. German law provides, subject to certain qualifications, for automatic indexing.[32] French law empowers the courts to insert a variation clause: *"selon les circumstances de l'espece."*[33]

In accordance with the *in praeteritum non vivitur* maxim, the orthodox rule in civil-law systems was that support could be ordered only for the future, never for the past. Exceptions applied if the father could not be found or otherwise evaded his obligations and the mother had to incur debts or use up her savings in órder to be able to feed her family. Most modern maintenance statutes expressly empower the courts to order support payments to be made for any period in the past. The Quebec provision contains important qualifications: support for preexisting needs may not be granted for more than twelve months, and then only if it is impossible for the creditor to act sooner or from the day the debtor was given formal notice.[34]

Everywhere the courts have powers to rescind, vary, or suspend an order for child support if a material change in the circumstances of the parents or the child occurs. That the order was made in terms of an agreement between the parties does not affect this power. Whatever the position may be regarding a nonvariation clause in an agreement for interspousal support, regarding child support, a contractual nonvariation clause is against public policy and therefore ineffective.[35] In deciding whether a variation is called for, however, an agreement between the spouses is one of the factors that the court will take into consideration.[36]

In most jurisdictions today, civil or common law, support orders can be modified retroactively concerning accumulated arrears. Thus, the Quebec Civil Code provides that "the debtor from whom arrears are claimed may plead a change after judgment in his condition or in that of his creditor and be released from payment of the whole or a part of them," but adds the qualification that "in no case where the arrears claimed have been due for over six months may the debtor be released from payment of them unless he shows that he was unable to exercise his right to obtain a review of the judgment fixing the alimentary pension."[37] Inflation, if not provided for by indexing in the original order, may be a factor justifying the variation of a support order.

A question to which no satisfactory answer can be given is what approach the court should adopt if a divorced man with a one-family income establishes a second family.[38] Is it better to condemn one family to poverty level while allowing the other one a comfortable existence or to reduce both to a spartan standard of life? And assuming that a choice has to be made, which family is to be preferred: the first or the second? Considering that a man ought not to feather his second nest at the expense of his first one and that his second wife, knowing of his previous marriage, must accept him subject to his commitments to his first family ("subject to a lien in favor of his first family," as some American judges have put it), some judges take the view that the needs of the children of his first marriage must always take precedence over those of the second one. This was also the view in England of the Archbishop of Canterbury's group, which took the stand that the claims of the first family were "inescapable."[39] On the other hand, the courts recognize that it would be undesirable to fix the support to be paid by the father to the children of his first family so high that he cannot pay it without reducing his second family to destitution.

In England the practice of the Supplementary Benefits Commission, in dealing with the man with two families, used to be to allow the man to keep for himself and his new family sufficient money to maintain them at supplementary benefit scale rates, with an additional element for housing costs plus a quarter of his net earnings, or five pounds, whichever was higher. His contribution for the maintenance of his former family had to come out of what was left.[40] However, everything must depend on the circumstances. In Tovey v. Tovey, the defendant had left his wife and three children and was living with an unmarried woman, who had two children and whom he intended to marry.[41] He argued that he should not be ordered to maintain his wife and children because if he had to pay them any maintenance, this would leave him with less than under the Supplementary Benefits Commission's formula. The court of appeal rejected this argument and held that he had to maintain his children even if, as a result, he would be put below subsistence level, let alone the commission's level. Said I.J. Ormrod:

> The question then was should he [the husband] be able literally to off-load the whole of his obligation to his wife and three children onto the State,

simply by taking over another woman with two children? It seemed to his Lordship, even in these days a startling proposition that a man who was in regular work should be required to make no contribution at all to the maintenance of his own children.

He went on:

> As a pure matter of public policy it was very undesirable indeed that a man should not, even in a purely formal sense, continue to contribute to the children who were his primary responsibility.

To paraphrase Mary Ann Glendon's remarks in *State, Law and Family,* why should the burden of other people's "serial marital adventures" be borne by the taxpayer?[42]

It is suggested that it is futile to look for a hard-and-fast rule and that every case must be decided on its own merits. Payment may be ordered to be made to the parent who has applied for support for the child, to an appropriate third person, to the court, to the welfare agency providing support for the child, or, in some legal systems (as in English law) to the child directly.[43]

If the mother fails to act, some official agency may intervene on the child's behalf. In Ontario application for an order for support of a dependent child may be made by a parent of the child, or, where they provide financial assistance for the child, by the Ministry of Community and Social Services or the municipality concerned.[44] In Quebec it may be made by the holder of the parental authority, the child's tutor, or any person who has custody of the child.[45]

There is no obligation on the woman to sue the child's father for child support before she can apply for social benefits for the child.[46] Where the father is able to pay, a social agency that had to provide support for the child because the father defaulted on his obligations is given in virtually all legal systems the right to recoup itself from the father.

In civil-law systems, a parent who had to bear the whole burden of support because the other parent could not be found or defaulted on his obligations has a right of recourse against the other parent, and a trader who supplied the child on credit with the necessities of life has a claim for recovery on the basis of having conducted someone else's business (*negotiorum gestio*—management of another's affairs) against the defaulting parent. In Ontario, the Family Law Reform Act 1978 makes provision to the same effect.[47] On the same principle, a stepfather who found himself compelled to provide the child with maintenance because the father failed in his duties may have a claim for reimbursement against the father.[48]

Everywhere it is provided that a child's claim to support may not be ceded or attached for debt.

The central problem in child support is the matter of enforcement. In all legal systems, the mother of the child may enforce the court's order by ordinary execution, and this generally works where the father is well off. Here the mere threat of attachment of goods or garnishment of wages will usually be sufficient to make him pay up. Nor, though for different reasons, do difficulties arise where the father of the child or children is destitute. Here, the mother of the child, if unable to maintain the child out of her own earnings or income, will have to make do with whatever social assistance she can obtain. The problem father is the man who, at little sacrifice to himself, can afford to provide the child of a previous marriage or extramarital union with support but who resents having to do so, perhaps because he dislikes his former wife or considers that she is not doing enough herself, perhaps because he feels that he no longer has any real ties with his son and daughter. Many fathers, no doubt, realize their responsibilities and pay as ordered. But many will go to any length to evade their obligation. In almost all countries, the success rate in enforcing child-support obligations is dismally low.

Recognizing that in most instances lack of means and legal understanding make it impossible for the deserted mother of a child to force the delinquent father to pay, all Western countries have set up public agencies that, automatically or at the mother's request, enforce support orders. In Ontario there is automatic enforcement by the clerk of the Unified Family Court or of a provincial court.[49] In Quebec a collector of support payments, appointed by the Minister of Justice, enforces support payments.[50] In Israel, National Insurance acts in the dual role of the provider of social assistance and the enforcer of support obligations. In France the Treasury enforces support orders,[51] in Michigan, the Friend of the Court.

Judging by well-nigh universal experience, the following are the main factors making for success in the enforcement of child support orders.

First, and most important, the officer or agency entrusted with enforcement must have the determination of a particularly tenacious bulldog, with the will to pursue the delinquent father, if need be, to the ends of the earth, and (to change metaphors) to use every weapon in the armory to make him pay.

Second, the law must provide a simple, speedy, and inexpensive garnishment procedure. For fathers steadily employed, garnishing their wages has proved to be the most effective means to make them live up to their obligations. The English Attachment of Earnings Act 1971 and the French Loi No. 73-5 of January 2, 1973, *relative au paiment direct de la pension alimentaire* (law regarding the direct enforcement of maintenance obligations), supplemented by *decret* 73-216 of March 1, 1973, may serve as models of efficacious procedures. Under the French act, all the person entitled to support under an order of court has to do, if the debtor fails to pay within the time fixed by the court, is to have a demand for direct payment served on his debtor's debtors by a *huissier de justice* (bailiff, executive officer of the court).

Third, everything should be done to make it possible to trace a delinquent father who has vanished. In most countries the support debtor is obliged to notify the judgment creditor or the clerk or public agency entrusted with the enforcement of support orders, of any change in his residential address or employment.[52] In England, Social Security and National Health Services, the Passport Office, Supplementary Benefits Commission, and the Ministry of Defence are required to assist the courts in tracing defaulting breadwinners.[53]

Fourth, repugnant as it may be to modern notions, civil imprisonment must be available, and ruthlessly used, where the father, though able to pay, persistently attempts to evade his obligations. Some systems rely for this purpose on contempt of court proceedings; others have specific provisions dealing with debtors who fail to comply with a support order. In Ontario, the court may order the attachment of the debtor's wages, present and future, and may order the debtor to give security. Where there is default in payment, the clerk of the court may require the debtor to file a statement of financial information, submit to an examination as to his assets and means, and appear before the court to explain his default. If he does not appear as ordered, a warrant for his arrest may be issued, and if he fails to satisfy the court that his default is owing to his inability to pay, the court may order his imprisonment. This order may be made conditional upon continuing default.[54]

Routine procedure in South Africa is to sentence a defaulting father to imprisonment, suspended on condition that he pays in the future as ordered and reduce arrears in whatever installments the court deems appropriate. The procedure is an effective way to make stubborn defaulters comply. Proof that failure to pay was due to lack of means and that such lack of means was not due to unwillingness to work or misconduct on the part of the debtor is a good defense.

As Alec Samuels remarked in the August 1981 issue of the English *Justice of the Peace,* "At the end of the day imprisonment must be the ultimate sanction. Everything else has been tried and has failed. . . . He [the debtor] is deliberately and continuously flouting the order of the court. He must go to prison."[55]

How has the problem of child support assumed, almost overnight, its present dimensions? The reason is the short-term marriage. By the laws of God and humanity, parents are required to take care of the needs of their children until they can look after themselves. But the children of *Homo sapiens,* unlike the offspring of animals, take a long time to grow up—anything from sixteen years upward. The divorce rate is ascending steadily, and where a marriage breaks up, it is usually before it has lasted ten years, long before any children born of it have reached man's (or woman's) estate.[56] More short marriages mean more one-parent families.

It has been suggested that broken marriages should be regarded, like motor accidents, as the unavoidable detritus of life in modern society and that, when a marriage breaks down, leaving destitute children in its aftermath, the state should assume responsibility for them. "In this way, energy and resources would not be utilized in enforcement proceedings which may result in little, if any, success."[57]

As early as 1968, Neville Brown of the University of Birmingham, England, prophesied that before long,

> the private law of maintenance will tend to wither away and its place be assumed by social security legislation. In other words, by the year 2000 the law will have abandoned as socially undesirable, frequently ineffectual and wholly uneconomic the hounding of spouses through the courts for non-support of their families. Non-support by spouse or parent will be ranged alongside those other vicissitudes of life—unemployment, sickness, industrial injury, child-birth, death itself—for which social insurance should make provision.[58]

Others have suggested insurance schemes, public or private, to provide for the children of broken marriages. In France, it was proposed to set up a public insurance program through which payment of support would be guaranteed by the state, which would then try to recover the sums paid by it from the debtors. This scheme was rejected on the ground that nothing should be done that might have the effect of diminishing the individual's sense of personal responsibility for his children.[59]

I am inclined to associate myself with this view. Children are produced by the deliberate acts of men and women. As an old German saying has it, to become a father is not difficult, but to be a father is. To shift responsibility for a child from the man who has fathered it to the community would offend against the basic moral and legal principle that a man is responsible for the consequences of his own intentional acts. So far from relieving him from liability, everything possible should be done to make him face up to his obligations, and only if both father and mother are destitute should social assistance be resorted to.

Notes

1. Arntzenius *Institutiones* 1.13.5 (1783).
2. A.H. Manchester, A Modern Legal History of England and Wales 1750-1950, 389, 390, 393 (1980).

3. *See e.g.,* arts. 203 and 334 of the French Civil Code (hereinafter referred to as C.C.), and paras. 1601 and 1615a of the German *Burgerliches Gesetzbuch* (Civil Code—hereinafter referred to as B.G.B.); also, M. Glendon, State, Law and Family 274 (1977); Thomson, The Parental Obligation to Maintain 9 Fam. L. 71 (1979).

4. B.G.B. para. 1602 (II).

5. *Id.* at para. 1603 (II).

6. *See, e.g.,* MacDougall, "Alimony and Maintenance," *Studies in Canadian Family Law* 293 (1972), 92 (Supp. 1977).

7. C.C. art. 203 (author's free translation).

8. *Id.* at art. 208 (author's free translation).

9. Art. 342-2 (author's free translation).

10. Quebec C.C. art. 633.

11. *Id.* at art. 594.

12. *Id.* at art. 635.

13. B.G.B. para. 1601.

14. *Id.* at para. 1602.

15. *Id.* at para. 1603.

16. *Id.* at para. 1615a.

17. *Id.* at para. 1615c.

18. The tariff is laid down in an ordinance: *Regelsunterhalts-Verordnung.*

19. Matrimonial Causes Act 1973, § 25(2).

20. *Id.* at § 24(1).

21. *Id.* at § 24(2).

22. Divorce Act 1967/68 (Canada) § 11.

23. *Id.* at § s. 2.

24. Family Relations Act R.S.B.C. 1979 c 121, 556.

25. Family Law Reform Act 1978 (Ont.) § 16.

26. (1972) 29 D.L.R. (3d) 641 (S.C. of Canada) at 650. See also B.G.B., para. 1610, C.C. arts. 342-2, and see note 6 *supra* at 348-349, and 141 (Supp. 1977).

27. (1979) 9 Fam. Law 15.

28. Barnes v. Barnes [1972] 3 All E.R. 872; Walker v. Walker (1978), 8 *Fam. Law* 107.

29. Matrimonial Causes Act 1973, §§ 23, 24; Domestic Proceedings and Magistrates' Court Act 1978 § 2.

30. Matrimonial Causes Act 1973, § 23, 24. *See* Thomson, *supra* note 3, at 17.

31. Quebec C.C. art. 638.

32. B.G.B. para. 1612a.

33. C.C. art. 208.

34. *See, e.g.,* § 19(f) of the Ontario Family Law Reform Act, 1978; and art. 643 of the Quebec C.C.

35. *See, e.g.,* B.G.B. paras. 1614, 1615a, and the House of Lords case of Hyman v. Hyman 1929 A.C. 601.

36. Note 6 *supra* at 137.

37. Quebec C.C. art. 644.

38. Note 6 *supra* at 340-341.

39. Glendon, *supra* note 3, at 278.

40. Thomson, *supra* note 3, at 108 (referring to Finer Report on One-Parent Families (1974) Cmd. 5 no. 29, paras. 206-9).

41. (1978) 8 *Family Law* 80. *See* Thomson, *supra* note 3, at 108.

42. 279.

43. *See, e.g.,* The English Domestic Proceedings and Magistrates' Courts Act 1978 § 32; the Ontario Family Law Reform Act 1978 § 19.

44. Family Law Reform Act 1978 § 18.

45. Quebec C. C. art. 634.

46. Thomson, *supra* note 3, at 108.

47. § 33.

48. *See, e.g.,* the Canadian case of Stere v. Stere [1980] 30 O.R. (2d) 200.

49. Family Law Reform Act 1978 (Ontario) § 27, as substituted by the Family Law Reform Amendment Act 1979.

50. Quebec Code of Civil Procedure, §§ 659.1ff.

51. Loi No. 75-618 du 11 juillet 1975.

52. *See, e.g.,* the English Attachment of Earnings Act 1971 § 15, and the South African Maintenance Act 23 of 1963, § 14.

53. (1978) 8 Family Law 117.

54. Family Law Reform Act 1978 (Ontario) §§ 28-31.

55. (145 *English Justice of the Peace* 456 1981).

56. Statistics show that the fifth through seventh years are the critical years in marriage. The marriages of teenagers are especially vulnerable.

57. Kloppenburg, Enforcement of Maintenance, 40 Sask. L. Rev. 231-232.

58. Neville-Brown, Maintenance ad Esoterism, 31 Mod. L. Rev. 137, (1968) 59. Glendon, *supra* note 3, at 276-277.

14

The Maintenance Jungle: A Comparative Review of Findings Related to the Effectiveness of Child-Support Laws in Various Developed Countries

Alastair Bissett-Johnson

The object of this chapter is to offer some comparative insights into child support and alimony in Canada, England, and Australia so that those who are reformulating the state and federal laws in the United States may see those points worth pursuing or discarding.

In practice there are common problems in all jurisdictions. Women generally do not receive equal pay for work of equal value even when they continue to work full time after childbirth. Often their careers are interrupted or their work is part time, and the child-care facilities necessary to enable them to work are often unavailable.

In other areas different problems emerge. For example, although child support is not tax deductible in the United States, it is in Canada.[1] In Canada, the taxpayer, typically the father, may deduct support payments from his tax. The payments then become taxable in the hands of the recipient, typically the mother, subject to the usual range of personal exemptions or deductions.[2] Typically the mother will have a lower marginal tax rate than the father, so the net effect is to allow income splitting and to increase the free funds available in the hands of the father to pay maintenance or support. Thus to a father with a marginal tax rate of 50 percent, support orders of $12,000 per year will reduce his take-home pay by only $6,000 per year and the mother, assuming a 20 percent tax rate, will pay only $2,400 tax on the payments. Although the role of tax as an instrument of public policy cannot be ignored, the present proposals have attracted some criticism, and the tax system in Canada at least, by a system of tax exemptions rather than flat-rate tax credits, rewards the richer parent with a higher marginal tax rate to a greater extent than those on lower marginal tax rates or those who do not pay tax at all.[3] Thus in the example, if the father who is ordered to pay $12,000 in support payments has a marginal rate of 20 percent his take-home pay will be reduced by $9,600.

Social Assistance

The first person to whom the custodian in charge of a child will turn for support is the state.[4] Even where those providing welfare or assistance have a direct action against a liable relative (usually the husband or father),[5] they seem to prefer to force[6] or encourage[7] the custodian (usually the wife or mother) to institute proceedings. Usually the wife or mother has little heart for such proceedings, which are, at the least, painful reminders of a failed relationship and usually produce no net financial return to the recipient since any payment is deducted dollar for dollar from social-welfare payments. Moreover, whereas welfare or social-assistance payments are regular, if modest, the wife or mother waiting for support payments from her child's father will testify that such payments are irregular or even nonexistent. Diversion or assignment of the support payments from the recipient to the welfare authorities (who then take over enforcement of the order in return for assuming the responsibility of paying the sums due under the order to the mother), has been advocated or achieved in some countries, but in Nova Scotia, although Guaranteed Income Payments seemed to work well in a pilot project in Cape Breton, the allegation that wives and mothers are the best enforcers of support orders has prevented the extension of the scheme throughout the province.[8]

Even when some part of the social-assistance burden is transferred to the liable relative, in many cases the amount that the payer can afford still leaves the recipient dependent on the payments from welfare authorities in order to meet a minimum standard of living.[9] Moreover, emergency needs can rarely be covered out of private support orders. However, public-welfare payments for the mother and children may be lost if the wife and mother is cohabiting with another man.[10] Despite the difficulty of defining such a term and the fact that the termination of public support, especially that for children, may inhibit the mother's building up new relationships that would ensure somebody else would assume the support obligation, cohabitation assures (often on dubious evidence) loss of support.[11] In Britain the tendency is to allow the continued payment of social assistance for a period for children after that for the mother has been terminated.[12]

The Order Itself

In Anglo-Canadian-Australian experience, support for both wife or common-law wife and child is often included in the same order, though the mother of an illegitimate child has only limited rights.[13] Cassetty's justified recognition of the blurring between alimony and child support is worth emphasizing and is a suitable topic for further study.[14] When maintenance for both wife and child is possible, some judges allege that psychologically the liable relative is more willing to support children than an estranged spouse, and they manipulate their orders accordingly. If alimony is unavailable under state law, as in Texas, the role of child support becomes even more pressing.

English and Australian experience suggests that even when support orders are made, such orders are for small amounts and almost always go quickly into arrears.[15] There may even be a tradition for magistrate's courts or family courts operating below the superior-court level to "think small" since they rarely deal with higher socioeconomic groups. Even in inflationary times, upward variations are rarely encountered, accounting for no more than 25 percent of the variations found by Finer, while the other 75 percent of variations were downward.[16]

Making and Quantum of Orders

There are few extant data available from cross-sectional surveys that tell much about the lives, circumstances, and resources of fathers who do not live with their children. What data we do have are not very encouraging. The Finer Committee Report indicated that in 1965, 70 percent of defendants in the inferior courts in England were receiving less than the then-average wages in manufacturing industries.[17] And the amounts the defendants were ordered to pay were less than half of what a woman with two children would have received on social assistance. The follow-up study in 1971 suggested that the purchasing value of orders actually went down between 1966 and 1971.[18] Variation of such orders rarely took place (the woman has little incentive given that any increase in support is usually deducted dollar for dollar from her support). The first experiments with not taking the whole of a woman's income into account in calculating her social assistance have involved earnings disregards. Extensions of this principle to maintenance may be worth pursuing. The same position holds true in Australia where Sackville demonstrated that in 1971, the average affiliation order was only $6 per week.[19] Even with inflation it is hard to resist the conclusion that such orders involve the most economically deprived sections of the community (and often the youngest). Small though the payments may be, they represent a disproportionate part of family income of poorer families. Moreover, the men were often left by the courts with less money than if they had made an informal arrangement with the social assistance authorities.[20] All of this led the Finer Committee to suggest that administrative means of resolving payments outside the court structure would be preferable.[21] The involvement of courts and lawyers may make the process slower, more expensive, less flexible, and more psychologically intimidating than an administrative process.

Recently two more detailed Canadian studies have been published on support obligations. Evidence that women who have the least years of schooling,[22] are poor, or who have a large number of children find that they have difficulty in obtaining orders or that any orders they obtain are small is hardly surprising, though the importance of the number of children in ensuring a payer's commitment to pay is interesting.[23] Nor is it surprising that nonwhite women find awards too expensive to seek or not worth the trouble because of the absent father's inability to pay. However, the caution on the possibility of underreporting of receipt by mothers or wives of support is timely and shows the difficulty of obtaining accurate statistics.

The fact that support for illegitimate children is less may be associated with the increase in teenaged pregnancies and anecdotal evidence that child abuse and neglect is encountered in such cases.[24] The teenaged fathers are unable to provide support, and the pregnancy may have been an attempt to secure social assistance to enable the mother to live separately from her parents with whom she may not be on good terms. In Nova Scotia the government has considered refusing social assistance to such mothers unless they have the emotional and financial support of their parents. No doubt the effect of such a change would be to increase the children available for adoption and to effect certain financial savings in social assistance. Its social consequences would be much more difficult to predict. The mere abolition of the legal distinction between legitimacy and illegitimacy may founder in practice on increased problems of proof of paternity, since the more casual the relationship, the more difficult paternity is to establish, as may be the enforcement of any resulting order.[25]

The question of the quantum of support may be related to the mechanism for securing that support. In practice we may have two separate systems of support, and the Finer Report may have been correct in questioning whether an administrative rather than legal solution is more appropriate for poorer families.[26] In wealthier families in Canada, the wife may be able to take advantage of the newer matrimonial property laws in all provinces to get a fair division of family property, or by use of secured lump-sum maintenance powers on divorce to receive support in a form that does not require constant enforcement.[27] The English courts have achieved similar results under the so-called clean-break principle.[28] Where the family income is smaller, the need for continuing maintenance and its proportion of the family budget increases. As Krause has pointed out, the distinction between poor and nonpoor families does not coincide with the distinction between AFDC and non-AFDC families if state support does not measure up to the poverty line.[29]

Length of Payment

In Canada, maintenance may go on until age twenty-four (if the child is undergoing postsecondary education), or longer (in special circumstances such as disability).[30] In England payments cease at eighteen unless the child is undergoing further education or training or there are special circumstances, such as disability.[31]

Enforcement

Once an order is made, there remains the problem of enforcing it. Even though in federal countries such as Canada and Australia, reciprocal enforcement of support is possible from state to state, it is quite another matter to locate a recalcitrant payer.[32] Statistics Canada relates that subsequent to the breakup of relationships, men become unprecedentedly mobile.[33] Anecdotal experience from Australia suggests that much of the developing areas of Australia, such as the north of western Australia, is populated by estranged husbands and fathers. Locating such men would be easier if federal data banks such as those of taxation agencies, as in the United States, were made available. In England such information is made available through the courts to the woman's lawyer. The information is not, however, made available to the woman herself for fear of causing harassment.[34] This practice has no counterparts in most of Canada or the United States. Quebec has recently added a new article, 546.1, to its Code of Civil Procedure by which a judge is empowered, where a support order is in arrears, to order a person, such as a relative of the defaulting payer, to furnish the address or work place of the defaulting payer.[35] Noncompliance attracts penalties. The only exceptions permitted are for those such as lawyers entitled by professional privilege to keep their clients' whereabouts secret. In practice a man's right to privacy may translate into a man's right to neglect his children or leave them destitute, since in neither Canada nor Australia is the existing reciprocal enforcement of maintenance legislation working well. Enforcement of orders under the federal divorce act is easier (if the defaulting parent or spouse can be found), but regrettably, the federal government in Canada is talking of a constitutional amendment to return the federal power over divorce back to the provinces. Since the federal government has the most complete data bases of residents in all parts of Canada, its involvement in the area of enforcement of support is essential. Although some Canadian provinces have provisions making their own data bases, such as vehicle registration and medical insurance, available to spouses wishing to trace their former partners, such provincially created powers cannot bind the federal govenment or have extraterritorial effect on other provincial government agencies.[36] Only the Manitoba Attorney General's Department routinely makes a crown counsel available to help persons with custody orders from another Canadian province or a divorce order, including custody and maintenance, made elsewhere in Canada, to enforce them in Manitoba.[37] However, in light of the Alberta survey, the problems of locating defaulting men should not be overexaggerated.[38]

Even if the whereabouts of the payor is known, garnishing of wages seems to work only against those who have a desire to pay but fritter away their wages.[37] It does not work well with those who are constantly prepared to change jobs. Even deducting at source depends on the new employer's knowing of the existence of the order.

Imprisonment has the undesirable effect of transferring the cost of supporting payor, recipient, and children to the taxpayer. Chambers is no doubt correct in claiming that "jailing kills a host of geese (or should it be ganders!) for a few golden eggs." No doubt there is a case for the retention of jailing to enforce maintenance, but it is questionable, despite Chambers's research, whether the cost of jailing a man produces a commensurate increase in support by encouraging other potentially recalcitrant men to meet their commitments.[40] The cost to the state includes the cost of keeping the man in jail plus possible additional social-assistance payments to the wife children.

In neither England, Australia, nor Canada does the collection rate reach the 80 percent payment in full referred to by Chambers[41] in Flint County or the lower figure mentioned by Sørensen and MacDonald.[42] In England half the orders in 1966 were in arrears, and one may doubt whether things have changed for the better since then.[43] In Canada, Wachtel and Burtch found that in a small sample the orders were in arrears on average by $2,000, though this varied with the life of the order and the court that made it (extraprovincial orders had higher arrears).[44]

Recent Canadian Studies

Recently two significant empirical studies on maintenance within Canada have been published. The first, by Wachtel and Burtch, was sponsored by the Policy Planning Department of the British Columbia Ministry of the Attorney General and the Social Planning and Research Department of the United Way of the Lower Mainland, and was based on court watching at the Vancouver family court in 1980 and a quantitative examination of court files from the same court.[45] The second study was an in-depth study by the Alberta Institute of Law Research and Reform.[46] Sponsored by the Federal Health and Welfare Department, Alberta Social Services Department, and the Institute of Law Research and Reform, it consisted of various components involving maintenance cases and the parties to it in Alberta.

The Vancouver Study

The median order in the sample had been made in 1975, and one-third of the orders covered mothers as well as children. The authors estimated an expected life for child-support orders of nine years, though the recovery of arrears might extend that estimate.

Original awards averaged $157 per month, though the median was $110. Typically there were two dependent children, and the awards averaged three-fourths of the comparable basic welfare rates.

Arrears was a feature of these cases. The median arrears was $1,950, which tended to rise with the life of the order. Orders originating in other provinces had significantly higher arrears.

The authors' court watching identified a number of responses among defaulting payors. In cases where payors had fluctuating incomes arising from seasonal factors, they were reluctant to save in periods of high income to have resources available to meet commitments, such as maintenance, during periods of reduced earnings. The authors also commented on the well-known problems of the interrelations of maintenance and access and the problem of the relative priority of first and second families.[47] The authors claimed that the court tried to avoid detailed accounting disputes and that it worked with a few simple premises:

a. in practice, two households are more expensive to maintain than one, so the standard of living must fall after separation if there is no additional income;
b. sacrifice cannot be demanded by the father, only prudence or, at least, no conspicuous waste;
c. that is, the respondent can expect to live at a reasonable level himself before he is expected to provide support for the divided family. The significance of this position, however worldly wise and reasonable, is that the "best interests of the children" are strongly prejudiced because the court accepts the notion (held also by the respondent) that separation had fundamentally changed the position of the children as dependent. After separation there are two households and two sets of expenses. In the intact household, the father's expenses on rent, food, utilities, and the like, also maintained his dependents; after separation, his income goes first to maintain himself. Maintenance payments thus come out of residual income.

Parallel ambivalence in the court's posture vis-a-vis indebtedness further erodes the dependent children's position. The court could be seen as affirming three general propositions:

i. that respondents must not beggar themselves to avoid their maintenance obligations;

ii. that support payments have first priority among debts; and

iii. that persons without the ability to manage their debts should be directed to counseling and legal relief. Nevertheless, some men countered successfully that it was in no one's interests to pauperize them or ruin their chances of future income by forcing them to liquidate their remaining assets.

The authors concluded that as long as the business code, which stresses that a man must meet his business obligations, takes social precedence over (and has more severe personal consequences than) private family responsibilities, the court should expect some resistance. Certain defaulters clearly saw it as in their best interests to choose the less-threatening road of neglecting family obligations. At present, maintenance enforcement hardly compares with general debt collection, restricted credit, and so forth in its personal implications. The court's only option to restore the family to its preferred creditor position, if personal bankruptcy seems warranted, is to put the respondent in touch with financial counselors.

The report concludes with a number of suggestions for procedural reforms and research follow-up. Some of the suggestions on the form of the order and record keeping are so straightforward and sensible one wonders how they have escaped implementation before now.[48] Other suggestions such as the first-family-first rule may require considerable public education. The report made the following recommendations:

Form of the Order:

1. Child Support orders should be payable only through the court and automatically monitored for enforcement unless the parents specify another suitable arrangement;

2. One or two standard payment dates, say the 1st and 15th of each month, should be adopted for all orders, to aid in remembering to pay;

3. Payments should be payable monthly, this practice to be standardized. Suitable redrafting of the payment schedules to conform to local practice should take place when an award is registered for enforcement in a reciprocating jurisdiction;

4. In keeping with recent practice, orders should specify how support is apportioned among the various dependents; and

5. Standardized information dossiers on the orders should be exchanged by reciprocating jurisdictions where an order is registered for enforcement. These should include the financial information available to the originating courts and the considerations taken into account in setting the award.

Recordkeeping:

6. Records should contain all significant enforcement initiatives and be reviewed to check for terms of dispositions; and

7. Where appropriate, records should be computerized for easier access and transferability. (An important secondary benefit is improved management control.)

The Alberta Study

The Alberta study consists of the following components:

1. Profiles of the individuals in maintenance cases.
2. An examination of factors relating to the granting of maintenance awards and the amount of such awards.
3. The incidence of payment and nonpayment.
4. The relationship of court orders to payment performance.
5. Factors relating to, and the reasons for, payment and nonpayment of maintenance orders.
6. The adequacy of the system of court administration relating to the granting of orders and their subsequent enforcement.
7. Marriage breakdown and the social system.

The investigation of these components involved a study of Supreme Court (now called the Court of Queen's Bench) records in Edmonton and Calgary, a study of family court records in Edmonton, Calgary, Lethbridge, and Grande Prairie, door-to-door surveys of the men and women involved with maintenance orders, and a study of defaulters.

The major findings of the study, among many, follow:

1. Slightly more than half of the women surveyed were employed full time at the time of the study and about one woman in five was on social assistance. About a third of the women said that they had been employed for less than half of the time since their divorce or separation;
2. Over 80 percent of the women surveyed reported net monthly income of less than $1000;
3. Eighty five percent of the men surveyed were employed or self-employed at the time of the study. Nearly two-thirds reported that they had been employed continuously since their divorce/separation;
4. About a third of the cases involving dependent children did not contain a maintenance award;
5. The income of the husband was strongly associated with the amount of awards to both the wife and children. There was no association between the income of the wife and the amount of the award;
6. The amount of awards to children in cases in which the wife was receiving social assistance tended to be lower than in other cases;
7. The survey of women indicated that about half of all maintenance orders in Calgary were paid up at the time of the study. However, only about a third of the ex-husbands paid their orders every month and in the full amount. About 30 percent of the women interviewed said that their husbands/ex-husbands had paid nothing in the past year;

8. There was some evidence that enforcement proceedings are not followed through in many instances. Forty percent of the Edmonton cases contained unserved summonses and 14 percent contained unserved warrants;

9. About 70 percent of a random sample of defaulters in Edmonton and Calgary were traced without using extensive tracing procedures;

10. The survey of women indicated that there is a lack of faith in the efficiency of enforcement among many women and that this may cause some not to file a complaint;

11. Low income appeared to be associated with irregular payment of maintenance orders but not with nonpayment in the survey of men;

12. Maintenance orders for marriages of long duration were better paid than for marriages of short duration;

13. There was some evidence that large maintenance orders were better paid than smaller orders;

14. There was no statistical evidence that dissatisfaction with access arrangement was associated with irregular or nonpayment. However, there were some respondents in the men's survey who gave this as their most important reason;

15. Fear of enforcement proceedings was not a major reason for payment among men;

16. Inability to afford payments was a major reason given by men for nonpayment. However, the question of affordability is relative: it depends upon the priority accorded by men to maintenance obligations relative to other financial obligations; and

17. Information relating to income, assets, debts, and employment was recorded very rarely in the files of all four Family Courts visited.

Apart from highlighting the fact that there is room for improvement in court record keeping of maintenance and child-support records and that more-vigorous enforcement might produce results, some of the most interesting data are those of the ease of location of fathers (or husbands) who are in default of court support orders. Canada has no parent-locator service such as exists in the United States, and the burden of finding a disappearing parent or spouse rests on the wife or mother. The report examined the allegation that "maintenance order defaulters are a difficult group to locate." This hypothesis was examined in the study of the defaulters. In this study, a systematic tracing procedure was followed using common sources such as telephone directories and addresses from the Motor Vehicle Licensing Branch, then the resources of the search unit of the Department of Social Services and Community Health, and finally the services of a professional tracing company. Nearly half of the defaulters were traced easily, and another 25 percent were found without using extensive tracing techniques. The conclusion seems to be that the problem of tracing defaulters is not of sufficient order to explain the weak follow-through of enforcement proceedings.

Although there can be no doubt of the worth of this study, one might caution how representative Alberta is of the whole of Canada. Its burgeoning economy may make estranged husbands reluctant to leave Alberta for provinces whose economy is less buoyant, and it may attract estranged husbands from other provinces whose wives may be unable to locate and obtain orders against them under the reciprocal enforcement of maintenance order legislation.

Payors with Two Families to Support

As divorce becomes more common, the increasing problem is one of dividing an inadequate cake between two families. This raises problems of social priority. In England the position appears to be that

> if a man can afford to support both families, even at subsistence level, he must do so. He is not entitled to claim that any maintenance that he pays to his wife will merely reduce any social security payments made to her by the Supplementary Benefits Commission without leaving her any better off. To permit this argument would be to allow a husband to transfer to the taxpayer a burden that is rightly his. Where, however, a man cannot support both families at subsistence level, the court takes the realistic view that the loss will have to fall on the wife (or former wife) and the court will take notice of the fact that any hardship to the wife, or former wife, will be mitigated by the social security system. The case of *Billington v. Billington* suggests that, for the purpose of fixing the "protected earnings rate" in attachment of earnings proceedings, there is an unofficial link between the "protected earnings rate" and the supplementary benefits that a man, and the family with whom he is now living, would receive were they to qualify for supplementary benefits. One assumes that similar reasoning would apply when it became necessary to establish what would be subsistence level for a husband and the family with whom he is now living in connection with maintenance proceedings.[49]

In Canada the position is more complicated. There is a strong feeling in regard to some of the cases that the first family has priority to support over the second family.[50] Often censorious statements are made about men who voluntarily incur additional obligations. If the second wife works, her income may be regarded as helping share the man's expenses and thus freeing up more of his income to pay support payments.[51] This gives the second wife a clear incentive to leave the work force.

Although remarriage is clearly not a ground for downward variation in support payments, the courts may be reluctantly forced to allow it when there is no alternative, though usually the variation is accompanied by censorious statements from the courts.

Where children are concerned, there has been a view expressed in some cases that where a man is the father of children in two families, the children should be treated equally. Unfortunately the arithmetic of some of these cases hardly bears scrutiny.[52] In New Zealand, encouraging the success of a second marriage has been an accepted criterion in quantifying maintenance for the first family.[53] Where the second union is de facto only, the moral question becomes more acute.

Remarriage by the recipient may bar her right to continued support but the childrens' rights may continue.[54] The stepfather may have a reserve obligation to support his stepchildren, but this does not necessarily terminate the natural father's responsibilities.[55] The paradigm case is one where the first marriage is short, but the second marriage breaks down after an appreciable period during which the stepfather becomes the psychological parent. Who, then, is the financial parent? For children born in and out of wedlock, adoption by the stepfather will bar the natural father's support obligations, though one must question if the natural father's desire to sever his maintenance obligations is necessarily a good reason to encourage him to give his consent to adoption.[56]

The problem of blended families and serial monogamy does, however, warrant further research on questions of support, Burgoyne and Clark have done some work in England that shows the complexity of the problem.[57] Among these complexities are financial problems, high emotional investment in the second marriage, including possible desire to have more children, and the problems for stepparents who acquire ready-made families comprised of their new spouse's children by a prior union.

It may be important to discover the extent to which the stepfather assumes a significant portion of the cost of supporting his step children in second marriages. We have little empirical data on this. It is also important to discover how many stepfathers have prior obligations to their previous families and are also supposedly helped to support their stepchildren by means of child support from a previous marriage. The problem can be shown in diagram form.

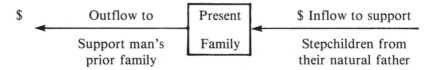

If the outflow and inflow cancel one another out, a great deal of court time and paperwork has been wasted. If the man's support payments to his natural children exceed those received from their natural father to support his stepchildren, this is, no doubt a source of friction in the present family. If the man punctiliously meets his support payments to his children but his stepchildren's natural father is not so punctilious, then the present family sees a hemorrhage out of funds and no corresponding transfusion into their total family budget. This last possibility has the potential to create a financial disaster for the current family. The truth is, however, that we need more data on what is actually happening in such families. Many existing legal rules seem based on assumptions about the primacy of support obligations being laid at the door of the absent parent or former spouse. We need to know whether these legel assumptions are shared in practice by families as they live their everyday lives.

A number of key policy issues, not unique to the Canadian experience, can be summarized as follows:

1. Whether the present Canadian income-tax system produces fair treatment for both parents under a support obligation and parents entitled to child support.
2. Whether adoption or other alternatives such as compulsory support by parents, are proper alternatives to society's paying social assistance to unmarried teenaged mothers and their children.[58]
3. Whether improved means can be found for the enforcement of visiting rights, since the failure to allow visiting may precipitate a withholding of child support.[59] The mere fact that the courts may see no interrelationship between access and support does not mean that fathers share this view.
4. The actual sources of support of children in blended families needs scrutiny to see whether it is more in accord with peoples' expectations to place the primary support obligation on stepparents with whom children live rather than to maintain ties with noncustodial parents who may themselves have support ties to the stepchildren with whom they now live.
5. The mobility of families after breakdown and the extent to which reciprocal enforcement of maintenance legislation is effective.
6. That improved procedures for tracing liable relatives be investigated, including the use of federal data banks and requiring persons knowing the whereabouts of such people to disclose this information.
7. That consideration be given to integrating or producing closer cooperation between courts (or an administrative alternative) that make support orders and the authorities that are supporting the recipients by means of welfare or social assistance and may also have an interest in securing enforcement of the order. Such a procedure might deal more expeditiously and less expensively with temporary reductions in men's income, which are such a factor in the buildup of arrears that the courts

do not seem to handle well.[60] Is a sure chance of collecting a modest sum from a man better than a near certainty of collecting nothing if the order is unrealistic?

At the end of the analysis, however, one might conclude that Cassetty is correct, at least for deprived families, in asserting that the legal-judicial enforcement system is ineffective in its well-intentioned but limited ability to enforce the parental child-support obligation.[61] For these families, it may be that administrative extralegal procedures would be more flexible, less expensive, and more likely to produce results. Tinkering with the legal system ultimately will produce only limited results. Probably the best hope for the poorer women and their children is through the provision of day care and jobs that provide an economic incentive to self-sufficiency. Remarriage of the recipient may also be a partial solution, but the man-in-the-house rule, if insensitively handled, may actually inhibit this by frightening men off before they are ready to make the necessary commitment.

Notes

1. *See also,* E.C. Harris, Canadian Income Taxation (1979).
2. Income Tax Acts. 109(b).
3. *See* Canadian National Council of Welfare Report on Welfare, The Working Poor—People and Programmes, (March 1981).
4. M. Glendon, *The New Property and the New Family* 53 Tul. L. Rev. 697 (1979).
5. *E.g.*, Family Maintenance Act, 1980 S.N.S. c. 6 § 23.
6. *See* Reg. 15(3) Family Benefits Regs. N.S. No. 178.
7. Finer Committee Report on One Parent Families (1974) Cmd. 5629 (1974). For the Australian position, see Sackville, *Social Issues for Fatherless Families*, (pts. 1 & 2), 46 Austl. L. J. 607 (1972), 47 Austl. L. J. 5 (1973). Jollimore v. Sandra Ford, the City of Halifax and the Minister of Social Services for Nova Scotia, S.C.A. 00722 of 1981 decision dated March 12, 1981.
8. See Finer Report, *supra* note 7, at 144; D. Chambers, Making Fathers Pay (1980).
9. Univ. of Alberta. Inst. of Law Res. Ref. Law Centre. Matrimonial Support Failures: Reasons, Profiles, and Perceptions of Individuals Involved (1981).
10. Similar experience can be found in the United States. *See* Note, 83 *Harv. L. Rev.* 1370, 1970, in Australia, Sackville, 47 Austl. L. J. at 18, and in Canada see Nova Scotia Family Benefits Reg. 15(3).

11. Rafuse v. Family Benefits Appeal Board 41 N.S.R. (2d) 345 (Cowan, C.J.). *See also* Finer Report, *supra* note 7, at 342, R. Lister, Child Poverty Action Group study(1973).

12. Finer Report, *supra* note 7, at 135, 342.

13. *E.g.,* see the definition of spouse in the Nova Scotia Family Maintenance Act 1980 c. 6 § 2: "A person married to another and, for the purpose of this Act, includes a man and woman, who not being married to each other, live together as husband and wife for one year." In Ontario the definition of spouse includes a couple who live together in a union of some permanence and have a child. Family Law Reform Act, 1978, c. 2 § 14.

14. J. Cassetty, Child Support and Public Policy 115 (1978).

15. *See* Finer Report, *supra* note 7, at 102. *Supra* note 9 for recent Canadian research.

16. *See* Finer Report, *supra* note 7, at 95.

17. Finer Report, *supra* note 7, 92-94.

18. *Id* at 95-102.

19. Sackville, *Affiliation Proceedings in Victoria*, 8 Melb. U.L. Rev. 372.

20. *See further* Bissett-Johnson & Pollard, Maintenance and Social Security, 38 Mod. L. Rev. 449 (1976).

21. Finer Report *supra* note 7, at 153 *et seq.*

22. Ch. 4 *supra.*

23. *Id.*

24. The writer is a member of the Suspected Child Abuse and Neglect Committee for a large children's hospital in Eastern Canada.

25. *See* New Zealand, Status of Children Act 1969, and Ontario, Children's Law Reform Act S.O. 1977 c. 41.

26. Finer Report, *supra* note 7, at 152-342.

27. *See* A. Bissett-Johnson & W. Holland, Matrimonial Property Law in Canada (1980).

28. W.M. Harper, *Financial Implications of the Unequal Division of Property on Divorce*, 130 New L.J. 429 (1980); M. Rutherford, *Financial Provision: The Clean Break Principle,* 130 New L.J. 183 (1980).

29. *See* ch. 16 *supra.*

30. *See, e.g.,* Nova Scotia Family Maintenance Act 1980 § 2(c), Canadian Divorce Act § 2.

31. *See* Matrimonial Causes Act 1973.

32. *See* Further Studies in Canadian Family Law (Mendes da Costa, ed.) (1972) and H.A. Finley, Family Law in Australia 236 (1979).

33. *See* Statistics Canada, Frequency of Geographic Mobility in the Population of Canada 31-32 (1978).

34. *See* Finer Report, *supra* note 7, at 123.

35. Bill 183 (1980).

36. Family Maintenance Act, S.N.S. 1980 c. 6 § 51.

37. *See also* R.M. Diamond, Position Paper (unpublished Aug. 28, 1980).

38. Study sponsored by Policy Planning Department, Department of British Columbia Ministry of Attorney General and the Social Planning and Research Department of United Way, Lower Mainland, 1625 West 8th Avenue Vancouver, B.C., V6J 1T9.

39. *See* ch. 2 *supra*.

40. Chambers, *supra* note 8, at p. 101.

41. *Id.* at 79.

42. *See* ch. 4 *supra*.

43. Finer Report, *supra* note 7, at 102.

44. Note 38 *supra*.

45. A. Wachtel & N. Burtch, Excuses—An Analysis of Court Interaction in Show Cause Enforcement of Maintenance Orders (1981). Inquiries and copies of the research can be obtained from A. Wachtel, c/o United Way of the Lower Mainland, 1625 West 8th Avenue, Vancouver, B.C. Canada V6J 1T9. Phone 604-731-7781.

46. Note 9 *supra*.

47. *See* ch. 10 *supra*.

48. See note 45 *supra* at 17.

49. Bissett-Johnson & Pollard, *supra* note 20, at 450; *see also* Smethurst v. Smethurst [1977] 1 All E.R. 110 (Fam. Div.) and the qualifications of this Court of Appeal in Shallow v. Shallow [1978] 2 All E.R. 483 and Tovey v. Tovey [1978] 8 Fam. Law 80. For further comments, *see* J.M. Thomson [1979] 9 Fam. Law 108.

50. Kinghorn v. Kinghorn [1960] 34 W.W.R. 123 (Sask, Q.B.).

51. For an example of judicial sleight of hand, *see* Tobin v. Tobin [1975] 19 R.F.L. 18 (Ont H.C.); *c.f. In re* Felisa L., 7 Family Law Reform Reporter 1029.

52. *E.g. In re* McKenna [1974] 2 O.R. (2d) 263.

53. *See, e.g.*, Taylor v. Taylor (1974) 1 N.Z.L.R. 52, 8.

54. *See* N.S. Family Maintenance Act S.N.S. 1980 c. 6 § 6(3).

55. *See* Divorce Act, Canada R.S.C. 1970 c. D-8 §§ 2, 11. *But see*, Kerr v. McWannel [1974] 46 D.L.R. (3d) 624.

56. *See* Bissett-Johnson, *Children in Subsequent Marriages*, in Marriage and Cohabitation in Contemporary Societies (S. Katz & J. Eekelaar, eds. 1980).

57. J. Burgoyne, *From Father to Stepfather* in The Father Figure (L. McKee & M. O'Brien, eds., 1974).

58. *See* Cassetty, *supra* note 14, at 177.

59. *See also* Cassetty, *supra* note 14, at 116, Bissett-Johnson, *supra* note 56, at 384 and ch. 10 *supra*.

60. *See* ch. 16 *supra*.

61. Cassetty, *supra* note 14, at *id*.

15 Child Support: Some International Developments

Sheila B. Kamerman and
Alfred J. Kahn

Parents are legally responsible for the maintenance of their children. When they fail to provide payment for child support or when payments are irregular or inadequate, authorities in a growing number of countries find it necessary to intervene. Intervention may be designed to enforce payment obligations or to provide a guarantee or a substitute for support payments. The methods for implementing these interventions, as well as the goals, may vary, but the trend among the advanced industrialized countries seems clearly to be toward a greater involvement of public authorities, particularly the social security agencies and the courts, to ensure income to those rearing children of divorced or separated parents.[1]

For some years social (public) assistance has been used in many European countries, as in the United States, in such situations where low-income families were concerned; indeed this system increasingly assumed a primary role in providing support in these cases. In recent years, however, there has been growing dissatisfaction with social assistance in this role and a conviction that an alternative method of providing financial help should be developed. Three reasons are given for the search for an alternative.

1. Single parenthood is more extensive and more visible than in the past. Both the numbers of single-parent families with children and the proportions they constitute among families with children have grown enormously over the past two decades in all industrialized countries. As a consequence, more children are likely to live in families in which the absence of the other parent's income (usually the father's, and therefore the primary source of income), and the failure of that parent to contribute to the support of the child, creates a major financial hardship.

2. Providing a substitute for the income of the absent parent has emerged as a large and growing component of the costs of social assistance in several countries. As more single-parent families turned toward social assistance for financial support and as social-insurance benefits for the elderly become more adequate, thereby reducing the numbers of aged needing assistance, single-parent families became an increasingly large proportion of assistance claimants and beneficiaries.

Funding for this study was provided by the Office of Family Assistance, Social Security Administration, Department of Health and Human Services.

3. At the same time as both of the above were occurring, social assistance itself is increasingly viewed by many as an inadequate and/or inappropriate response to the need for child support because benefit levels were low, often inconsistently provided, and stigmatized.

Further contributing to a search for an alternative strategy in some countries—Sweden, for example—has been the change that has occurred in the life-styles of most women with children: the large-scale entry of women into the labor force. Increasingly the issue of child support is no longer viewed as the need to compensate a single-parent family for the loss of the income of the absent parent. Instead the need is for compensation for the absence of that parent's contribution toward the support of the child. The assumption is that except where very young children are concerned, under about age two or three, women will be working and support themselves, but those earnings may not be adequate to cover the full costs of a child as well. Thus, there is need for assured child support.

Still another factor in the development of a new policy is the increase in coverage and significance of family or child allowances (or child benefits) in many countries in recent years. These are cash benefits or payments made by the government to families with children, usually provided as flat-rate benefits, with a specific amount paid for each child in the family. In some countries the amounts vary by age, ordinal positions, and/or number of children. In contrast to most other public-income transfer payments, family allowances are usually not indexed. They are usually tax free and not income tested. In addition, they are generally awarded until a child completes compulsory schooling or reaches the end of compulsory school age; in some cases the benefit can be extended if the child is a full-time student.

Designed to compensate parents in a small way for the economic costs of rearing children, family allowances play a far more significant role in the income of single-parent families—where income tends to be low—than in the income of two-parent families. Moreover, some countries provide a supplementary grant for the first child in a single-parent family or for low-income families.

Thus, growing numbers of single-parent families, greater visibility, higher public expenditures, changing definitions of functions, and an expanded societal role in contributing to the costs of rearing children have led to a reexamination of existing policies and a search for alternatives.

There have been two developments in those countries implementing new policies. First, a public authority, often the social security agency, guarantees a specified level of child support by advancing support payments to the custodial or caretaking parent if payment is not regularly provided by the absent parent or if payment is not made at all. In addition, the same or another public agency assumes responsiblity for the collection of child support from the absent parent, crediting what is collected against the payments advanced. Within this framework, policies vary depending on whether the public authority acts for all single parents or only low-income women, whether a court order is required for the process to be initiated, whether the support is for mother and child or only the child, and whether the primary concern is with reducing the burden on the public purse or assuring adequate support for the child.

Four countries that have moved in this direction are Sweden, France, the Federal Republic of Germany (FRG), and Israel.[2] The French and German policies are only just now being implemented, and a few details are available. The Israeli program is designed as an improvement on social assistance. The assumption is that the sole mother with a child under fourteen should not be expected to work, a consistently provided benefit at the poverty level should be available to support mother and child, and a public authority should assume responsibility for collecting support from the absent parent in order to offset public expenditure for the benefit. In contrast, the Swedish policy assumes labor-force participation by women (but does not require it), views the benefit as a child's entitlement, and is designed primarily to ensure an adequate level of support for a child. Only secondarily is it expected to compensate for public assumption of the financial burden. Both of these programs contrast with the U.S. policy development as illustrated by Title IV-D of the Social Security Act, where the primary goal has been to recover money so as to effect a reduction in public expenditure for public assistance.

The Countries and Their Programs

The descriptions of what these countries provide and the comparisons of the situations of single-parent, female-headed families across countries draw upon data from an eight-country study of income-transfer policies (social insurance, public assistance, personal income tax) as they affect the incomes of families with children in industrialized countries: Australia, Canada, France, FRG, Israel, Sweden, United Kingdom, and the United States. The comparisons are based on 1979 data for taxes, transfer payments, and earnings. Study findings include a picture of how sixteen prototypical families fared in 1979 in each of the countries studied. Each family was given a particular family composition (number of parents and of children), a work history, a place of residence, and so forth. Included among the sixteen family types were four single-parent, female-headed families, each with two children aged two and seven. In one family, the mother was not working and was dependent on transfer payments for all her income. In a second family the situation was the same, although we posited a court order (not complied with) requiring support by the absent father at two times the value of the child benefit for one child. The result in all countries, for different reasons, was that the two families ended up with the same income. In the third family the mother worked part time and earned the equivalent of half an average production worker's wage in that country. In the fourth family, the mother's earnings were supplemented by a voluntary payment of child support by the absent father equal to what the courts had ordered in the other case, twice the child-allowance benefit.

Israel

Alimony, or child support, is provided through the National Insurance Institute (the organization responsible for administering social insurance and supplementary benefits) to those women who have a court order for child support. The National Insurance Institute (NII) acts, in effect, as a collection agency for women with a court order who are income eligible for supplementary benefits. The national means-tested income-maintenance program for pensioners, the disabled, and widows is comparable to SSI in the United States. As of January 1, 1982, the social-assistance program was replaced by a new income-support program, administered by the NII and delivered through the same local office as earlier handled the social insurance benefits and the supplementary benefits. The benefit is provided these women through the NII, which then seeks reimbursement from the father. If the court order is higher than the benefit provided and the agency collects it, the woman will receive the difference. If less is collected, she will receive the equivalent of the supplementary benefit. If the court order is lower, she will receive only the amount ordered.

The benefit, which is set nationally and is identical to the survivor's benefit under the national social insurance scheme, is equal to 25 percent of average wage for the mother, 37.5 percent for a mother and one child, and 42.5 percent for a mother and two children. No addition is made for more children since child support for third and subsequent children is covered by the level of the child benefit (child allowance), which at a lower benefit level also provides partial support for first and second children. The benefit is indexed and tax free. Payments continue as long as the court order is in force or until the child reaches age eighteen, unless the child is disabled.

The program is financed out of general revenue and costs less than 1 percent of social-welfare expenditures. It is administered nationally as a separate part of the social-insurance system along with the maternity allowance. About 15 to 20 percent of the social-assistance recipients qualified for the program in 1978, the first full year it was in effect. About half the costs were met through recovery from fathers.

In assessing the Israeli child-support program, it should be noted that single-parent, female-headed families constitute only 4 percent of all families with children. Similarly, although an important component of the social-assistance beneficiaries, they constitute only a relatively small proportion of that population now receiving the new income-support benefits, which include the former social-assistance recipients as well as those who received supplementary benefits. Most supplementary-benefit recipients are the elderly; another important group among younger families are widows and survivors; divorced, separated, and single mothers are a much smaller proportion of beneficiaries than either of these groups.

When the program was first established, it was viewed as a means of assuring women access to a nonstigmatized income-transfer system and provision of a somewhat higher benefit than that available through social assistance. Coincidentally, the hope was that some portion of the expenditure would be offset by collection of payment owed from the responsible parent, the father. Thus far only about one-third of the costs have been recovered from the father.

With the new income-support program replacing social assistance fully in place and delivery of the benefit integrated with the supplementary-benefit system, the value of a special system for the child-support benefit could be questioned. Indeed the new program was expected to replace the alimony program, but this has not occurred. One advantage the alimony program has is that no work requirement is imposed. In contrast, under the new income-support program, there is an employment or work requirement unless the mother has at least one child under age five or two or more children, at least one of whom is under age ten. A second advantage is that it continues to carry a more positive image than the new income-support program. Moreover, as the alimony program becomes available to nonincome-eligible claimants as well as those who are income eligible, it may still help to reduce stigma and, perhaps equally important, make coming for financial help by women not receiving support from absent (present and former) husbands more acceptable.

Except for those awarded a specific benefit by the court that varies from the standard, there would be no difference in benefit levels between those receiving supplementary benefits and alimony payments. Nor is the work incentive now any different than for all benefit recipients. Supplementary benefits are reduced at a 60 percent rate for earned income and 100 percent for unearned income. Only the label placed on beneficiaries would be different.

Federal Republic of Germany

Following legislation passed July 1, 1979, and implemented beginning January 1, 1980, a cash, tax-free maintenance allowance, in an amount related to a specified standard per child, can be provided by the government to any single parent, male or female, having a support order from the court requiring payment of child support when the payment is not forthcoming and when the parent requests help. In such cases, public funds can provide a guarantee for child support for very young children. This support is available only for a maximum of three years, or until a child reaches age six.

About 8 percent of all families with children are single-parent families in the FRG, and these families constitute less than 20 percent of the total number of social-assistance recipients.

As of January 1, 1980, the child-support benefit was equal to 11.6 percent of the 1979 net wage of a German average production worker (APWW). Since receipt of this benefit leads to a 50 percent reduction in the child allowance, child support for a single mother and two children would constitute one-third of APWW (net), somewhat more than the individual maintenance component in social assistance would provide. It is anticipated that 70 to 90 percent of the claimants may be nonworking mothers and thus would be entitled to social assistance if this new benefit were not available. In effect, the child-support benefit is a somewhat more generous alternative to social assistance, supplemented further by a housing allowance. It is also available as a supplement to earned income for working mothers and thus, in theory, could provide a modest work incentive. An alternative interpretation is that it provides a more generous benefit for just those women who are not expected to work, those with preschool-aged children.

The advance maintenance payments (child-support benefit) are financed equally by national and state government and probably will be administered by state child-welfare departments. States are expected to use the court system to recoup a portion of the monies expended from the responsible parent. At the time of writing, the benefit was still in the process of implementation. It is expected that there may be extensive variations across state lines, at least until there is more experience in administering the program.

Sweden

Advance maintenance payments are a tax-free cash benefit equal to 40 percent of the Swedish reference wage, an indexed amount used as the basis for setting all social benefits. Payments can be made by the social-insurance office as child support to a single parent for each child up to the age of eighteen. The program was instituted to prevent children from being penalized as a consequence of a parent's inability or failure to pay a maintenance allowance (child support) for the child. The program was established in its present form in 1964 and represents the most significant development in the child-support field among those countries now exploring alternative ways to provide financial support for children.

The parent, usually the mother, applies for advance maintenance in person, by phone, or by mail to the local social-insurance office. (The father is the initiator in 10 to 15 percent of the cases.) Payment is made to the person responsible for the care of the child regardless of whether paternity has been established, a court order is in effect, or the court-ordered child support is lower than this amount, and regardless of the custodial parent's income or marital status. The custodial parent is required by law to assist in the establishment of paternity, however, and paternity is established in a high percentage of cases. In effect, the benefit level represents a normative standard and is viewed as the equivalent of what one parent would contribute to support a child, or a little more.

Social-insurance offices administer the program. About 38 percent of the costs were offset by collection from the responsible parent in 1979. This is expected to reach 50 percent soon. The philosophy underlying the program, however, is to provide adequate support for the child, not to impose a penalty or even a difficult burden on low-income fathers no longer living with their wives.

Approximately 27 percent of all families with children are single-parent families. About 11 percent of all Swedish children and 53 percent of those in single-parent families are supported by these advance maintenance payments—some 220,000 children. (There are 310,128 single-parent families in Sweden, but advance maintenance payments are paid in some two-parent families too.) In almost all single-parent families, children are supported either by the absent parent's voluntary contribution of support, or by advance maintenance payments, or by a combination of the two. Only a very small proportion of children, including children of newly arrived immigrants, are not eligible for this benefit.

Only 20 percent of the social-assistance recipients in Sweden are single mothers. (Forty-five percent are males divided evenly between middle-aged alcoholics and unemployed youths or substance abusers; 23 percent are single women, largely young; social assistance accounts for only 1 percent of social-welfare expenditures and benefits 5 percent of the population at most.) Less than 20 percent of single mothers receive assistance. Moreover, when they do, benefits are generally small and are provided for a brief period to cover a temporary or transitional need or an emergency. Two-thirds are on assistance for fewer than three months. Furthermore, despite the substantial increase in the numbers of single-parent families, these women, like all other Swedish women, are likely to work outside the home, even if only part time.

For instance, in 1978, 59 percent of all female heads of families were employed full time outside the home and another 16 percent were employed half-time or more. Only 14 percent were not working outside the home at all.

United States

In the United States, 17 percent of the families with children are single-parent families; 20 percent of all children live in these families. About half of these families receive public assistance, constituting about half of all public-assistance recipients (AFDC and SSI together). Assistance recipients equal a little more than 7 percent of the population.

In contrast to the child-support program in other countries, Title IV-D is designed to facilitate the collection of support payments from the absent parent in order to offset the cost of AFDC benefits to the single mother and her children. No nationally uniform standard benefit has been set. Moreover, because of the variation in AFDC benefit levels and eligibility criteria, as well as the difference in the way income is counted, the same family receiving the same amount in child support might be entitled to a partial AFDC benefit in one state and no benefit in another. This creates still further problems for the latter family since loss of eligibility may lead to loss of entitlement to Medicaid. Thus, a family could receive child support from an absent parent and end up in a worse situation than without it.

How the Families Fare

How do single-parent families fare in those countries experimenting with alternative approaches to providing child support? What difference does it make if the government advances or guarantees payment of child support if the father does or does not contribute?

We compared how four typical female-headed families—mother and two children aged two and seven—would fare in each of these countries, both in comparison to two-parent families in each of the countries studied and to the same type of families across countries.

The Nonworking-Mother Family

The nonworking mother lives on a very tight income level in each country except Sweden. Despite the economic hardships this mother faces, all of the countries assure this family type greater income protection than is assured two-parent families with only one breadwinner when that wage earner is unemployed for a long time and unemployment insurance benefits have run out. A variety of programs ensure that the Swedish family receives income the equivalent of or close to the equivalent of an APWW. The APWW is the benchmark used in each country. It is not comparable across countries but serves to describe how families fare in relation to the same country standard even though that standard does not represent the same level of living across countries. The figure 93.8 for Sweden in table 15-1 for family 1a signifies a year-end 1979 income of 93.8 percent of the average production worker's net wage. In the FRG, the family's income is well above half of APWW (60 percent) and would have been higher for family 1b (where the court orders support but the father does not pay it) if the advance maintenance program were in place. In Israel and in New York State, a state with high AFDC benefits, family 1a's income would be about half APWW. (Food stamps represented the equivalent of a family allowance for these income-eligible families in the United States in 1979.) In Pennsylvania, a state with maximum possible AFDC benefits at about the median level, the family has far less income than half an APWW. Thus, in over half the states in the United States, families of this type would fare still worse. In Israel, the mother awarded support by the court would have been better off except that we specified an amount for the support below the supplementary benefit level, and in the Israeli program, the family's benefit was limited to the amount of the order. In the Swedish program, in contrast, if the order were viewed as too low (as in this case), the child-support payment made by the government would be at the higher level set as a standard by the government.

In Israel, the FRG, and Sweden, this family receives a family allowance and social assistance (see table 15-2 for the benefits the family receives and the contributions each makes to family income). In the FRG and Sweden, a housing allowance is provided, and subsidized housing is likely to be available to this family in Israel. In addition, in Sweden, the child-support benefit makes a significant difference.

Table 15-1
Net Income of Families, after Earnings, Transfers, and Taxes, as Percentage of Net APWW: Intercountry Comparisons and Rankings

	Family Type[a]					
	1a and 1b	Ranking	2a	Ranking	2b	Ranking
Sweden	93.8	1	123.1	1	123.1	1
FRG	60.0	2	70.9	4	76.3	4
Israel	50.0	4	71.5	3	80.1	3
United States						
New York	54.8	3	100.6	2	100.6	2
Pennsylvania	43.9	5	69.0	5	75.1	5

[a]1a = nonworking mother, two children aged two and seven; 1b = same as 1a, but court orders father to contribute child support in the amount of twice the child benefit for one child (or the AFDC budget allocation), but the father does not pay; 2a = mother works and earns half an APWW; 2 b = same as 2a but the father voluntarily contributes child support equal to the amount ordered by the court for family 1b.

Table 15-2
Percentage Contribution of Various Transfer Programs to Yearly Income, Families 1a and 1b

Programs	Sweden	FRG	Israel	New York	Pennsylvania
Family allowance	13.3	15.5	17.1		
Housing allowance	22.0	18.4	a	b	b
Social assistance	36.1	66.1	82.9	79.5	77.6
Food stamps				20.5	22.4
Child support (advance maintenance)	28.6				
Father's contribution					
Earned income minus deductions					
Total	100.0	100.0	100.0	100.0	100.0
Percentage of APWW	93.8	60.0	50.0	54.8	43.9

[a]Extensive housing subsidies exist in lieu of housing allowances.

[b]Although some public housing and rent subsidies exist, these are not entitlement programs and benefit only a small minority of the eligible families. In contrast, the benefits in Sweden and FRG cover all families who have children or all income-eligible families.

For a single mother with two children, advance maintenance payments equal 27 percent of a net APWW in Sweden. Coupled with the nonincome-tested child allowance, equaling 12.4 percent of APWW, almost 40 percent of APWW is provided to the mother. A generously income-tested housing allowance adds another 21 percent. All of these together, in addition to a special tax benefit, comprise a significant income package that is close to the net value (after taxes) of an APWW. Yet few families of this type are receiving social assistance in Sweden. To understand why, we turn to assess the financial status of the working single-parent families.

The Working Mother's Family

What happens to the income of a family of this kind when the mother finds work and earns a salary equal to half an average wage? (See table 15-1.) The basic benefits that are provided are the same (table 15-3): family allowances, housing allowances, tax benefits (like the earned income-tax credit in the United States), and food stamps in the United States. Social assistance is eliminated in all countries but the United States for this family (2a), and only in New York does it remain an important part of income. For this working single-parent family, the social-assistance supplementation is the equivalent of only a little more than the child-support benefits provided in Sweden. But in addition, the Swedish family then receives more than that

Table 15-3
Percentage Contribution of Various Transfer Programs to Yearly Income, Family 2a

Programs	Sweden	FRG	Israel	New York	Pennsylvania
Family allowance	10.1	13.1	12.0		
Housing allowance	16.7	8.2			
Social assistance				28.5	6.9
Food stamps				8.2	4.7
Child support (advance maintenance)	21.8				
Tax credit (refundable)				3.6	5.2
Father's contribution					
Earned income minus deductions	51.3	78.7	88.0	59.7	83.2
Total	99.9	100.0	100.0	100.0	100.0
Percentage of APWW	123.1	70.9	71.5	100.6	69.0

through the family allowance and the housing allowance. The former is available to all families with children regardless of income, and the latter is available to a large proportion of these families—half in 1979—even though the benefit is income tested. As a consequence, the Swedish family is significantly better off than this family type in all other countries, and the Pennsylvania family is the worst off of all.

When the father contributes each month a sum equal to twice the monthly child allowance for a first child (or a second child where the first is not covered) or the AFDC budget amount for the child in the United States, the ratios are of interest (see tables 15-1 and 15-4). The family income remains the same in Sweden where the father's voluntary contribution merely reduces the advance maintenance payment. It stays the same in New York, where the father's contribution is collected by the agency to meet half the costs of APWW. The family is somewhat better off in Pennsylvania where the father's contribution is greater than the family would receive from AFDC and food stamps combined, so that even though the family loses eligibility for public benefits, it is slightly better off. The family is better off in the FRG and Israel because the father's contribution is added on to receipt of family allowances (and housing allowances in Germany) as well as the mother's earnings. However, this single-parent family with earned income is treated relatively less generously in Germany as compared with other working families because the tax system takes an unusually large amount of the woman's earnings.

Regardless, for these working families as well as for the nonworking families, the Swedish families are the best off of all. Family income for the

Table 15-4
**Percentage Contribution of Various Transfer Programs to Yearly Income,
Family 2b**

Programs	Sweden	FRG	Israel	New York	Pennsylvania
Family allowance	10.1	12.1	10.7		
Housing allowance	16.7	6.6			
Social assistance				14.1	
Food stamps				8.2	
Child support (advance maintenance)	10.5				
Tax credit (refundable)				3.6	4.7
Father's contribution	11.3	8.1	10.7	14.4	18.8
Earned income minus deductions	51.3	73.2	78.6	59.7	76.5
Total	99.9	100.0	100.0	100.0	100.0
Percentage of APWW	123.1	76.3	80.1	100.6	75.1

nonworking family is 56 percent higher than for the next best-off family (the German family) and 114 percent better off than the Pennsylvania family. The difference is accounted for by the availability of the child-support payment in addition to the family allowance and the housing allowance, all of which continue despite the existence of earned income.

Of more importance, by far most families of this type in Sweden are working. One consequence of the Swedish approach is the existence of a significant work incentive provided single mothers through these benefits in a society that emphasizes work and expects women, even mothers, to be in the labor force. To illustrate, the difference in income between that of a nonworking sole-parent family (which receives social assistance in addition to the other benefits) and a similar family in which the mother works part time and earns half an APWW is 43 percent. The family retains almost the entire net earned income of the mother. Eighty-five percent of the difference is attributable to the advance maintenance payments, clearly an important benefit, and available to all sole mothers, regardless of whether the woman is in receipt of a court order.

Conclusion

In recent years, public authorities in several countries have become more actively involved in establishing a program whereby payment of child support at a specified national standard can be guaranteed if the absent parent fails to contribute, or his contribution is inadequate, or payment is made irregularly.

In addition, these authorities have assumed primary responsibility for collecting these funds from the absent parent, using the court system as necessary. Although the efforts at collection are serious and in varying degrees successful, the primary objective in moving in this direction has been not only to reduce the burden on the public purse but, more important, to assure a more-adequate provision of child support to a deserving child. In some countries, the movement represents a move from a more discretionary benefit to a more-objective and uniform national benefit like SSI in the United States. In others, it represents part of a long-term trend away from means-tested benefits and toward more universal provision. Regardless, the movement away from social assistance further underscores the trend observed in many countries toward use of transfers to provide a supplement, rather than a substitute, for earned income or other benefits and thus to incorporate a work incentive into the income-transfer system.

Sweden is an excellent example of a country in which all of these trends are occurring: a move toward universalism, toward using income transfers—even where income tested—as an income supplement, toward actively encouraging work and incorporating a work incentive into the income-transfer system. The child-support or advance maintenance program includes all of these elements, and in addition, is aimed at guaranteeing children a minimum standard of living regardless of their parents' ability to pay. Although not all aspects of the Swedish program are appropriate for the United States (paternity is readily acknowledged and absent fathers relatively easily identified and located in Sweden), there are important lessons to be learned. Concern for the well-being of children, for the role of parents in assuring this, as well as encouragement for mothers to work and to earn underlie the Swedish approach. These concerns would seem salient for the United States too.

Notes

1. See Christinia Cockburn, "General Report on the Roundtable Meeting," Social Security Provisions in the Case of Divorce (Geneva: International Social Security Association, 1978).

2. Other countries that have moved this way include Austria, Denmark, Norway, Poland. For a brief description of what these countries do, see Elizabeth K. Kirkpatrick, "Alimony and Public Income Support: Fifteen Countries," *Social Security Bulletin*, January 1977.

**Part VI
Reforming the Child-Support
System: Options and
Constraints**

16 Child-Support Enforcement: Legislative Tasks for the Early 1980s

Harry D. Krause

In 1934, the American Law Institute's Restatement of the Law of Conflicts characterized support obligations and their enforcement as "of no special interest to other states and since the duty is not imposed primarily for the benefit of an individual, it is not enforceable elsewhere."[1] In theory, this notion was laid to rest by the widespread enactment of the Uniform Reciprocal Enforcement of Support Acts of 1950, 1958, and 1968.[2] In practice, however, American law remained deeply insensitive to the enforcement of child-support obligations.

In the last two decades, several social trends merged to change this situation. Increasing rates of divorce, family abandonment, and illegitimacy combined to leave unprecedented numbers of children in single-parent homes, typically without adequate or any support from the other parent.[3]

The New Frontier and the Great Society of the 1960s brought new emphasis on welfare programs for the poor, so many of whom are children. Thoughtlessly, the basic eligibility criterion of the AFDC program—absence of a parent—was carried forward from a program originally intended to deal primarily with orphans. Perversely, the aid program began to encourage fathers to leave their needy families so they would be entitled to state support. Indeed, the program made it financially attractive for single and poor women to have children.[4]

Riding the constitutional equality wave, some twenty U.S. Supreme Court decisions demanded substantial equality for children born out of wedlock, a mandate seeking implementation in terms of support enforcement.[5]

Family policy, in terms of public versus private responsibility, came to be a national concern.[6] As welfare costs soared out of control, the federal government moved into the child-support vacuum left by the states in their traditional preserve—family law. By 1975, initiatives of the Senate Finance Committee that had extended over several years had resulted in amendments to the Social Security Act that mandated federal and state cooperation in the strict nationwide enforcement of parental support obligations. Now some $1,500 million is transferred annually under this extension of cooperative federalism.

The Senate Finance Committee reports that in the first forty-seven months of the child-support program (August 1975 through June 30, 1979), states reported total collections of over $3.6 billion, of which $1.6 billion was for AFDC families and $2.0 billion was for families not on welfare, at a total cost of $1.0 billion, or 28 cents per dollar collected. In the first forty-seven months of the child-support enforcement program, 1,573,000 absent parents were located, there were 970,000 support obligations established, and paternity was established by the courts for 323,000 children.

The heavy impact on the court systems of the cities, counties, and states is apparent from statistics showing the tremendous increase in child-support activity in these areas since the program's inception in 1976. In fiscal year 1976, 184,000 parents were located. The number of parents located in fiscal year 1978 was 519,000, an increase of 182 percent in two years. In fiscal year 1976, 76,000 support obligations were established. The number of support obligations established in fiscal year 1978 was 350,000, an increase of 361 percent in two years. In fiscal year 1976, 15,000 paternities were established. The number of paternities established in fiscal year 1978 was 123,000, an increase of 820 percent in just two years.[7]

This seems a good time to pause and review our position in this important area of law and ask where we should go from here. The discussion here will not address the more practical issues of public funding for child-support enforcement services[8] or the wisdom and justice of child-support enforcement services.[9] Whether one is for or against enforcement, the reality of the federal program must be faced in specific terms. Instead, I suggest that thought be given to several issues that have not been much considered. Three that are important and present a realistic approach to change are:

1.   Setting reasonable support obligations.
2.   Reinstatement of a support disregard in setting AFDC benefit levels.
3.   According due process to men named as fathers in paternity cases.

Defining a Realistic Child-Support Duty

A cynic may hypothesize that state child-support laws, both in terms of substance and enforcement procedures, have been permitted to survive in their present state of disarray, unevenness, and consequent unfairness only because they have not been enforced with any degree of regularity. Indeed the irresponsibility of many fathers may be partly explained in terms of unrealistic obligations being imposed under unrealistic laws. This is a matter of state law. And what have the states done?

They have not risen to this challenge. Perhaps it is time to conclude that the federal initiative should not stop at the sudden activation of these inadequate state laws but that a corresponding responsibility rests on the federal authorities to ensure that the states develop more sensible, more uniform, and more predictable support laws. So far, Washington has not provided much leadership. The Office of Child Support Enforcement (OCSE) states that its goal "is to assume a greater role in improving the child support laws in the states. However, our role is to encourage, not mandate, the states to adopt model legislation, and effective enforcement procedures."[10]

Current federal law provides considerable room for OCSE to play a more-important role in defining standards for more-acceptable state law in the support enforcement area. In the context of OCSE-sponsored support enforcement, federal minimum standards should mandate less arbitrary and diverse conceptions of the needs of the child and the father's ability to pay than are now applied in the courts; set standards for automatic and, where appropriate, even retroactive modification of existing orders; and insist on less counterproductive methods of support enforcement than are now the rule. In sum, it should be an important goal of federal involvement to assure that state enforcement efforts do not reach the point of increasing, instead of reducing, social disorganization. First and foremost, this involves manageable levels of support.

In general, the issue is relatively simple: the father must be assured a standard of living that does not impair his earning capacity, his work incentive, or his ability to provide for himself and his current functioning family (if he has established one). There are three problems in this area: (1) the case against arrears; (2) the idea of imposing flexible support obligations; and (3) the proper balance between the father's former and his current family.

Even if the initial order may have been reasonable, it is the overwhelming accumulation of unpaid past support that persuades many a basically willing father to flee from unrealistic responsibilities. Mandatory wage deduction and careful monitoring of compliance provide at least a partial answer.

Beyond that, two major steps would cure much of what else is obviously wrong with the arrears problem. First, in appropriate cases, retroactive modification of accumulated arrears should be allowed, and indiscriminate enforcement of arrears should not. Second, flexible child-support obligations should be imposed that are geared directly to the fluctuating earnings with which most of our population lives.

Regrettably, support judgments with automatic adjustment clauses to take into account temporary fluctuations in income are still rare, as are automatic child-support escalator clauses. Of course, such clauses run the risk of overemphasizing one or the other side of the support equation. On the paying parent's side, an adjustment clause geared to decreases in income will avoid the accrual of large arrears—possibly with interest—that very likely will never be paid. On the other hand, an increase in the supporting parent's income does not necessarily entitle the child to more support, nor does an income decrease necessarily signal inability to pay (as when the obligated parent has assets). Because of these problems, the rare court decisions concerning automatic adjustment clauses have not favored such clauses. The courts remain jealous of their discretion in this area.[11]

Despite all legitimate doubt, however, some intelligent use can be made of automatic adjustment clauses. We should assign clearly defined consequences, in terms of support to be rendered, to clearly ascertainable, objective events such as inflation (measured by a variation on the consumer price index specifically geared to the needs of children), and the child's foreseeably increasing needs based on increasing age.[12] On the father's side, we should focus on fluctuations evidenced by his income-tax return or, for quicker response, wage data, including the temporary fluctuations that typically do not support modification, such as short-term unemployment. These consequences should be assigned in presumptive, not conclusive, terms, so that only the average case would take care of itself. In the less usual case, the party to whom compliance with the automatic adjustment clause would bring inequities should shoulder the burden of proof and take the initiative of invoking the court to obtain an appropriate modification. This approach would go some distance toward the important goal of reducing the too frequent, expensive, and wasteful recourse to the courts that our present system invites.

The question of whether, in an appropriate case, modification should be allowed retrospectively, thus eliminating or reducing accumulated arrearages, has been answered variously. The better view, it seems, would permit the elimination of impossible arrearages, which some courts achieve under specific or general statutes.[13] Other courts steadfastly refuse to consider retroactive modification.[14] A related question is whether the obligated parent's support liability can be discharged in bankruptcy. As to future support, the answer clearly should be, and is, "no."[15] Normal support arrears, not dischargeable, are thus elevated to a preferred level. It is interesting to ask whether the Bankruptcy Reform Act of 1978, which permitted the discharge of child-support obligations that have been assigned to the welfare authorities, when seen in the light of the prevailing non-modifiability of arrears, was altogether as unreasonable as it was made out to be. In 1979, the American Bar Association's (ABA) Section on Family Law considered proposing a resolution to the ABA's House of Delegates urging Congress to repeal the appropriate sections, reasoning that, "In an effort to clarify the bankruptcy laws and carry the 'clean sweep' concept of bankruptcy to an extreme conclusion, Congress permitted discharge of such assigned sums. In so doing, it failed to realize that the analogy to ordinary debts did not apply, that these were statutory debts like taxes and punitive damages. In carrying the 'clean sweep' concept to this extreme conclusion, it failed to recognize that from the debtors' side, this concept is not being as fully applied, there being numerous exemptions for real and personal property. It also failed to consider the time-consuming and judicially burdensome method by which the bankruptcy can be frustrated by a modification upward of future payments. Congress also failed to consider the numerous state court devices for relief from hardship caused by support burdens. Finally, because of drafting failures it threatens also to permit discharge of substantial sums owed the custodial parent and threatens to dismantle the protective shield from abuse by absent parents that the welfare assignment concept provides the custodial parent and child.''[16] In May 1981, Public Law 97-35 ended the dischargeability in bankruptcy of assigned arrears.

The third specific question that involves the father's ability to pay is, What if a second, current, family is in the picture? Is it unreasonable to conclude that support enforcement for the former family becomes socially counterproductive when it threatens to deprive the second family of a realistic basis for economic survival? To ask the question in these loaded terms is to answer it. However, we must first define a realistic basis for economic and social survival.

Current state law draws no bottom line relating to the father's income below which support obligations will not be enforced, nor does OCSE. That such a line should be set seems clear. The unanswered question is where that bottom line should be drawn. Traditional state law would consider the needs of the prior family first and either ignore or discount the father's new responsibilities.[17] This approach seems untenable in terms of policy, as well as in the light of decisions equalizing the support rights of legitimate and nonmarital children. If discrimination on the basis of illegitimacy is not permissible, discrimination on the basis of priority seems equally untenable.[18]

The logical conclusion would be to put all children on an equal footing regardless of priority (although age would figure quantitatively in terms of need).[19] The support award for children would thus be determined on the basis of full equality of each child's claim on the father's resources. The next question, however, is, What resources? And it seems obvious that the term must be refined to encompass disposable resources only.

Inevitably the definition of disposable resources turns us back to whether the analysis of the father's ability to pay gives priority to his current responsibilities and arrives at a support duty regarding earlier responsibilities only after the needs of his current family are satisfied. Despite the constitutional considerations that favor equality, it is a permissible, even a compelling, state purpose first to ensure a basis of economic and social survival for the current family before a payment to other dependents is exacted.[20] This argument would seem to permit some inequality of support apportionment between old and new dependents in favor of the new. The open question remains, how much?

Under contract with OCSE, the Greater Community Council of New York developed in 1977 a *Guide for Determining the Ability of an Absent Parent to Pay Child Support*, which OCSE transmitted to all state agencies.[21] This guide is a sincere attempt to take into account various factors that should be considered in fixing support obligations. It adopts the reasonable principle that enforcement must stop at a certain point and fixes that point by reference to federal definitions of budget standards that are automatically adjusted for inflation and changes in living patterns.[22]

The proposed budget, however, posits an unrealistically high income level before requiring any payments to a former family. This is not surprising since the budget proposed for the father's new family is derived from actual income and consumption figures in normal (presumably undivorced) U.S. households. On this basis, the study bootstraps itself to reach a conclusion that would prevent significant amounts of child support from being collected from absent parents who earn less than middle-class incomes.[23]

At the other extreme, we might consider equalizing the situation of the father's old and new families by reference to the AFDC benefit level. This idea has a certain plausibility; it would provide true equality. This approach, however, is not tenable. AFDC benefits do not reach the poverty level in any state.[24] Indeed, the House of Representatives voted in the fall of 1979 to set a first-time national standard for minimum AFDC benefit levels at 65 percent of the poverty line.[25] (Some caution is indicated, however, in view of substantial in-kind benefits flowing to AFDC recipients. Appropriate adjustments would be in order.[26])

If AFDC support for the old family were more adequate (and more uniform nationally), it might possibly be defensible to give the father's current family the overriding weight the New York study recommends. Given the current state of affairs, however, application of the council's recommendations would produce potentially enormous differences between the standards of living of the father's first and second families. By excusing contributions from a father who enjoys the relatively satisfactory standard of living proposed in the Community Council's budget, the proposed formula unacceptably relegates earlier children to the relative squalor of inadequate AFDC support.

A more realistic but still difficult formula might define the father's disposable resources (those to be shared equally by all of his children) as any amount above the federally defined poverty line. With appropriate adjustments for age and special needs, such as health, that formula would ratably apportion the father's earnings in excess of the poverty level between his old and his new responsibilities. A similar formula was recommended to, but not adopted by, the Senate Finance Committee Staff when a predecessor bill of Public Law 93-647 was under consideration.[27] Most people would agree that the bottom line below which there is to be no support enforcement relating to earlier responsibilities should not be drawn lower. Some may wonder whether the poverty line is not too low and whether this approach would provide an acceptable balance between the earlier and the current family, whether it will avoid the worst of all possible consequences of the enforcement program—two broken families where previously there was only one.

A Support Disregard in Setting AFDC Benefit Levels

While society's interest in the economic and social survival of the currently functioning family admittedly is great, even overwhelming, it does not follow that this social interest should be asserted at the sole expense of the earlier children.

If we agree that it would not be sound policy to take the father's new family down to the AFDC level, we should consider an alternative that would help move the father's earlier children up to a budget similar to that allowed his current family, even if that is only a partial solution.

A new formula would apply the father's support payments under which more would go to his children and less for reimbursement to the state. The resulting inequality between AFDC families with paying fathers and those without can be justified more easily than the inequality now threatened in the balance between the father's earlier and current dependents.

Specifically, the absent father's support payment could be used first to bring his AFDC family up to a federally defined minimum standard, such as the poverty level (adjusted by regional cost of living factors), before the state insists on reimbursement for aid previously rendered or deducts the father's payments from current aid payments. If this solution is not feasible in the political tug of war between state sovereignty and federal influence (and money), there is the intermediate—truly minimum—position that the father's support payment should at least be used to bring his family up to state-defined AFDC need standards before it is applied to assistance reimbursement. This compromise would help in those twenty-odd states that pay less than their own standard of need.

This clearly is the less desirable—if politically perhaps the more feasible—route. Twenty-two states pay full need so nothing would change in those states; only the twenty-eight states that pay less than need would be affected by this compromise proposal. The trouble is that the problem of inadequacy of AFDC benefits is not necessarily more serious in the states that pay less than their own definition of need than it is in those states that pay full need. By employing a lower definition of need, some states that pay full need actually pay less aid than some states that pay less than full need. To illustrate, on October 1, 1978, Delaware paid all of a need of $287 and California paid $423 of a need of $444; Illinois paid $300 on a need of $300 and Idaho paid $344 on a need of $395. Further distortions result from the fact that some of the states that pay less than need apply their percentage reduction after deducting income and others do so before. Assuming a state-defined need of $250, a support payment of $100, and an 80 percent factor applied to the need standard, the first method would yield monthly aid of $120 ($250 − $100 × 0.8). The second method would produce aid in the amount of only $100 ($250 × 0.8 − $100). While the states in the first category thus give the family a greater benefit from the father's payment than do the states in the second category, the state-defined need standards and percentage reductions in the states that pay less than need vary so widely that even a state with a less-advantageous reduction formula may provide more total aid to a family than another state with a better formula.[28]

What do we do now? Leaving aside complex technicalities, payment for current child-support and payments on arrears are withheld until all assistance, past and present, is reimbursed.[29] This was not always so. For the first fifteen months of its operation, the new federal law allowed 40 percent of the first $50 of each monthly payment to be disregarded; that is, a maximum of $20 per month was given to the children over and above their AFDC allowance.[30] This provision expired in 1976. No new efforts are in sight to revive this or any similar practice.

The revival of a limited support disregard would have four important policy dimensions. First, allowing the children a tangible net benefit from the father's contribution will provide an incentive to the mother to cooperate in locating (and ascertaining) the father. Second, if fathers saw their payments moving their families into a somewhat better position than that of families for which no support is collected, there probably would be a salutary effect on many fathers' willingness to pay. Moreover, the idea of a support collection disregard is not new or foreign in principle to existing AFDC policy. It would be closely analogous to the earnings disregard current law allows AFDC mothers and students to encourage them to go to work. Unfortunately, the current administration's policy is moving in just the opposite direction in this analogous situation.

Third, allocating some of the father's support contribution to the children over and above their AFDC allowance would help alleviate the serious problem of dealing equitably with both the father's current family and his "earlier" dependents.

Finally, giving children (in appropriate cases) a direct net benefit from their father's support payment would help reduce the most blatant inequity of the AFDC system: the widely different benefit levels provided in the several states under varying state formulas for determining need, as accentuated further by each state's own choice as to what percentage of the state-defined need actually is paid to recipients.[31]

Due Process for Men

Improved paternity procedures raise the issue of collateral enforcement costs—especially for blood tests—that may threaten a program's collection-cost ratio. Worse, a fair trial for men named as fathers of nonmarital children is costly not only because of the expense of blood tests, but if the test excludes the accused as a potential father, the enforcer has lost a potential support obligor. Prosecutors (and support enforcement authorities generally) have been understandably reluctant to commit scarce funds to activities that seem to work against their own interests.

A judge from a large southern city explains that "95 percent of the suspected fathers admit paternity even before the case comes to trial," and a state IV-D official boasts that "75 percent of the people I interview admit paternity and we have no problem getting payments from them."[32] Similar reports come from all over the country. But how many of these men are truly the fathers? What causes these men to admit paternity so freely and incur up to eighteen years of support liability? Is it what the judge thinks—"most of these guys feel pretty good afterward about having done the right thing"—or do these men simply admit sexual access to the mothers and feel uncomfortable with the idea that their partner may have had concurrent relationships with other men at the probable time of conception? To identify the error rate, full blood tests should be run on a representative sample of men who readily admit paternity. It is by no means inconceivable that the results of such a study would be sobering and compel the conclusion that voluntary admissions of paternity should be accepted only upon careful investigation and, if there is any doubt, blood tests.

The federal government is now putting its resources and initiative behind ascertaining paternity, and it should not abdicate its responsibility for monitoring the means by which these obligations are established. The program's primary concern with giving the child and the taxpayer their due must now be matched with an equal commitment to verifying that the man accused of being the father really is the father. Fundamental reform of the paternity action has become the most-pressing task in this entire area. Reform is needed as much to facilitate finding a responsible father for the nonmarital child as to protect the possibly considerable number of men who are falsely accused of paternity.

Reform should move on two interrelated levels: a new procedural framework for the paternity action must improve the quality and the volume of adjudication, and more-efficient and speedier proceedings must provide fuller safeguards for possibly falsely accused men. Within that framework and to achieve both objectives, medical evidence must play a cardinal role.

The Uniform Parentage Act,[33] now enacted in nine states,[34] was developed specifically in response to the U.S. Supreme Court decisions securing the nonmarital child's substantive rights.[35] The act sets out a framework in which traditional paternity practice is superseded by a more efficient and constitutionally sound procedure. The central goal is fairness to the child as well as to the accused man.

In the area of paternity, perhaps nothing is as urgently in need of attention—and as easily accessible to constructive federal involvement—as blood testing. True, blood typing tests will reduce the number of men now held liable for child support, but only by eliminating the nonfathers ordered to support the children of other men. Moreover, not all aspects of blood-typing tests work against the child-support enforcer. In many cases probability calculations may provide circumstantial evidence that positively indicates paternity.[36] The 1976 joint AMA-ABA guidelines on paternity testing are a promising development and are finding increased acceptance in the courts.[37]

The enactment of proposed federal legislation (actually passed by the Senate several times in the early 1970s) that mandated centralized blood-typing facilities at federal expense would have been useful.[38] On the other hand, in its assigned role as developer and supervisor of state plans for ascertaining paternity, OCSE could now do more than it does. OCSE should concern itself with the designation and accreditation of qualified laboratories in cooperation with an appropriate private or public agency so that we may get away from the dangerous current practice of some enforcement agencies, which simply assign paternity testing to the lowest bidder without effective quality control.[39]

OCSE also might give early consideration to recommending or requiring (as a part of state plans) adherence to standard procedures, including forms, that would facilitate the introduction of blood-typing evidence into the courts, which in many states still faces expensive technical obstacles under the law of evidence.[40]

Notes

1. Restatement of the Law of Conflict of Laws §458, comment (a) (1934).

2. 9A U.L.A. 647, 747 (1979).

3. Senate Committee on Finance, Staff Data and Materials on Child Support, 96th Cong. 1st Sess. 4 (1979) (CP 96-7).

4. Joint Economic Committee, Income Security for Americans: Recommendations of the Public Welfare Study, 93rd Cong., 2d Sess. 80 (1974). *Cf.* Janowitz, *The Impact of AFDC on Illegitimate Birth Rates*, 38 J. Marriage and the Family 485 (1976).

5. H. Krause, Child Support in America: The Legal Perspective 115-162 (1981).

6. E. Califano, American Families: Trends, Pressures and Recommendations. A Preliminary Report to Governor Jimmy Carter, Jr. (September 17, 1976) (mimeograph manuscript).

7. Senate Committee on Finance, Social Security Amendments of 1979, 96th Cong., 1st Sess., 66-67 (1979).

8. *See* generally, D. Chambers, Making Fathers Pay: The Enforcement of Child Support (1979); *Testimony before the U.S. Senate Subcommittee on Public Assistance,* 96th Cong., 2d Sess. 204-217 (1980).

9. Krause, *supra* note 5, at 281-306.

10. Letter of December 26, 1979, from Louise B. Hays, Esq., Deputy Director, OCSE, to Harry D. Krause.

11. *E.g.,* Stanaway v. Stanaway, 70 Mich. App. 294 N.W.2d 723 (1976); *cf.* Hagbloom v. Hagbloom, 71 Mich. App. 257, 247 N.W.2d 373 (1976); Moore v. Moore, 173 Conn. 120, 123-124, 376 A.2d 1085, 1087 (1977); Wilcox v. Wilcox, 242 Ga. 598, 250 S.E.2d 465 (1978); *In re* Mahalingham, 21 Wash. App. 228, 584 P.2d 971 (1978).

12. In Branstad v. Branstad, 400 N.E.2d 167 (Ind. App. 1980); *In re* Stamp 300 N.W.2d 275 (Iowa 1980); *see* DuCanto, *Indexing of Marital Settlement Agreements,* 68 Ill. B.J. 808 (1980); Note, *Inflation-Proof Child Support Decrees,* 66 Iowa L. Rev. 131 (1980) and Annot., 75 A.L.R. 3d 493 (1977).

13. Emanuel v. Emanuel, 5 Fam. L. Rev. (BNA) (D.V.I. 1978).

14. Ferry v. Ferry, 201 Neb. 595, 599-600, 271 N.W.2d 450, 453-54 (1978); *accord,* Jahn v. Jahn, 67 Ind. 377, 385 N.E.2d 488 (1979); Gomez v. Gomez, 92 N.M. 310, 587 P.2d 963 (1978); Sistare v. Sistare, 218 U.S. 1, 30 S. Ct. 682, 54 L. Ed. 905 (1910)(dictum); Worthley v. Worthley, 44 Cal. 2d 465, 283 P.2d 19 (1955)(dictum); Gamble v. Gamble, 258 A.2d 261 (D.C. 1969); Robertson v. Cason, 203 So.2d 743 (La. Ct. App. 1967).

15. 11 U.S.C. § 523(a)(5)(1978).

16. 11 U.S.C. § 523(a)(5)(A)(1978).

17. Krause, *supra* note 5, at 20-21.

18. Gomez v. Perez, 409 U.S. 535, 93 S. Ct. 872, 35 L. Ed. 2d 56 (1973); *cf.,* Zablocki v. Redhail, 434 U.S. 374, 98 S. Ct. 673, 54 L. Ed. 2d 618 (1978).

19. 45 C.F.R. § 302.53(b) (1981).

20. Shapiro v. Thompson, 394 U.S. 618, 89 S. Ct. 1322, 22 L. Ed. 2d 600 (1969).

21. M. Sauber & E. Taittonen, Guide for Determining the Ability of an Absent Parent to Pay Child Support (1977) (OCSE-IM-77-12).

22. Krause, *supra* note 5, at 437-441.

23. U.S. Dept. of Commerce, Bureau of the Census, Statistical Abstract of the Untied States 455 (1978).

24. H.R. Rep. No. 45, 96th Cong., 1st Sess. 92 (1979); Krause, *supra* note 5, at 465 n. 89.

25. Congressional Quarterly 2534 (November 10, 1979).

26. Krause, *supra* note 5, at 461-464.

27. H. Krause, Family Law: Cases and Materials 503-504 (1976).

28. H.E.W. Social Security Administration, Family Assistance Characteristics State of Plans for Aid to Families with Dependent Children 234-35 (1978); OCSE-AT-76.5 at 21 (1976), 44 Fed. Reg. 29122 (1979); Hays, *supra* note 10.

29. 45 C.F.R. § 302.51(b)(3), (4) (1979).

30. 42 U.S.C. § 657(a)(1) (1976).

31. 45 C.F.R. § 233.20 (1978). Joint Economic Committee, Studies in Public Welfare, Paper No. 20, Handbook of Public Income and Transfer Programs; 1975, 93rd Cong., 2d Sess. 161-166 (1974); H.E.W. Social Security Administration, Family Assistance Characteristics of State Plans for Aid to Families with Dependent Children 236-237 (1978); Jefferson v. Hackney, 406 U.S. 535, 92 S. Ct. 1724, 32 L. Ed. 2d 285 (1972). *Cf* Krause, *supra* note 27, at 459-476.

32. U.S. New and World Report, Feb. 12, 1979, at 50, 1 OSCE Child Support Report 4, (Sept. 1979).

33. 9 U.L.A.

34. 9 U.L.A. 579 (1979), enacted as Cal. Civ Code §§ 7000-7018 (Cum. Supp. 1979); Colo. Rev. Stat. §§ 19-6-101 through 19-6-129 (1978); Haw Rev. Stat. §§ 584-1 through 584-26 (1976); Minn. Laws 1980, ch. 589; Mont. Rev. Code Ann §§ 61-301 through 61-334 (Cum Supp. 1977); Nev. Rev. Stat. §§ 126.031/126.231 (1979); N.D. Cent. Code § 14-17-01 through 14-17-26 (Supp. 1977); Wash. Rev. Code Ann, §§ 26.26.010-26.26.905 (Supp. 1978); Wyo. Stat. Ann §§ 14-2-101 through 14-2-120 (1977). See Comment, *Washington's Parentage Act: A Step Forward for Children's Rights*, 12 Gonzaga L. Rev. 455 (1977); Note, *The Uniform Parentage Act: What It Will Mean for the Putative Father in California*, 28 Hastings L.J. 191 (1976). In 1980, the Act was pending in the legislatures of Delaware, Florida, Idaho, Kansas, New Jersey, and Ohio.

35. Krause, *supra* note 5, at 119-160.

36. *Id*. at 219-243.

37. 10 Fam. L. 2, 247 (1976), *reproduced in* Krause, Appendix C, 537-82, *See*, e.g., Little v. Streater, 452 U.S. 1, 101 S. Ct. 2202, 2206, 68 L. Ed. 2d 627 (1981); Mills v. Habluetzel, 102 S. Ct. 1549, 1554, 1557 (1982).

38. H.R. 17045 93rd Cong., 2d Sess. (Dec. 14, 1974) (Senate version).

39. 45 C.F.R. § 303.5(c)(1979).

40. *See* K. Broun Producing Blood Tests in the Course: The Law of Evidence in Krause, *supra* note 5, at 246-271.

17 A Proposal for Reform of the Child-Support System

Harold W. Watts

For nearly fifteen years the category of assistance aimed at ensuring material support for rearing children in the social security system through AFDC has been in a state of crisis. Various reforms have been proposed and some have been tried, and still the program is a popular subject for attack, carrying a notoriety far out of proportion to its size within our social-benefit system and discordant with the crucial purposes that AFDC aims to serve.

The policies outlined in this chapter do not aim at a complete solution to the problem of low-income in families that are rearing children. In particular it is assumed that some sort of income-tested transfer is likely to continue to be needed and provided even for families that have two parents who are fully engaged in the task of supporting and nurturing their children in cases where their productive capacities are not sufficient for the needs of their children. There may also be noncategorical programs such as food stamps that offer benefits to persons of all ages and that can fulfill part of the needs of family units that are rearing children.

The policies considered here aim at the part of the public income-transfer system that is most directly related to the private transfers that must also be considered as part of the full system of support for child rearing. In the normal or ideal situation, a child has two parents who are present and active in providing nurture. This situation may not prevail for any one of several reasons.

In the case of death, there exists a social insurance provision for children who are survivors of a covered worker. These benefits are related to prior earnings of the worker, and they are not related to the income of a surviving parent or to any other available private insurance benefits. Benefits are not discontinued if a stepparent or surrogate parent enters the household. But for children who are orphaned by parents who are not in covered employment, have not worked long enough to be fully covered, or are not part of the paid labor force, the survivors' insurance does not provide any coverage.

For the other reasons for a "parent shortage" and for uninsured parental death cases, the means-tested public-assistance category of AFDC provides the principal source of public income support. This program was designed to fill the remaining need, as self-defined in each jurisdiction, after the parent who cares for the child has sought support from the absent parent and, if the youngest child is old enough, has entered or sought employment aimed at eventual self-support. The extreme impairment of incentive to work that that simple make-up-the-difference strategy entails was somewhat reduced in 1967 when the "thirty and a third" rule enabled AFDC recipients to retain part of their net earnings from work. But the same rule applies to any private transfer (or other receipts) and similarly leaves no direct incentive to seek child-support judgments or to pursue regular payment of judgments entered. Regulations may and typically do require such efforts, but the only available sanction for insufficient effort is complete denial of benefits. Compliance is predictably uneven, and the effect of the regulation is more often harassment than genuine encouragement of support responsibilities.

A key point of this proposal extends social insurance of the sort now provided to children of covered workers in the event of death to a wider range of hazards that may deprive children of one or both parents. It attempts to insure each child against such deprivation regardless of the reason and to maintain or even expand the incentive and reinforcement for parental support responsibility.

But let us start a bit further back and consider the problem of determining normative standards for basic levels of child support expected from an absent parent and for equitable sharing conventions where circumstances allow support beyond the minimum standard. These are the levels that should be informing family court proceedings where support orders and awards are made. The same standards ought to be pertinent to the question of support levels provided by social insurance when the support cannot be or is not provided by an absent parent. One part of the proposed reform of child support mandates a mechanism to determine appropriate support levels consistent with prevailing standards in our society and to review and update them periodically in the light of social and economic changes that may affect such norms. Possibly a small commission could be instituted to perform this function and to provide annual reviews and reports on the status of children who are not living with both parents. Such a commission could also supervise or even conduct a continuing program of research on the special needs and hazards of child rearing in one-parent circumstances.

The social-insurance part of the child-support reform would take basic support standards prescribed by this commission, which would specify the amount of monthly payments appropriate for different numbers and ages of children as target levels for support and would pay no benefits for cases where parental support or alternative public child-support benefits equal or exceed the basic standards. Where these sources fall short, however, the child-support insurance program would pay benefits equal to a major fraction of the difference or, say, 80 percent. If there were no other sources of child support, the program would pay 80 percent of the basic standard—the maximum benefit. It should be emphasized that every child who is not living with two parents would be eligible for a support claim if other sources, such as survivor's insurance, court-ordered support, or voluntary support, do not provide as much as the basic standard. The support claim would be filed by the custodial parent and would be a joint claim if more than one unsupported (or not fully supported) child were in custody. In the case of children living with neither parent, claims would be made by a guardian or foster parent; a different schedule of benefits might be appropriate for such cases. Adoptive parents would stand fully in the place of the biological parents they have replaced. Stepparents, on the other hand, would not assume the support responsibility for stepchildren, nor would the support obligation of an absent parent be reduced by the presence of a stepparent in the custodial family.

Finally, the benefit payments should represent a form of taxable income for the custodial parent. In cases where the family unit is poor, this provision will not substantially reduce the value of the benefit—but the "clawback" of a benefit that is not income tested seems quite appropriate for those who pay substantial amounts of net taxes. It is also recommended that the existing tax code be amended to make child-support payments (whether court ordered or voluntary) deductible for the payor and countable as income for the recipient. At present the treatment of alimony follows that pattern, but child support is not deductible for the payor. There appears to be no sound reason for this different treatment (it is not connected with the rules for counting dependents' exemption), and the practice probably leads to substitution of alimony for child support in order to reduce overall taxes. In the content of a linear credit tax system or constant marginal tax rates over most income categories, there would be some net administrative gain in taxing all factor income at the source and allowing interpersonal transfers to be untaxed. As long as there are sharp differences in marginal rates, however, it seems wrong to tax child allowances at higher rates than alimony. This is what typically happens at present.

Besides a commission to set support standards and a social insurance benefit scheme to augment support payments that are below the standard, the next component aims to provide a regular reminder and reinforcement to absent parents for meeting child-support responsibilities, and, as necessary, to exact prompt and sure penalties for willful neglect or abandonment of these responsibilities. A report on parental responsibility should be made a standard part of the income-tax reporting process. Since exemptions and some sort of deductions now depend on accurate reporting about children and their level of dependency, the added information would not seem out of place on a tax form. Each adult or filer (including both joint filers) would have to list all minor children for which he or she is responsible as a parent, and for each child the parent would have to indicate how support responsibilities were being met. The nominal possibilities are: living and sharing household with child; paying court-ordered support payments; paying voluntary amounts at least as large as basic standards unless court-ordered support is larger; or some combination of these in intervals covering a full year.

For each child and for each fraction of a year that support is not being provided in one of these ways, a schedule of penalty tax rates would determine a surtax on the tax bill. These payments would be calculated as a fraction of adjusted gross income reduced only by a single personal exemption and standard deduction. The penalty payments would not be deductible, and nonpayment or late payment should be handled like any other tax delinquency. The statements on the report of parental responsibility would be subject to the same sort of audits as other income-tax report items, and the penalties for fraudulent reporting could also be extended to these matters.

The surtax provision will not yield a substantial revenue. Most noncustodial parents who have substantial amounts of taxable income would probably find it advantageous to meet their support requirements in the prescribed ways. But whatever revenue is obtained should be channeled to the social insurance fund that pays supplemental child support. The bulk of the fiscal support for the child-support insurance will have to come from some general revenue source. There does not seem to be any self-evident special group that should be asked to support this cause as the benefits to taxpayers from fewer casualties of deprived childhood are spread widely. It is at least arguable that the childless are a group that should contribute differentially to the support of partially abandoned children. They are not directly involved in nurturing their own children to take a place in future generations, but they will depend, as will all of us, on the children who are produced to carry on the work of society while they are collecting their retirement benefits.

Finally, there should be careful consideration of the merits of a centalized registry of birth, death, and parenthood that could facilitate the enforcement of judicial awards and promote more-impartial administration of support responsbiltiy laws. A registry could be established by recording the parents as from a birth certificate by name and social security number, at the time of birth. The mother would have responsibility for naming the father, subject to appeal by the named father. Upon petition, a mother would be allowed to accept undivided responsibility for a child at birth and hence decline to name a father. This registry would need to be updated whenever an adoption alters legal parental status. Deaths would also be entered from death certificates. The parental and ancestral status of immigrants could be entered at official points of immigration.

It is now possible to determine with near certainty which of a group of candidates is the biological parent of a child. To the extent that this is relevant to acceptance of responsibility by a father or to the willingness to share it by a mother, there are now more-reliable tests than in the past. Similarly, the technology available for recording and updating such files and for performing the sorting operations needed to identify family groups has made such a registry feasible and relatively inexpensive.

Besides its use as a means of auditing and even prompting responses on the statements of parental support, such a registry would have other uses. It would be an authoritative source of genealogical information, it could provide independent control totals for census and other survey designs, and it could provide a sample frame for sampling family networks, a topic that has been neglected in the prevalent study of easy-to-sample household units. There are also potentials in such a registry for invasion of privacy and other official meddling. As a consequence, the issue needs further study to explore possible safeguards against abuse, as well as a more-complete review of the benefits. A more-specific assessment of the kind of data system required and its costs is also needed.

In summary, the proposal outlined here takes the incremental step of expanding social-insurance coverage to include all forms of loss of parental support. The notion is that society is insuring the child because the child has no control or responsibility over such events and should consequently be given equivalent treatment in each of them. It largely separates the assignment and enforcement of responsibility of absent parents from the immediate issue of support for the child and enables such encouragement or sanctions to be carried on without the active or initiating participation of the custodial parent. Finally, it aims at securing and maintaining social consensus around standards of parental responsibility, both as to when and how much support should be provided. It aims to do this in a humane and consistent way that is not linked with welfare and the associated stigma. While these reforms would not solve all of the low-income problems of families with children, with either one or two resident parents, it can make a contribution to solving that problem for the difficult one-parent cases and for some of these may be all that is required for them to be self-supporting, including a more dependable private transfer from absent parents.

18 A Proposal for Comprehensive Reform of the Child-Support System in Wisconsin

Irwin Garfinkel, David Betson, Thomas Corbett, and *Sherwood K. Zink*

In the summer of 1980, a research team from the Institute for Research on Poverty under contract with the Wisconsin Department of Health and Social Services engaged in a project to examine the existing Wisconsin child-support system and design and evaluate alternatives to it. This chapter presents the preliminary findings of our research, design, and evaluation effort.

Weaknesses of the Current Child-Support System

One of every five children in the United States is potentially eligible for financial support from a living parent who is not residing with them.[1] Sixteen percent of these children live with their fathers and 24 percent with their mother and a stepfather; most however—60 percent—live in female-headed households.[2]

Because of increasing rates of divorce, separation, and out-of-wedlock births, the proportion of children in female-headed households increased from 8.5 percent in 1965 to 12.6 percent in 1978. Estimates indicate that nearly half of all children born today will spend part of their first eighteen years in a single-parent home.[3]

The economic support of this large and growing number of children who live apart from at least one of their natural parents is problematic. Both natural parents living with their children unavoidably share their income with them. In contrast, when a parent lives apart from his child, it requires a conscious act to share his income with the child. Does the absent parent contribute to the support of his children?

Data published by the Census Bureau indicate that of those women potentially eligible to receive child support, only 59 percent were awarded payments.[4] Of those awarded such support, only 49 percent received the full

This research was supported by the Institute for Research on Poverty with the Division of Economic Assistance of the Department of Health and Social Services, State of Wisconsin, and by the Graduate School of the University of Wisconsin.

amount due them and 28 percent received nothing. In short, the U.S. child-support system fosters parental irresponsibility.

The current child-support system is highly inequitable. A recent article on child support began by noting that two men, each with $450 net income per month, paid $60 and $120 per month in child support, while yet a third man with $900 net income paid only $50.[5] Whether and how much a man pays or a child receives in child support depends not just on the man's ability to pay but on the attitudes of local judges, district attorneys, and welfare officials, the beliefs and attitudes of both parents, the current relationship between the parents, and the skills of their respective lawyers. Even in those cases settled in court, the factors taken into account depend on the judge, the jurisdiction, and a number of incalculable circumstances. Nearly every absent parent can find someone earning more who pays less. In many cases how much a man is expected to pay depends on whether he or his ex-wife has remarried. In many other cases remarriage has no effect on support orders. Whichever is more just or better social policy, this unequal, arbitrary treatment of people in similar circumstances is inequitable.

Child support is a major source of continuing tension between many former spouses. Because there are no firm guidelines, ex-spouses quarrel over what is a fair amount of child support. The tax structure adds to the friction. A man in a high-income tax bracket will prefer paying alimony (which is deductible) to child support (which is not). His former wife will prefer to receive child support (which she does not have to include in her taxable income) to alimony (which she must and which is likely to cease should she remarry). Ex-husbands often would rather give gifts to their children (to buy their affection) than supply cash (which may benefit their former wives). The adversarial atmosphere of the divorce extends throughout the minority of the children. When ex-husbands fail to pay support, the ex-wives often deny visitation, and vice-versa, an action that is bound to worsen what is usually a bad relationship between the ex-spouses and may weaken the bonds of affection between the absent parent and his children.

Finally, nearly half of all children living in female-headed households are poor and on welfare. The widespread failure of the system to ensure that absent parents pay child support impoverishes these children and shifts the burden of financial support to the public sector.

Welfare is no longer the best way to provide aid to children living in single-parent families. When AFDC was enacted in 1935, in the midst of the Great Depression, women were not expected to work. The program was designed to enable single mothers to stay home to raise their children. In view of that objective, reducing benefits by one dollar for each dollar of earnings—a 100 percent tax rate on earnings—made sense. Now that half of married women with childen work, expectations have changed, and a new consensus is emerging that single mothers are expected to work. Welfare programs, however, are not good vehicles to aid those expected to work, for in order to confine welfare benefits to the poor, the benefits must be reduced as income increases. This has the effect of discouraging work effort because earnings are virtually confiscated by high benefit-reduction rates. In response to the changing expectations, tax rates in AFDC were reduced in 1962 and 1967 to encourage work. But reduced tax rates also had the effect of raising the amount a mother could earn before she lost eligibility for AFDC. Welfare took on the role of providing income supplementation, as well as the role of providing a minimum income to those who could not or were not expected to work. This dual role has never, throughout the history of welfare dating back to the Elizabethan Poor Law, proved to be stable. After short episodes, the income-supplementation role has been shed. Now the Reagan administration is raising tax rates in the AFDC program. Unfortunately, there is now no program in place to provide supplementation to single-parent families.

Goals, Constraints, and Design Decisions

Goals and Constraints

A number of goals and constraints shaped our efforts to design a better child-support system. The goals were to:

1. Establish equitable parental financial responsibility for child support.
2. Collect the resulting obligation.
3. Cushion the economic loss to children of single parents resulting from the absence of a parent.
4. Guarantee a minimal level of economic child support for all children with a living absent parent.
5. Reduce both welfare costs and case loads and minimize the stigma associated with guaranteeing economic support for children with absent parents.
6. Integrate single-parent families into the main-stream of American economic and social life.
7. Reduce the adverse effects of the current system on the behavior of both absent and custodial parents.

Our constraints were to:

1. Avoid taxing absent parents for the support of children other than their own.

2. Avoid imposing excessively high tax rates on absent parents.
3. Avoid making existing and potential AFDC beneficiaries worse off.
4. Achieve these changes with little or no increase in the general revenues that now are being spent on AFDC.

Program Design Decisions

Evaluation to date leads us to conclude that these goals and constraints would be best obtained by enacting a new program to collect and distribute child-support payments. The objective of equitably establishing parental financial responsibility is best served by legislating a simple normative formula for child support. The most effective way to collect the support obligation of the absent parent is to treat it as a tax and collect it through the withholding system. The best way to guarantee a minimum level of child support for all children with a living absent parent and simultaneously reduce welfare costs and case loads and minimize the stigma of welfare is to pay benefits to all children (rich and poor alike) with a living absent parent who is legally liable to pay child support and to supplement the benefits up to a minimum out of general revenues (that would otherwise be spent on welfare) when the ability of the absent parent to pay cannot yield child support equal to the minimum. Finally, it is our judgment that the preferred way to increase the economic well-being of female-headed families on welfare is to offer them an alternative opportunity, a nonwelfare benefit that, when combined with even part-time work, will be superior to welfare.

The child-support program that we envision can be best described in terms of our recommendations about:

1. Which children are entitled to or eligible for child-support payments.
2. Which absent and custodial parents are obligated to make child-support payments.
3. How much absent and custodial parents are obligated to pay.
4. How much children are entitled to receive.
5. How the system will be administered.

Which Children Are Entitled to or Eligible for Child-Support Payments?
All the children who are Wisconsin residents, under the age of eighteen (under nineteen if in secondary education), and have at least one living absent parent legally liable for paying child support are eligible.

Which Absent and Custodial Parents Are Obligated to Make Child-Support Payments? All parents not living with their children have a legal obligation to share their income with their children. Low income is not a sufficient cause to exempt anyone from the system. No matter how low the income, the state will enforce the responsibility of the absent parent to share part of his income with the child. Even absent parents in prison will be required to share what little income they earn with their children. The unique circumstances that apply to very wealthy people will be accommodated not by exempting them from the system but rather by exempting income above $50,000 from the system. If the family-court judge finds that it is in the best interests of the child or custodial parent for the child, and therefore the absent and custodial parents, to be excluded from the system, all three parties will be excluded from the system. The statutory clause on the best interests of the child should be narrowly worded to include such specific examples as cases where there is a property trust settlement for the children, which guarantees them at least as much as the tax structure described here. Custodial parents whose children receive a public subsidy will be liable for a child-support subsidy tax.

How Much Absent and Custodial Parents Are Obligated to Pay: The legislated child-support formula for absent parents will apply up to $50,000 per year in 1982 dollars. Each year thereafter the $50,000 figure will be adjusted by the average real growth in the economy. Custodial parents will be free to seek supplementary child-support orders through the courts on absent-parent income in excess of the tax base. The tax rate will be a proportionate rate starting with the first dollar of income. Neither the tax base nor tax rate will be altered in the event of remarriage of either parent or the parenting of additional children by the absent parent. The tax rate for the initial child will be higher than that for subsequent children. The tax rate will approach, but not reach, zero by the fifth child. The tax base for custodial parents liable for the public subsidy child-support tax will be gross income, which, when multiplied by the tax rate, will be sufficient to recoup the public subsidy. The average tax rate on custodial parents will be lower than that on absent parents. Whether this is achieved through a lower rate or an exemption has not yet been decided.

How Much Each Child Will Receive: The amount to be disbursed will be equal to the amount paid by the absent parent or a minimum, whichever is larger. The program will pay benefits for children alone and not for the caretaker. The amount collected and paid out will get smaller per child as the number of children increases. The benefit will be increased annually by either the increase in the absent parent's income, or, if the child receives only the minimum benefit, by the average growth of the economy (GNP). The benefit will be invariant with respect to the marital status of both the custodial and absent parent.

How the System Will Be Administered: The responsibility for collecting child support from absent parents and disbursing those payments should be shifted from the county clerk of courts to the separate unit responsible for child support within the Wisconsin Department of Health and Social Services (the state IV-D agency). The state IV-D unit should develop as rapidly as possible the computer capability to administer the system. This division will also be responsible for notifying employers of additional withholding requirements. Each county IV-D program will have a computer terminal by which they may enter all new cases into the state system and get information from that system on old cases. The intake process will be automatic for all new cases. Once the program is established, most eligible persons will be incorporated into the system by virtue of the court's disposition of a family-dissolution, separation, or paternity decision.

It is possible to design such a program that would cost the general taxpayer no more and probably less than is currently spent on AFDC yet make no AFDC beneficiaries worse off. Indeed such a program would improve the status of many beneficiaries and reduce welfare costs and case loads without imposing unfair or excessive tax rates on absent parents. Although the analysis of behavioral effects is not yet complete, our preliminary judgment is that on balance, the incentives of the new system would be less adverse than those of the existing system.

Rationale for Selection of Specific Alternatives

Eligibility for the New Child-Support Program
Would Not Be Income Tested

If income is made a condition of eligibility, the program will not be very different from AFDC and thus would suffer from the same drawback of high benefit-reduction rates. Currently AFDC beneficiaries pay higher tax rates than most other Americans by virtue of the reduction in benefits they suffer as their earnings increase. Research indicates that how much they work is more sensitive to economic disincentives than is the labor-force participation of male heads of families.[6] Placing high tax rates on AFDC mothers, therefore, discourages them from working, at least in the regular labor force where earnings are reported routinely to government officials.

By their nature, income-tested programs segregate beneficiaries from the mainstream society by creating special institutions that serve only the poor. This institutional segregation is exacerbated by the economic disincentives that encourage beneficiaries to avoid the conventional labor market.

AFDC also stigmatizes beneficiaries. There is evidence that many beneficiaries accept the negative characterizations of welfare recipients held by others and therefore feel less worthwhile.[7] A child-support program that provides benefits as a matter of right to children with absent fathers from all income strata would not stigmatize beneficiaries.

Income-tested programs are more expensive per case to administer than nonincome-tested programs because of the need to determine eligibility and vary benefits by income. On the other hand, even though they are cheaper per case, nonincome-tested programs may be more costly to administer because they serve so many more people (cases) than do income-tested programs. However, in situations where the state deals with an entire population group (rich and poor alike), even if the benefit program is only for the poor (income tested), a nonincome-tested program will be cheaper to administer. Such is the case with the income tax considered in conjunction with the food stamps program. It costs at least $2 billion more to administer these two programs than it would to administer a credit income tax, which would both pay benefits to and collect taxes from everyone in the population in a unified nonincome-tested cash program.[8] A nonincome-tested approach appears to have the same potential for administrative cost savings in the child-support area, at least in Wisconsin and other states in which all child-support payments are channeled through government agencies. That is, while a nonincome-tested child-support program may be more expensive to administer than the benefit and tax sides of AFDC, it is likely that it will be cheaper to administer than the combined AFDC, IV-D, and judicial systems that now serve rich and poor in different systems.

The administrative cost savings of having a single, unified, and therefore nonincome-tested system distributing child-support benefits will probably be dwarfed by the greater efficiency of a single, unified system in child-support collections. By making child-support obligations a tax and using the withholding system to collect it, we should improve collections dramatically. If the state collects payments from all absent parents, it will have to distribute those payments to the children. Thus if a single collection system is more efficient than a bifurcated system, a nonincome-tested program will not only be cheaper to administer but will collect more as well.

The arguments put forward for income testing have both philosophical and cost considerations. Society's interest in ensuring support for children diminishes as the income of the family in which they live increases. Closely related is the fact that income testing ensures that benefits have some relation to need. On the cost side, it is argued that a nonincome-tested program would increase costs or general revenue financing in at least two ways: those children currently on AFDC whose mothers work would not have their benefit reduced, and some children not now on AFDC whose absent parents have low incomes would be eligible for the minimum child-support benefits.

These additional costs could exceed the administrative savings and larger collections resulting from the greater efficiency of a non-income-tested approach.

We disagree with both these philosophical and cost assumptions. Although it is true that society's interest in assuring support for children diminishes as the income of the family in which they live increases, it is not true that there is a social interest in only those children who live in poor families. Although the involvement of the federal and state governments in the enforcement and provision of child support has increased in the last fifty years, local governments have been heavily involved in child-support enforcement and provision for centuries, and appropriately so. When someone parents a child, he or she incurs an obligation to contribute to the support of that child. Governments are responsible for enforcing this obligation.

A nonincome-tested program will pay benefits to children who would be ineligible under an income-tested program. In some of these cases, the absent parent's income will be insufficient to pay for the minimum. This will increase the public subsidy and increase costs. This problem arises frequently in the proportion of cases where the custodial parent is the father and the absent parent is the mother.

Whether the extra costs of having a nonincome-tested program in terms of eligibility lead to an increase in financing from general revenues, however, depends upon the combination of benefit levels and tax rates that are chosen for the program, as well as the improved collections and administrative savings of a nonincome-tested program. It is possible to choose combinations of benefit levels and tax rates that lead to either increases or decreases in costs.

Indeed one of the advantages of contemplating a nonincome-tested approach is that it makes explicit the trade-offs in keeping tax rates on both absent and custodial parents reasonably low, making benefits to children that are decently high, and keeping costs to the general public reasonably low.

For example, suppose that we concluded that the custodial parent should help finance the public child-support benefit by paying a special surtax on her income like the absent parent. How high should that surtax be? Suppose further that we conclude that the appropriate surtax rates on the income of the absent parent are 20 percent for the first child, 10 percent for the second child, and half the previous rate for each successive child. It is difficult to think of a convicting justification for charging the custodial parent higher surtax rates. Yet this is what AFDC has done since its inception. Even at its lowest, the implicit tax rate on earnings in the AFDC program nationwide was 40 percent. Throughout most of AFDC's existence, the tax rate was closer to 100 percent. The Reagan administration's welfare reforms bring the rate closer to 100 percent once again. The option of a net tax on all custodial parents is not considered because such a tax would violate our fourth constraint: that the child-support tax not exceed the benefit to the child (except possibly to offset administrative costs). This does not rule out the option of taxing all custodial parents and refunding the tax in cases where there was no public subsidy. The issue of how to administer a tax on custodial parents if there is one and of whether to offset the absent-parent liability for above-minimum payments through a custodial parent tax have been considered but are not discussed here.

Public Subsidies

The argument for a tax on custodial parents is threefold: it will increase the equity of and public support for the program, reduce the public subsidy to split families, and reduce incentives for low-income families to split or feign splitting.

Most people feel that it is unfair for all of us to finance a public subsidy to a child whose custodial parent is very wealthy—for example, if the custodial parent's annual income is $50,000 or more and the absent parent makes little or nothing. Is it fair to tax low- and middle-income people so the state can pay up to $3,000 to subsidize the child-support benefit? It is hard to make a case that such subsidy is just.

A tax on custodial parents in cases where the absent parent does not earn enough income to pay for the minimum benefit will reduce the public subsidy. Our estimates indicate that the revenue that can be raised by a tax on the custodial parent is substantial. For example, for a program with a $3,000 minimum for the first child and a $1,500 minimum for the second and tax rates on the absent parent of 20 percent and 10 percent for the first and second children, a tax on the custodial parent of 10 percent and 5 percent for the first and second children will raise $82 million, or about one-fifth as much as the tax on the absent parent.

Finally, by virtue of reducing the public subsidy, the tax on custodial parents will reduce the incentive for families with at least one low earner to split or feign splitting. While the guarantee of a minimum payment unavoidably creates such an incentive, and while in our judgment the economic security for children achieved by the minimum outweighs the adverse incentive, reducing this adverse incentive is a gain.

There are four arguments against imposing a surtax on the income of custodial parents to help finance the child-support benefit. First, since the custodial parent is living with the child, the state must assume, as we do in the case of intact families, that the parent is sharing income with the child. Just as the state does not enforce a transfer from married parents to children with whom they live, the state should not intervene with a single parent living with the child.

Second, the custodial parent, unlike the absent parent, is providing custodial care for the children. At the least, this suggests that the custodial parent should pay a much lower surtax than the absent parent.

Third, a tax on custodial parents will decrease their incentives to work, reduce the number of families that leave welfare, and reduce the economic well-being of children in such families.

Finally, it would complicate administration of the program to impose a tax on custodial parents. If a separate income test is used to administer the tax, we are back to the AFDC system. If not, one would have to match tax records of the absent and custodial parents to ensure that the sum of their surtaxes did not exceed the child-support benefit. Moreover, either the custodial parent would have to pay a tax at the end of the year or the state would have to collect, through the withholding system, the tax from all custodial parents and then refund it in some way to most. Neither option is attractive.

The first two counterarguments may be dealt with easily. The purpose of the tax on the custodial parent is to reduce the unnecessary public subsidy when the child's needs are met, not to enforce a transfer from the custodial parent to the child. While provision of custodial care may justify a lower tax on custodial than absent parents, it does not justify no tax.

The charge that a tax on custodial parents will reduce their economic well-being, may reduce incentives to work, and will reduce the number of families who leave welfare is true. It is also true, however, that a tax on custodial parents will reduce the public subsidy. Just as disincentives to work, reducing the well-being of single mothers and their children, and driving more people to rely on welfare should be avoided where possible, a big public subsidy should also be avoided where possible. The severity of both evils to be avoided depends upon the severity of the tax rate. The higher the tax rate, the greater the reduction in economic well-being, the number of people who leave welfare, and probably the work effort of custodial parents.[9] On the other hand, the higher the tax rate on custodial parents, the lower the public subsidy. Having no tax on custodial parents gives zero weight to the value of avoiding large public subsidies where possible. A relatively low tax rate will give great value to this objective at little cost to the objectives of avoiding adverse work incentives, reductions in the well-being of single mothers and their children, and reliance on welfare.

Finally, a tax on custodial parents will complicate administration, but the complications are not fatal. The extra costs may be justified by the objective achieved.

Publicly Distributed Benefits Would Be Related
to the Income of the Absent Parent

The child-support program is designed to serve children with absent parents from all economic strata. If there is only a flat benefit, the program will not serve children from middle- and upper-class families very well. Indeed in many cases the program will worsen their situation.

For two reasons, the flat minimum benefit will tend to become a maximum benefit. Some absent parents will argue that the minimum benefit represents the cost of a child. Undoubtedly some judges will accept this interpretation. Consequently, in some cases child-support orders for children from middle- and upper-income families will be less than if there were no program.

Second, and more important, the efficiency of public collection of support up to the minimum will weaken private collection above the minimum. Unless the absent parent can afford to pay a great deal more than the minimum benefit, the monetary and psychic costs of privately pursuing supplementary child-support orders will discourage custodial parents from doing so. Similarly, the rewards for lawyers will also be reduced. Currently the reward for pursuing child support is the full amount of the order. Once the program is enacted, the minimum will be guaranteed. Consequently the reward to the custodial parent will be reduced to the total order minus the minimum. The reward to the lawyer will be some proportion of that. Because of this, in practice the minimum will tend to become a maximum.

Although it would be easier and cheaper to administer a program that paid only flat benefits, the administration of the entire child-support system would be far more complex and costly. A flat-benefit program would be accompanied by a parallel part-private, part-public system for families with middle incomes and above. These families would be served by both the new child-support tax-benefit program and the supplementary payment system. In Wisconsin and other progressive states, the state already plays a large role in collection and disbursement of child support for all families. All payments are supposed to go through the office of the clerk of courts. If there were a flat-benefit program, we would have the absurd situation of two different public agencies collecting and disbursing child-support payments for the same people.

In addition to the extra complexity and public costs that would arise from this duplication of efforts produced by a flat-benefit system, there will also be extra monetary and psychic costs to both the absent and custodial parents. In the absence of a predetermined child-support formula, exspouses now quarrel over the appropriate amount of support. This potential source of continuing tension would remain in all cases where the absent parent had income in excess of the amount required to finance the minimum. Moreover once supplementary orders were established, many custodial parents would incur additional costs to enforce them.

A flat-benefit system would also perpetuate the horizontal inequities of the current system. How well custodial and absent parents fared in terms of supplementary award collection and payment would vary even for people in identical circumstances with respect to income and family size.

Finally a program that pays benefits and collects taxes above the minimum will appear to be more equitable than a flat-benefit program because the tax on absent parents for a flat system would be highly regressive on incomes in excess of that required to finance the minimum. Consequently, a flat-benefit program is open to the charge of being highly inequitable to low-income absent parents. In contrast, a program that took the same percentage of income from all absent parents (except those with exceptionally high incomes) for child support is not open to this charge. Furthermore by making middle- and upper-middle-income absent parents liable for the same proportion of their incomes for child support, the low-income absent parent will gain some political protection, for if some percentage of income seems too high or unfair for middle-income absent parents, the case would seem even stronger for low-income absent parents.

Our rationale is countered by the following arguments. The more income and other resources the custodial parent has, the better able she (or he) is to take care of herself and her children on her own through the courts. So if a case can be made for child support in excess of the minimum based on higher-than-average ability to pay of the absent parent, custodial parents can be expected to make such a case in court.

Second, it will be easier to administer a program that pays flat benefits than one that pays benefits related to income of the absent spouse. In the latter case, it is necessary to know the income of the absent spouse in order to determine the benefit the custodial parent is entitled to receive for the child. Benefits must be adjusted to reflect increases (and perhaps decreases) in the income of the absent spouse for those whose absent spouses pay more than the minimum

If upper-income absent parents become unemployed, or ill, or lose income for any other reason, the income-related program would have to let benefits drop to the minimum, which would be disruptive to the family and further complicate administration, or continue to pay the higher benefits, which would increase costs. The additional cost would have to come out of either general revenues or additional revenue raised from absent parents whose incomes exceeded the amount necessary to fund the minimum.

Third, there is no need to have a duplicative system. Custodial parents could be given the choice of either participating in the public system or collecting child support from the absent parent on their own. This would promote choice, further simplify administration, and reduce costs.

Fourth, it is not clear that horizontal equity is best served by eliminating the courts entirely, or nearly entirely, from the process. Not fixing a tax rate up to a very high level of absent-parent income leaves room for other financial arrangements to be made, such as leaving assets to children. It could be that the percentage tax imposed by the public system would become the norm for those who sued for supplementary support but that judges could then deviate from that norm where individual circumstances warranted such a deviation. The burden on the courts will be alleviated substantially by a flat-benefit program.

Finally, it may be that expenditures on children in married families increase less than proportionally with income. Epenshade's numbers, for example, suggest this.[10] If this is so, a regressive tax structure would not be so inequitable in that it would only be reflecting the pattern of support of parents who live with their children.

We are not convinced by such arguments. Although some custodial parents whose former spouses have above-average income would get supplementary court orders, others would not. Similarly, while some would encounter no enforcement problems, others would. The issue boils down to whether we want to improve collections from lower-income absent parents at the cost of lowering payments to children of many middle-and upper-income absent parents. The option of letting custodial parents choose between an efficient public-enforcement system with a fixed benefit and a higher support order backed by the inefficient private-enforcement system poses this trade-off most starkly. To withdraw public support for enforcement for the benefit of children in middle- and upper-income families could be a huge step backward in Wisconsin. It would weaken even further the position of children from such families, who now must depend on the dual public-collection system.

Finally, the data do not indicate that expenditures on children increase less than proportionally with income. And if this were the case, it would provide no justification for a flat benefit. Studies differ substantially on how expenditures on children vary by income. Perhaps the best indicates that up to a very high income level, expenditures are relatively proportional to income.[11] But the major point is that one can find a good study to justify either a proportional or regressive tax structure. No study, however, indicates that additional expenditures on children drop to zero after a certain income is reached. Yet this is the pattern that a flat-benefit structure would imitate.

No Disbursements Provided under this Program Would Be for the Explicit Needs of the Custodial Parent

The program is for child support. Paying custodial benefits does not fit with the program's rationale and concept. Furthermore, we do not propose to resolve the alimony issue or to take alimony settlements out of the courts. Consequently, if there were a custodial-parent benefit, it would have to be funded entirely by general revenues. Although there is already a custodial benefit in the AFDC program, it is income tested. The child-support benefits are not income tested. Extending the custodial benefit to all parents or child-support beneficiaries therefore would be quite costly. This could be avoided only if we taxed absent parents for alimony as well as child support.

It is true that AFDC has paid custodial benefits since 1951, but program integrity and cost considerations argue strongly against a custodial-parent benefit in a program of child support. The objective of reducing welfare rolls as much as possible can be better accommodated by making the benefit for the first child higher than might otherwise be desirable than by having an explicit custodial-parent benefit. The child-support benefit structure we are considering has a higher benefit for the first than for subsequent children. The major rationale for this kind of benefit structure is that there are economies of scale: the first child costs most than subsequent ones. It is possible and perhaps desirable to stretch the difference even more to make up for some of the custodial benefit in AFDC.

But it is not likely that we could justify a benefit structure of $4,000 for the first child and $1,000 for each subsequent child, which is approximately what would be required to replicate and therefore replace the AFDC benefit structure in Wisconsin. Differences in the cost of first and subsequent children do not appear to be nearly this large.[12] Furthermore, it is likely that the cost in terms of general revenue will increase as the benefits for the first child, relative to subsequent children, increase.

This raises the question of why the AFDC benefit structure pays so much more for the first than for subsequent children. Is this benefit structure simply a remnant of a time when it was assumed that the mother would not and should not work? From a social and economic point of view, it is better for a mother with one child than for a mother with two or more children to work. One of the major rationales for adopting a new nonincome-tested child-support program is to reduce the implicit tax in AFDC on poor mothers and thereby encourage work. Therefore replication of the existing AFDC benefit structure may not be appropriate.

If we come within $1,000 or even $1,500 of the benefit for a one-child family, many current AFDC beneficiaries will not obtain AFDC supplementation because they will work and earn enough to be ineligible or discover that the supplement to which they are entitled is too small to be worth the bother.

Cost Estimates

The cost estimates for several variants of the program are based upon the 1975 Survey of Income and Education (SIE) data base for the state of Wisconsin. Income figures have been inflated to 1980 dollars by the cost-of-living index.

The most difficult part of the exercise is to estimate the income of the absent parent because these are not available in the SIE. Based upon relationships in the married population, we assumed that the race of the absent and custodial parents was the same and calculated the probabilities for years of schooling and age being the same, higher, or lower. We then estimated income distributions for thirty-six race, age, and years-of-schooling groups for both males and females. The probabilities were then put together with the income distributions to give us estimates of absent-parent income.

The cost estimates are derived for both the portion of the program that involves the minimum of flat benefit and for benefits above the minimum, which will be paid exclusively by the absent parent. Administrative costs are also ignored.

Table 18-1 presents estimates for a number of plans with different minimum benefit levels. Minimum benefits, given in the first two rows of the first column of each plan, range from $4,000 to $2,000 for the first child and from $1,500 and to $1,000 for the second and subsequent children. The tax rates are 20 percent for the first and 10 percent for each subsequent child, with a maximum of 40 percent no matter how many children. Tax rates on custodial parents, not shown in the table, are one-half those on the absent parents. Net savings equal gross benefits minus the sum of absent- and custodial-parent tax revenues and AFDC savings. All of the plans in tables 18-1 and 18-2 assume that 100 percent potential of absent parent-tax revenue is collected.

Savings range from a low of $49 million to a high of $118 million. Not surprisingly net savings decrease as the level of the minimum benefit increases. An increase in the minimum benefit increases total benefits paid out. Absent-parent tax revenues remain constant. (The small increases in the table are a result of rounding.) Increases in the minimum benefit, however, do lead to offsetting increases in the custodial-parent tax and AFDC savings. Thus, while increasing the minimum benefit from $2,000 for the first and $1,000 for subsequent children to $4,000 and $1,500, respectively, increases total benefits paid by $152 million. Net savings decrease by only $70 million.

One other aspect of table 18-1 is worth noting: the custodial-parent tax is a significant source of revenue. The more generous the plan, the more significant the role of the custodial-parent tax. In the most generous plan, for example, the custodial-parent tax is equal to 25 percent of the absent-parent tax, while in the least generous plan, the percentage is only half that.

Table 18-2 is identical to table 18-1 except that the tax rates rather than benefit levels are varied. The benefits in all plans are equal to $3,500 for the

Table 18-1
**Fiscal 1980 Savings from Wisconsin Child-Support Program as a Function of
Alternative Minimum Benefit Levels**

	Benefit	Tax Rate	Benefits (millions)	Tax on Absent Parent[a] (millions)	Tax on Custodial Parent (millions)	AFDC Savings (millions)	Net Savings (millions)
1st child	$4,000	20%	$626.6	$398.7	$102.9	$173.6	$ 48.7
2d child	1,500	10					
Maximum:		40					
1st child	4,000	20	591.8	398.5	93.8	173.1	73.6
2d child	1,000	10					
Maximum		40					
1st child	3,500	20	590.3	398.5	92.6	169.3	70.2
2d child	1,500	10					
Maximum		40					
1st child	3,000	20	556.9	398.3	82.1	164.2	87.7
2d child	1,500	10					
Maximum		40					
1st child	3,000	20	526.7	398.2	72.6	158.6	102.7
2d child	1,000	10					
Maximum		40					
1st child	2,500	20	499.0	398.0	61.7	151.4	112.1
2d child	1,000	10					
Maximum		40					
1st child	2,000	20	474.7	397.8	50.4	144.9	118.4
2d child	1,000	10					
Maximum		40					

[a]Differences in tax revenue from absent-parent tax across plans are due to rounding.

first and $1,500 for each subsequent child. Savings increase with tax rates.
Indeed, when tax rates are low enough, savings turn into costs.

The tax rate on the first child is a more important determinant of net
savings than either the tax rate on the second child or the maximum tax rate.
For example, plans 4 and 7 are identical except that the maximum tax rate in
the former is 40 percent, while in the latter it is 30 percent. The difference in
savings is small—less than $6 million. In contrast, plans 1 and 5 are iden-
tical except the tax rate on the first child is 25 percent in plan 1 and only 15
percent in plan 5. Savings fall from $87 million to $39 million.

For at least two reasons, the estimates of revenues from absent parents
and therefore of net savings in tables 18-1 and 18-2 are too high. First, some
absent parents are in jail or another public institution; second, no matter
how great the collection system, less than 100 percent of potential revenue
will be collected. In both cases, the problem will be most serious for absent
parents with low earnings. In table 18-3, therefore, we present additional

Table 18-2
Fiscal 1980 Savings from Wisconsin Child-Support Program as a Function of Alternative Tax Rates

	Benefit	Tax Rate	Benefits (millions)	Tax on Absent Parent[a] (millions)	Tax on Custodial Parent (millions)	AFDC Savings (millions)	Net Savings (millions)
1st child	$3,500	25%	$623.1	$446.1	$91.0	$172.6	$87.1
2d child	1,500	10					
Maximum:		40					
1st child	3,500	25	601.3	413.6	92.0	172.4	76.8
2d child	1,500	05					
Maximum		40					
1st child	3,500	20	590.3	198.5	92.6	169.3	70.2
2d child	1,500	10					
Maximum		40					
1st child	3,500	20	561.0	345.1	93.2	168.9	46.2
2d child	1,500	05					
Maximum		40					
1st child	3,500	15	557.1	338.0	93.6	164.7	39.1
2d child	1,500	10					
Maximum							
1st child	3,500	15	531.5	276.6	92.4	163.7	
2d child	1,500	05					
Maximum		40					
1st child	3,500	20	558.3	337.1	92.4	168.9	40.5
2d child	1,500	05					
Maximum		30					
1st child	3,500	15	544.7	309.6	92.7	164.7	22.4
2d child	1,500	10					
Maximum		30					
1st child	3,500	15	531.5	276.6	92.4	163.7	1.1
2d child	1,500	05					
Maximum		30					
1st child	3,500	10	530.0	261.5	90.4	161.6	−16.5
2d child	1,500	10					
Maximum		30					
1st child	3,500	10	517.2	208.1	85.5	160.4	−63.2
2d child	1,500	05					
Maximum		30					

[a]Differences in tax revenue from absent-parent tax across plans are due to rounding.

estimates for a few plans where we assume that 20 percent and 40 percent, respectively, of the poorest absent parents do not pay anything at all.

What stands out from table 18-3 is that the estimates of net savings are very sensitive to assumptions about collection effectiveness. Estimates range from a savings of $62 million to additional expenditures of $48 million.

Table 18-3
Fiscal 1980 Savings from Wisconsin Child-Support Program as a Function of Percentage of Potential Absent-Parent Tax Revenue Collected

	Benefit	Tax Rate	Benefits (millions)	Tax on Absent Parent[a] (millions)	Tax on Custodial Parent (millions)	AFDC Savings (millions)	Net Savings (millions)
Collect 100% of Tax on Absent Parents							
1st child	$3,500	20%	$590.3	$398.5	$ 92.6	$170.1	$71.0
2d child	1,500	10					
Maximum:		40					
1st child	3,500	20	558.3	337.1	92.8	170.0	41.7
2d child	1,500	05					
Maximum		30					
1st child	3,000	20	526.7	398.2	72.6	164.0	108.1
2d child	1,000	10					
Maximum		40					
1st child	3,000	20	484.2	336.8	74.0	153.7	80.3
2d child	1,000	05					
Maximum		30					
Collect Nothing from Poorest 20% of Absent Parents							
1st child	3,500	20	581.0	337.2	98.4	168.1	22.8
2d child	1,500	10					
Maximum		40					
1st child	3,500	20	553.2	286.7	96.7	168.3	− 1.6
2d child	1,500	05					
Maximum		40					
Collect Nothing from Poorest 20% of Absent Parents							
1st child	3,000	20	512.4	338.7	80.2	155.7	62.2
2d child	1,000	10					
Maximum		40					
1st child	3,000	05	475.5	286.4	79.5	148.8	39.2
2d child	1,000	05					
Maximum		30					
Collect Nothing from Poorest 40% of Absent Parents							
1st child	3,500	20	568.5	260.0	116.1	167.1	− 25.2
2d child	1,500	10					
Maximum		40					
1st child	3,500	20	546.8	223.2	106.9	167.1	− 47.5
2d child	1,500	05					
Maximum		30					
1st child	3,000	20	492.4	261.6	100.8	149.7	19.7
2d child	1,000	10					
Maximum		40					
1st child	3,000	20	464.0	222.9	95.2	145.4	− .6
2d child	1,000	05					
Maximum		30					

[a]Differences in tax revenue from absent-parent tax across plans are due to rounding.

The current system collects about 65 percent of the liability of absent fathers. We think that this is a lower-bound estimate of the effectiveness of the new system. Of course, it is probable that the current system excludes those from whom it is hardest to collect. Still, we believe that effectiveness can be substantially improved, perhaps to as high as 80 percent of the absent parents. The fact that this is a guess highlights the need to get more information on the effectiveness of alternative collection mechanisms.

There are many other shortcomings in our cost-estimating methodology. For two reasons, AFDC savings are underestimated: because some AFDC beneficiaries will, as a result of the lower tax rate, work more, and some potential AFDC beneficiaries will fail to claim the AFDC supplement to which they are entitled once they are receiving the child-support benefit. On the other hand, AFDC savings are overestimated because the reduced benefits of existing beneficiaries who now work are not taken into account. In addition, the demographic data are for 1975. Due to increases in divorce, separation, and out-of-wedlock births, the number of eligible children has increased, which should increase both gross benefits and tax revenues. The net effect is unknown. We plan to use a new data base, the Wisconsin Basic Needs Study, to address this issue.

Despite these and other weaknesses, we believe the estimates give us reliable orders of magnitude. They suggest that the proposed reform has great promise, and they point to the need to get better information on the effectiveness of alternative collection mechanisms.

Summary and Conclusion

The U.S. child-support system condones parental irresponsibility, is inequitable, exacerbates tensions between former spouses, and impoverishes children in female-headed families. Our reform proposal shows promise of correcting these ills. By legislating a normative formula for child support and enforcing the obligation to pay child support as we enforce the obligation to pay taxes, parental responsibility would be fostered, glaring inequalities eliminated, and one important source of continuing conflict between ex-spouses removed. Enactment of a child-support program would also lead both directly and indirectly to improvements in the economic status of children in single-headed families. In many nonwelfare cases, child-support payments will be higher than they would have been in the absence of the program. In some welfare cases, the child-support payments will be high enough by themselves to obviate the need for welfare. In even more cases, the child-support payment combined with a small amount of earnings will obviate the need for welfare. In all of these cases, economic well-being will be improved directly. In addition, by substituting the much-lower custodial-parent tax for the implicit welfare tax rate, greater incentive for work will be created. To the extent that this incentive is effective, economic well-being will be improved indirectly.

Our intermediate, best-guess cost estimates suggest that these desirable objectives can be achieved with, at worst, a very slight increase and, at best, a slight decrease in the public tax burden. The contrast between the dismal reality of the current system and the bright promise of the proposed reform is sufficient to warrant experimentation with, or demonstrations of, this reform proposal.

Notes

1. Estimates derived from *Child Support and Alimony: 1978 (Advance Report),* Current Population Reports, Special Studies Series P-23 No. 106, Bureau of the Census; *Statistical Abstract of the United States*, 100th ed. U.S. Department of Commerce. Details as to how these estimates were derived may be obtained from the authors.

2. *Child Support and Alimony,* table I.

3. See the statistical appendix in Daniel Patrick Moynihan, "Welfare Reform's 1971-72 Defeat, A Historic Loss," *Journal of the Institute for Socioeconomic Studies* (Spring 1981).

4. *Child Support and Alimony.* Unfortunately these data refer to children under age twenty-one rather than age eighteen. In the absence of better microdata, we had to rely on the reported data for this age group.

5. Lucy Marsh Yee, "What Really Happens in Child Support Cases: An Empirical Study of Establishment and Enforcement of Child Support Orders in the Denver District Court," *Denver Law Journal* 57 (1979).

6. See Stanley Masters and Irwin Garfinkel, *Estimating the Labor Supply Effects of Income Maintenance Alternatives* (New York: Academic Press, 1977), chap. 8.

7. Lee Rainwater, "Stigma in Income Tested Programs," in *Income Tested Transfer Programs: The Case For and Against,* ed. Irwin Garfinkel (New York: Academic Press, 1982).

8. Jonathan Kesselman, "Taxpayer Behavior and the Design of a Credit Income Tax," in Garfinkel, *Income Tested Transfer Programs.*

9. Masters and Garfinkel, *Estimating the Labor Supply Effects.*

10. Thomas Espanshade, *The Costs of Children in Urban United States,* Population Monograph Series, No. 14 (Berkeley: University of California, 1973).

11. Jacques van der Gaag, "On Measuring the Costs of Children," *Children and Youth Services Review* (Spring 1982).

12. Ibid.

19 Child Support in the Twenty-First Century

David L. Chambers

Fifty years from now, or a hundred years from now, will absent parents still be held financially liable for the support of their children? Two forces have shaped our current system of private liability. The first is a perception, wholly accurate, of large numbers of children in need, children who cannot be adequately provided for by the single parent with whom they live. The second is a moral judgment about absent parents: that they can be justly required to contribute to their children's support throughout the children's minority. Change may occur in the laws of child support if there cease to be any substantial number of children in need—unlikely, but possible—or if there are changes in the perception of the degree of moral responsibility absent parents bear for their children's support or in attitudes toward the proper role of government in assuring the needs of children.

The issues of need and responsibility may seem separate but in fact intertwine. In our society, need is a relative, not an absolute, concept. A person who has less than she or he ought is in need. Children who have lived with both parents, both working, at a high standard of living but now live with one parent at a moderate standard may be perceived as in need even if they live today at as high a standard as the mean of American children. Whether we consider them in need turns in part on whether we consider them to have moral claims on the absent parent's income. Thus, changes in either perceptions of need or perceptions of responsibility, if they occur at all, may well occur at about the same rate. What is difficult to foresee is the rate or direction of change.

Picture America in 1910. A person living in the United States who was given a sudden glimpse of life in 1980 would have gasped at the increased number of divorces, at the numbers of children whose parents never lived together at all, at the changes in attitudes toward sexuality, and at the altered role of government, especially the federal government, in meeting people's needs for income. Even President Reagan might be labeled a bolshevik.

If we could glimpse the year 2050, we would surely experience the same sensation of beholding Sodom and Gommorah. Let us nonetheless try to forecast some of the changes that may occur over time in the factors that affect the shape of systems of child support.

Trends in Factors that Affect Laws of Support

Number of Children in Financial Need

Today most parents raising children on their own face serious economic difficulties. The great majority of single-parent children live with their mothers, and most such families are poor. In 1978, over half the children living in families maintained by women with no husband present lived below the federal poverty line, even after taking into account welfare benefits they received.[1] Even those children whose mothers earn enough to keep them above the poverty line typically have to maintain a far more frugal level of existence than they would if their fathers were living with them.

There probably will not be a decline in the number of children in need, at least in the short run. Daniel Patrick Moynihan, the senator from New York, has recently made some projections that will carry us to the beginning of the next century.[2] He has forecast that of all children born in 1978, roughly half will have lived in a one-parent, female-headed family before reaching eighteen and that of that group, two-thirds (or roughly one-third of all children) will receive AFDC before reaching eighteen, if eligibility standards remain comparable to today's. Those are stunning figures, each approximately 50 percent higher than the figures for children born around 1960 and reaching majority today.

Senator Moynihan's projections were based on trends in the rate of nonmarital births and in the rate of divorce and on the rates of participation of single-parent families in the AFDC system. In the short and long term, the number of children in need will also turn on other factors, many of which Senator Moynihan could hardly have tried to take into account: the nation's general prosperity, the reliability and degree of use of contraceptives, the incidence of abortion, the birthrate generally, the degree of women's participation in the labor force, the relationship of men's earnings to women's, the incidence of father custody and joint custody, and changing notions of the concept of need.

We are already beginning to see trends that may lead to a reduction in the number of children in need. For example, a greater percentage of women raising children on their own have jobs—about 65 percent in 1980.[3] On the other hand, as to some other relevant factors, very little change has yet occurred, even though many have expected it. Over the past few decades, for example, little change has occurred either in the proportion of single-parent families that are headed by men[4] or in women's average earnings as a percentage of men's average earnings.[5]

Whatever the changes over time, it seems highly probably that many children will continue to live in single-parent families; that, especially for the youngest such children, many of their custodial parents will not be employed full time; and, more broadly, that children who live in single-parent families will in general have less income available to them than children who live in two-parent families. Some sort of income-transfer system will thus probably continue to exist. The question is whether that system will remain a mixed public and private system—the AFDC system and the child-support system—or will become more wholly public or more wholly private. The answer will turn in large part on the perceptions of future generations about the responsibilities of absent parents for their children.

Changing Perceptions of the Appropriateness of Requiring Payments from the Long-Absent Parent

However reasonable the grounds are for assuming (and requiring) that parents who live with a child support the child, the reasons are substantially more fragile for imposing long-term financial liability on a parent who has never lived with a child or who once lived with a child but has not so lived for many years. The reasoning may seem increasingly fragile over the coming decades. Two sorts of grounds are offered today for rules imposing liability on parents for the care of their child: that they caused the child to come into being and more broadly that they are part of the child's relevant family.

Responsibility of Those Who Bring Children into Being. One jurisprudential foundation for governmentally imposed child support is remarkably simple and straightforward: parents cause children to come into being. They are capable of not causing children to come into being by merely refraining from intercourse. Having engaged in an act of their free will, they can justly be held responsible for the consequences.

Forty years from now, there will have been many developments in genetic engineering, but no doubt most children will still result from voluntary intercourse between a man and a woman. If so, the same reasoning will apply. It may nonetheless be less persuasive than it is today, at least in cases in which the parents have had no more than a dating relationship and have never lived together. How later generations will consider the children of such relationships may well turn on what changes of attitudes occur toward abortion and sexuality.

Today we are in a period of national ferment over the issue of abortion. In the United States today, three of every ten pregnancies end in abortion, yet at the same time, large numbers of people ardently believe abortion immoral. Where we will stand fifty or a hundred years from now is difficult to foresee. The nation may have adopted a constitutional amendment barring abortion altogether. If that occurs or if attitudes toward abortion remain in as much conflict as they are today, then attitudes toward the responsibility of each parent for a child may well remain the same. On the other hand, it is possible that attitudes will have moved far to the other extreme. Abortions may carry no moral stigma whatever. It will be nearly risk free to the woman and freely available, perhaps through a nonprescription, over-the-counter pill. If that time arrives, then a pregnant woman, particularly an unmarried pregnant woman, who knows that the father has no desire to participate in the child's upbringing may be seen as making a unilateral decision to bear a child, and the responsibility for raising it may be seen as hers alone.[6] Perhaps before such a view could develop, attitudes about intercourse, and especially extramarital intercourse, might also have to change. As long as intercourse carries the flavor of sin, many people will want to hold the male responsible regardless of the decision-making process of the woman. It seems likely that attitudes toward both sex and abortion will evolve together, but where they will both come out is hard to guess.

If attitudes toward sex and abortion do become more permissive, then it is possible that the male, in case of children born outside marriage, will eventually be seen in much the same way as the contributor to a sperm bank is considered today. Few today would wish to hold liable the sperm-bank donor, even though he is plainly the cause of a child's having come into existence because someone else's voluntary decision to bear a child is seen as the relevant decision.

Responsibility of Family Members. Changing attitudes toward abortion might alter people's sense of the appropriateness of holding a father financially responsible in a case in which he has not been living with the mother and the mother chooses to carry the child to term knowing that he has no desire to participate in raising the child. Parents involved in the common cases of divorce are in a quite different position, however. Their decisions to have had a child will be commonly viewed as joint. For them there is more than the causal link to justify holding the absent father liable; there is also the link of having chosen to live together as a family. There are many examples of laws imposing liability on one relative for another when only this link of family tie has been present.

Over the last hundred years, state laws in this country have at various times imposed financial liability on adults for their aged parents, on grandparents for needy grandchildren, and even on adult siblings for each other.[7] These laws have rested not on a judgment of moral fault and certainly not on a person's having caused a baby to be born but rather on a strong sense that family should take care of itself. As patterns of small-town residency have changed, and the notion of core family has changed, most of these laws have been repealed.

Today, in the public mind, a child's family includes the mother and father, wherever they live, and whether they live together until majority, death, or the entry of a court order terminating parental rights. Most of us do not regard the financial responsibility of a parent who lives with a child to be markedly different from the responsibility years after moving away.

The family of the future may be viewed instead as any group of people who live together in intimacy at a given point in time, whether related by blood or marriage. So seen, a stepparent or step-sibling would be regarded as part of a child's relevant core family and the stepparent would be held financially responsible for a stepchild during the period when they reside together. On the other hand, a blood parent who never lives with a child (like many fathers of children born outside of marriage) and a parent who once lived with a child but has long ago moved elsewhere would no longer be considered part of a child's relevant family at all.

Will such a change of view come about? Some forces point in this direction, and a few other forces point toward keeping current views—and financial responsibilities—in place. What points in the direction of a change? The principal force is not something new. It is the response of absent parents, typically fathers, to obligations of child support and rights of visitation. Without substantial prodding, most fathers who have never lived with their children never pay support at all, and even divorced fathers who have lived with their children typically pay regularly for only a short time, then pay less, and then pay nothing.[8] Neither love nor a sense of moral responsibility induces them to pay as much as they could. Current patterns of visitation are similar. Little statistical information exists on visitation by noncustodial fathers of illegitimate children, but every study of divorced, noncustodial fathers confirms patterns that are somewhat comparable to their patterns of support payment: visits begin with frequency and then typically taper off within a few years.[9]

Many people attribute men's low rates of payment to a general moral degeneracy. It is nonetheless possible to ascribe a more sympathetic cause than immorality for declining feelings of responsibility over time. A sense of responsibility grows from attachment nurtured by warm interaction. Although a significant minority of divorced, noncustodial fathers sustain a vital relationship with their children years after separation, more commonly fathers who see their children no more frequently than every other week gradually feel less and less a part of their children's lives.[10] Especially if a mother remarries, but even if she does not, most fathers inevitably participate less in the tiny events important to the sense of family, the events that impart the sense of being the child's protector, teacher, and companion. They would still say that they loved their children, but their feeling is not the same as it was. Under such circumstances, child-support orders are often experienced as a form of taxation without representation.

Over the coming decades, we can expect divorced noncustodial parents to become even more detached from their children by a previous marriage than they are today. What will affect them—so subtly that they will be unaware of it—is the ever-increasing incidence of children living with only one of their parents. We have seen a great change in the last thirty years from a view of divorce as a form of social pathology that breeds juvenile delinquency to a view of divorce as simply an unpleasant fact of twentieth-century life. In 1960, about 22 percent of all children under eighteen in the United States lived in a home without one or both of their biologic parents. By 1978, the figure had risen to 32 percent, and by 1990, according to estimates of the Bureau of the Census, the figure will rise to around 41 percent.[11] Shortly after the year 2000, half of America's children may be living with neither parent or with only one. When that day arrives, it seems likely that family units of a mother and children and, possibly, family units of a father and children will more and more be seen as family unto itself, a family that is in no sense incomplete. If a single parent and child living alone are family, then the long-absent parent is even more likely to regard his financial responsibilities as diminished or ended, and his perceptions of his responsibilities are more likely to become accepted as reasonable.

There are nonetheless reasons why legislatures might never accept the absent parent's point of view. One of these is that many children in single-parent families will remain in financial need, and taxpayers will remain disinclined to provide support through the welfare system without some contribution from those absent parents who can afford to pay.

Another reason exists: even if absent parents become increasingly disengaged from their children, such disengagement may nonetheless be unfortunate for children's emotional well-being. Adults may view the single-parent family as complete, but children, at least children of divorce, will still view their family as broken. Several recent studies of divorced children living with their mothers suggest that one factor strongly related to children's emotional health and development after divorce is the quality of their continuing relationship with their fathers.[12] It is at least clear that several years after divorce, children who rarely see their fathers still think about them a lot and yearn to see more of them.[13] If we decided that it is important to encourage continued contact between children and their absent parent, compulsory child support may possibly be an instrument for sustaining absent parents' sense of a stake in their child. If further studies indicate that children derive substantial benefits from visiting with their absent parents and that these parents are more likely to continue visiting if they are successfully prodded into maintaining payments of support, then good reasons would exist for resisting changes in the law.

The Issue of Gender

Today the overwhelming majority of children who live with only one of their parents live with their mothers. The anger that many such mothers feel when fathers fail to pay is often directed not merely at the moral laxity of individual men but also at the social position in which they view themselves as having been placed by men in general.

To appreciate the place of gender in the child-support process, one need only picture the different position today of a man with custody of his children. As an initial matter, we typically view him as being in his position by choice. Society has not prescribed child rearing as his lot in life. Few would depict him as a deserter if he had failed to fight for custody of his child when he divorced. The father with custody also typically stands in a different position economically. Upon becoming a single parent, he is far less likely to be entering the labor market for the first time and far more likely to have substantial seniority in his job. If women today were in the position men are—able in general to provide support for their children, regarding themselves as custodians by choice—there would be far less public concern about enforcing support against absent parents.

To be sure, many divorcing men today also see themselves as victims of their gender, discriminated against with regard to custody and subject to eviction from the home for which they strained for years to earn enough to pay. Moreover, men may resent being viewed as privileged for their position in the labor force. A life repairing streets, tightening bolts on an assembly line, or washing cars is not all fun. But as to child support, it is women who are justly perceived as the principal victim. Before a change will come about in perceptions about the duty of absent parents to support their children, changes may also have to occur in the comparative economic and social position of men and women in our society and in attitudes toward women's obligations to be the principal caretakers of young children.

Implications for Public Policies

The increasing numbers of children living with single mothers may inspire different reactions in social policy in the short run than in the long run. In the long run, as I have forecast, the support-enforcement system may shrink if men and women approach the labor market and parenting more nearly as equals and if a family is seen as the unit that lives together at a common point in time. But in the short run—the next twenty to twenty-five years—the state and federal governments are likely to engage in ever more ardent efforts to collect money from absent fathers. Ironically, one of the techniques most likely to be used in the future may lay the groundwork for undoing the current private system of support.

Today in most states, parents under orders of support receive their paychecks and then are expected to write a check for part of it to the former spouse. When they fail to pay, agencies or lawyers send warnings and threaten them with jail. If the Treasury depended on a comparable system for the collection of income taxes instead of relying on employers to withhold the amount due, the nation would be bankrupt. In this book, we have read of a plan for the state of Wisconsin to build the child-support system into a tax-withholding system through wage deduction by employers for all parents under orders of support. Eventually the federal government might participate in such a system. If such a system were created, it would pose many risks for individual privacy. Imagine a federal computer with records of everyone's failed marriages and illegitimate children. But there is little doubt that it would lead to vastly greater collections of support than are currently achieved.

If such wage-deduction systems were developed, the current one-to-one relationship between dollars paid in by absent parents and dollars received by their children might gradually disintegrate. Beginning perhaps with the federal government making payments for children as soon as it is notified that a wage deduction has gone into effect (and without awaiting the actual receipt of deducted payments from the employer), the federal government, over the very long term, might alter either the social security system or the AFDC system to serve as guarantor for more and more children being raised by single parents. The degree to which children's needs ever came to be met out of general public revenues would turn on both future income-earning capacities of custodial parents and on the perceived degree of moral responsibility of absent parents for their children. Somewhat ironically, the creation of a universal wage-deduction scheme could be motivated by a desire to implement more effectively a system wholly premised on notions of individual responsibility but plant the seeds for more public participation over time.

Any change in attitudes toward the responsibilities of long-absent parents is likely to be gradual. One change in the law, recommended by others in this book, would require courts to take custodial parents' earnings into account to a greater extent than they do today in fixing child-support awards.[14] Today in most states, child-support awards are fixed in terms of a percentage of the noncustodial parent's income at divorce. The percentages used—say, 30 percent of the noncustodial parents' earnings in the case of a couple with two children—impel custodial parents to work full time if they wish to approximate their former standard of living. In this important sense, custodial parents' earnings are already taken into account in fixing child-support awards. In most states, however, orders are fixed without reference to the custodial parent's actual earnings. She can earn as much as she is able without any decrease in the size of the child-support award. A change in the law that might occur would be that support orders would be fixed as they are today for the first few years of an order but that thereafter a tax would be imposed on the custodial parents' earnings—for example, by reducing the child-support award by one dollar for every three dollars the custodial parent earned above a certain base. In this way, in most families, the noncustodial parents' compelled contribution would decline after a few years.

A later metamorphosis in the law that seems plausible to expect is that at some point, states would change their laws to reduce altogether the number of years of financial liability of an absent parent. Today orders run throughout a child's minority. In most cases of divorce, orders today last longer than the marriages they follow.[15] In many cases of paternity orders, the orders run nearly as many years into the future as the young parents have lived up to this point themselves. In the system forecast, orders of support might run for only three or four years after their entry. Court-ordered visitation might also expire at the same point. After that time, parents would have to hammer out their own informal arrangements. For some families in this future world—more families than today—parents at the point of divorce would devise joint custodial plans with small transfers of income that might continue after the three-year period. In others, the mother would retain custody, but the father would continue to pay support voluntarily in much the same manner that they do in many states today where support is barely enforced. But in many other families, all links between the absent parent and his children would end.

Orders of shorter duration would respond to the problem of the psychological disengagement over time of most absent parents from their children. It would also respond to the most pressing financial needs of children, since, in this envisioned future economy, the difficulties custodial parents face in providing adequate income through their own earnings will typically be urgent only when the children are infants or, in cases of divorce, in the period immediately after separation. After a period of a few years, say three or four, the vast majority of custodial parents would have full-time, decently compensated jobs or remarry a full-time worker, or both. A law reducing the years of liability would closely resemble a change that is occurring in judicial practice regarding alimony. It is apparently becoming less common for courts to enter orders of long-term support for wives even after twenty- or twenty-five-year marriages and more common to enter orders to provide support and money for schooling or training for a fixed period of years.[16]

A final value of the termination of liability after a few years is simply that limiting the length of liability would remove government earlier from coercive involvement in people's lives. Americans today decry big government but are quick to use it to suppress undesired behavior. Child-support laws today fix for men and women the terms of their relationship many years after their lives have settled into other patterns. They are doing so on an increasingly vast scale. Half of the children born in the United States today can expect to be eligible for an order of support for their benefit during their childhood. Half can later expect, as adults, to be either the payor or payee of an order of support for their own children. The child-support system will reach perhaps two-thirds of all Americans born this year either as children or as adults.

Across the country, the web of court orders tying parents to children looks today like a map in an airline magazine showing all the places the airline flies. It will be even more eye dazzling in forty years. So long as children's basic needs can be met, I would prefer a world in which a few years after separation, adults worked out voluntarily the terms of their relationships just as we permit them to do today in nearly all matters when they live together. To be sure, it is distasteful to contemplate adults trading support for visitation with a child threatened with receiving neither after the bargain. But the current mechanisms for enforcing support are also distasteful. Maybe public-policy decision makers in later generations will make different choices than we are making today.

Notes

1. Chart 27, in *American Families and Living Arrangements,* Current Population Reports, Special Studies, Series P-23, No. 104 (May 1980).

2. D. Moynihan, *Children and Welfare Reforms,* 6 J. Inst. Socioeconomic Stud. 1 (Spring 1981).

3. *American Families and Living Arrangements, supra* note 1, chart 20.

4. *Id.,* chart 16.

5. U.S. Department of Labor, Bureau of Labor Statistics, *Handbook of Labor Statistics,* Table 60, at p. 118 (December 1980).

6. See chapters 5 and 6.

7. H. Clark, Domestic Relations 212-218 (1968).

8. D. Chambers, Making Fathers Pay (1979), ch. 5.

9. W. Goode, Women in Divorce (1955); J. Wallerstein and J. Kelly, Surviving the Breakup: How Children and Parents Cope with Divorce (1980); E. Hetherington, M. Cox, and R. Cox, *Stress and Coping in Divorce: A Focus on Women*, in J. Gullahorr, ed., Psychology and Women: In Transition; J. Fulton, *Parental Reports of Children's Post-Divorce Adjustment* 35 J. Social Issues 126 (1979).

10. Wallerstein and Kelly, *supra* note 9.

11. *American Families and Living Arrangements, supra* note 1, chart 16.

12. J. Wallerstein and J. Kelly, *supra* n. 9 at 171-172, 203, 217-219; Hess and Camara, *Post-Divorce Family Relationships as Mediating Factors in the Consequences of Divorce for Children,* 35 J. Social Issues 79 (1979).

13. J. Wallerstein and J. Kelly, *supra* n. 9; M. Hetherington, M. Cox and R. Cox, *supra* n. 9.

14. See chapters 7 and 9.

15. In a study of divorced couples with children in Genesee County, Michigan, the average age of the couples' youngest child was 3.3 years at separation. Thus a support order would be expected to last over 14 years. On the other hand, the average length of the marriages to the point of separation was 7.7 years. See Chambers, Making Fathers Pay, Table 31, p. 311 (1979).

16. The Uniform Marriage and Divorce Act, parts of which have been adopted in many states, directs courts in fixing the amount and duration of alimony (which the act calls "maintenance") to consider "the time necessary to acquire sufficient education or training to enable the party seeking maintenance to find appropriate employment" (Section 308).

About the Contributors

Barbara Bergmann received the Ph.D. in economics from the Radcliffe Graduate School, Harvard University, and is a professor of economics at the University of Maryland. She was senior economic adviser to AID, Department of State, in 1966 and 1967, on the senior staff of the Brookings Institution from 1963 to 1965, associate professor of economics at Brandeis University from 1962 to 1964, and senior staff economist for the Council of Economic Advisers, Executive Office of the President, 1961 to 1962. Dr. Bergmann has served as a consultant to the Council of Economic Advisers, the Ford Foundation, the Rand Corporation, the German Marshall Fund, and the Federal Communications Commission. She is the author of numerous articles and research papers concerning discrimination in employment and women's issues.

David Betson received the Ph.D. in economics from the University of Wisconsin at Madison where he is a research associate at the Institute for Research on Poverty. Dr. Betson has extensive experience in the development of microsimulation models to estimate the economic effects of alternative tax-transfer structures and is currently a member of the Wisconsin Child Support Project research staff.

Alastair Bissett-Johnson received the LL.B. from Nottingham University and the LL.M. from the University of Michigan at Ann Arbor. He is professor of law at Dalhousie University, and has previously taught at McGill University, Montreal, and Monash University in Australia. Professor Bissett-Johnson is the author of more than fifty scholarly articles. His books in the area of family law include *Matrimonial Property Law in Canada* (1980), *Materials on Family Law* (1976), and *Family Law in Australia* (1972).

Carol S. Bruch received the J.D. from the University of California at Berkeley in 1972 and is professor of law at the University of California at Davis. Professor Bruch was a U.S. Supreme Court clerk for the late Justice William O. Douglas and a Max Reinstein Fellow of the Alexander von Humboldt Foundation at the University of Munich and the University of Frankfort, 1978-1979. Professor Bruch has served as a consultant to the California Law Revision Commission and has published extensively in the area of family law.

David L. Chambers received the LL.B. from Harvard Law School in 1965 and is professor of law at the University of Michigan at Ann Arbor. He has served as president of the Society of American Law Teachers and is a member of the board of Michigan Legal Services, Inc. Professor Chambers's book, *Making Fathers Pay* (1979), an analysis of several aspects of the child-support enforcement system in Michigan, is one of few empirical studies on this topic to date.

Thomas Corbett, a doctoral candidate in social-welfare studies at the University of Wisconsin at Madison, is a member of the Wisconsin Child Support Project research team.

Martha J. Cox received the Ph.D. in developmental psychology from the University of Virginia at Charlottesville, has served as a Fellow at the Bush Institute for Child and Family Policy at the University of North Carolina at Chapel Hill, and is currently at the Timberlawn Psychiatric Research Foundation, Dallas, where she serves as a clinical research associate. Dr. Cox is well known for her research in the area of the social and psychological responses of children to divorce.

Irwin Garfinkel received the Ph.D. in social work and economics from the University of Michigan in 1970, is professor of social work at the University of Wisconsin at Madison, and served as director of the Institute for Research on Poverty between 1975 and 1980. Dr. Garfinkel has published widely in the areas of labor supply and income-maintenance policy, has been a consultant to state and federal government, and currently serves as principal investigator for the Wisconsin Child Support Project.

H. Robert Hahlo, professor emeritus, University of the Witwatersrand, Johannesburg, received the LL.D. from the University of Witwatersrand where he also served as the dean of the faculty of law and head of the Department of Law. Professor Hahlo also holds the D.J. degree from the University of Halle, Germany, and is formerly director of the Institute of Comparative Law, McGill University. He is currently professor of law, University of Toronto, president of the International Society on Family Law, and an associate member of the Academy of Comparative Law, Paris. Professor Hahlo is the author of numerous scholarly treatise and books, including *Law of Husband and Wife.*

Dorothy S. Huntington received the Ph.D. in clinical psychology from Harvard University, and is currently serving as director of research and evaluation for the Center for the Family in Transition, Corte Madera, California. Dr. Huntington has extensive research and clinical experience in the area of infant and child development and mental health and has held teaching positions at the University of California at Berkeley, Stanford University School of Medicine, and the University of California at San Francisco.

Alfred J. Kahn holds the D.S.W. from Columbia University where he teaches in the areas of social policy and social planning and is codirector, Cross-National Studies of Social Service Systems and Family Policy. Dr. Kahn has served as consultant to federal, state, and local agencies, to voluntary organizations, and to foundations concerned with the planning of social services, income-maintenance and child-welfare programs, and international collaboration in the social-policy area. The author of more than 170 scholarly works, Dr. Kahn's recent books include *Family Policy: Government and Families in Fourteen Countries* (1978).

Sheila B. Kamerman, codirector, Cross-National Studies of Social Service Systems and Family Policy Project, received the D.S.W. from Columbia University. Dr. Kamerman, whose research, teaching, and publications are in the areas of child welfare, social services, income-maintenance policy, and child care, is a professor at the Columbia University School of Social Work and the author of numerous scholarly journal articles and books, including *Child Care, Family Benefits, and Working Parents* (1981). Dr. Kamerman has served as advisor to the National Academy of Science and the American Public Welfare Association.

Sanford N. Katz received the J.D. degree from the University of Chicago and was a U.S. Public Health Fellow at Yale Law School. He has served on the law faculties of Catholic University of America and the University of Florida and is currently professor of law at Boston College Law School. The author of a number of scholarly articles and books on family law, including *Marriage and Co-Habitation in Contemporary Society* (1980), Professor Katz chairs the Family Law Section of the American Bar Association, is vice-president of the International Society of Family Law, and editor-in-chief of *Family Law Quarterly*.

Harry D. Krause received the J.D. from the University of Michigan and practiced law in the District of Columbia and Michigan before joining the faculty of the College of Law, University of Illinois, where he now is Alumni Distinguished Professor of Law. He serves on the Board of Editors, *Family Law Quarterly,* and formerly served on the Advisory Board of Editors of the *American Bar Association Journal,* on the Council of the Section on Family Law of the American Bar Association, and as vice-president of the International Society of Family Law, for which he now serves as a member of the Executive Council. Professor Krause drafted the Uniform Parentage Act for the Commissioners on Uniform State Laws and is the author of numerous scholarly articles and the following books on family law: *Illegitimacy: Law and Social Policy* (1971), *Family Law: Cases and Materials* (1976), *Creation of Kinship Relations* (1976), *Family Law in a*

Nutshell (1977), and *Child Support in America: The Legal Perspective* (1981).

Maurice MacDonald received the Ph.D. in economics from the University of Michigan and is an associate professor, consumer science, the University of Wisconsin at Madison. Dr. MacDonald is a research affiliate of the Institute for Research on Poverty, a member of the Wisconsin Child Support Project, and serves as a consultant to the Office of the Assistant Secretary of Education, the Urban Institute Project on Women and the Family, and the U.S. Department of Agriculture, Food and Nutrition Service. In addition to his book, *Food Stamps and Income Maintenance* (1977), he has published numerous articles based upon his empirical research in the areas of marital disruption, poverty, and child support.

Isabel Marcus received the Ph.D. in political science and the J.D. from the University of California at Berkeley. Dr. Marcus is a member of the Faculty of Law and Jurisprudence, State University of New York at Buffalo. Dr. Marcus has published books and articles in such areas as matrimonial support for U.S. military wives, sexual harassment, school-desegregation implementation, and health-care reform policy. In addition, she is a labor arbitrator for the U.S. Federal Mediation and Conciliation Service.

Neil J. Salkind received the Ph.D. in human development from the University of Maryland. Dr. Salkind was formerly a Fellow at the Bush Institute for Family and Child Policy at the University of North Carolina at Chapel Hill. He is currently associate professor of educational psychology and research, School of Education, and of human development and family life, University of Kansas at Lawrence. The author of numerous books and articles, many of which have addressed issues related to the father-child postdivorce relationship, Dr. Salkind has been the recipient of a National Endowment for the Arts Award for his work in the area of child development.

John J. Sampson received the LL.B. degree from the University of Minnesota, practiced law in San Francisco, and served as assistant general counsel to the U.S. Committee on Obscenity and Pornography. He is currently a member of the faculty of the Law School, University of Texas at Austin, where he is principal investigator for the Children's Rights Clinic and formerly member of the Resource Center on Child Abuse and Neglect at the School of Social Work. In addition to his numerous publications in the areas of conflict of laws in family-law cases, division of retirement benefits upon divorce, and conflict of laws between community law and common-law property states, Professor Sampson is editor and author of the "Family Law Section Newsletter" for the State Bar of Texas.

Isabel V. Sawhill received the Ph.D. in economics from New York University and serves as program director, Employment and Labor Policy, at the Urban Institute in Washington. Dr. Sawhill's distinguished career includes service as director of the National Commission for Employment Policy; program director of the Women and Family Policy project at the Urban Institute; policy analyst for the Department of Health, Education, and Welfare, Office of Management and Budget; and chair of the Department of Economics at Goucher College. The author of numerous articles and books based upon her research in areas such as the impact of income-distribution policies, economic productivity, and the impact of labor-market policy on inflation and unemployment, Dr. Sawhill's book, *Time of Transition: The Growth of Families Headed by Women* (1975), is considered by many to be the most important and widely cited effort of its kind in the recent history of social science.

Annemette Sørensen received the Ph.D. in sociology from the University of Wisconsin at Madison where she is a research affiliate with the Institute for Research on Poverty and the Women's Studies Research Center. Dr. Sørensen also serves as a research associate with the Institute of Applied Social Research, Oslo. Her research and publications have addressed such issues as the relationship between marriage, child rearing, and occupational achievement among men and women.

Judith S. Wallerstein received the Ph.D. in psychology from Lund University, Lund, Sweden, and is currently executive director of the Center for the Family in Transition, Corte Madera, California. In addition, Dr. Wallerstein is a senior lecturer, School of Social Welfare, University of California at Berkeley. She was formerly a Fellow at the Center for Advanced Study in Behavioral Sciences, Stanford University, and Edith G. Neisser Memorial Lecturer at the Erikson Institute, Chicago, and served as a member of the Advisory Commission on Family Law to the California Senate Subcommittee on Administration of Justice. Dr. Wallerstein's longitudinal study of postdivorce family relationships has led to numerous publications dealing with various aspects of this phenomenon, including her book, *Surviving the Breakup: How Children and Parents Cope with Divorce* (1980).

Harold W. Watts received the Ph.D. in economics from Yale University and later served as Irving Fisher Research Professor at that same institution. While professor of economics at the University of Wisconsin—Madison, Dr. Watts was instrumental in establishing the Institute for Research on Poverty and served as its first director. Dr. Watts participated in the design, administration, and analysis of the results of the New Jersey/Pennsylvania Guaranteed Income Experiment and has served as Guggenheim Fellow and a member of the National Research Council and the

Carnegie Council on Children. He has also served as assistant director of the Cowles Foundation for Research in Economics, an economist for the Division of Research and Planning in the Office of Economic Opportunity, and as a consultant to the U.S. Department of Housing and Urban Development, the Stanford Research Institute, the Rand Corporation, and Mathematica, Inc. The author of numerous studies and publications in the areas of poverty, income-maintenance policy, and negative income-tax experiments, Dr. Watts is professor of economics at Columbia University.

Edward M. Young received the M.A. from Fuller Theological Seminary in Pasadena, California, and currently serves as associate director for Health Services Research at the University of California, Los Angeles. Mr. Young's interdisciplinary research and publications have included various topics related to children's rights and welfare, particularly those related to paternity determination for children born out of wedlock, and court systems and administrative procedures for establishing and enforcing child-support obligations.

Sherwood K. Zink received the LL.B. from the University of Wisconsin—Madison and serves as legal counsel for the Wisconsin Bureau of Child Support, Division of Economic Assistance, Wisconsin Department of Health and Social Services. Mr. Zink is a member of the American Bar Association Family Law Section, for which he formerly served as chair of the Comparative Law Study Committee on International Support Laws. In addition, Mr. Zink served as an advisor to the National Conference of State Legislatures' Beneficial Support Laws Project, and as a member of the Finance Committee of the National Reciprocal and Family Support Enforcement Association. Mr. Zink was instrumental in the development of the Wisconsin Child Support Project and serves as its project manager.

About the Editor

Judith Cassetty received the Ph.D. in social-welfare studies from the University of Wisconsin—Madison in 1977. She is currently a member of the faculty of the School of Social Work at the University of Texas at Austin, where she teaches in the areas of social policy and public administration and planning. Dr. Cassetty was coordinator of the Wisconsin Workshop on Child Support Research and Public Policy, has served as a member of the Advisory Committee for the National Institute for Child Support Enforcement, and has been a consultant to the National Conference of State Legislatures. Her book, *Child Support and Public Policy* (1978), is considered a benchmark in this area of research.